The Values of Volunteering
Cross-Cultural Perspectives

NONPROFIT AND CIVIL SOCIETY STUDIES
An International Multidisciplinary Series

Series Editor: Helmut K. Anheier
> University of California, Los Angeles, California; London School of
> Economics and Political Science, London, United Kingdom

The Values of Volunteering
Cross-Cultural Perspectives

Edited by

PAUL DEKKER

Social and Cultural Planning Office
The Hague, The Netherlands
and
Tilburg University
Tilburg, The Netherlands

and

LOEK HALMAN

Tilburg University
Tilburg, The Netherlands

KLUWER ACADEMIC / PLENUM PUBLISHERS
NEW YORK, BOSTON, DORDRECHT, LONDON, MOSCOW

Library of Congress Cataloging-in-Publication Data

The values of volunteering: cross-cultural perspectives/edited by Paul Dekker and Loek Halman.
   p.   cm. — (Nonprofit and civil society studies)
   Includes bibliographical references and index.
   ISBN 0-306-47737-8—ISBN 0-306-47854-4 (pbk.)
   1. Voluntarism—Cross-cultural studies.   I. Dekker, Paul.   II. Halman, Loek.   III. Series.

HN49.V64V35 2003
361.3'7—dc21

2003044642

ISBN 0-306-47737-8 (hardbound)
   0-306-47854-4 (paperback)

©2003 Kluwer Academic/Plenum Publishers, New York
233 Spring Street, New York, New York 10013

http://www.wkap.nl

10 9 8 7 6 5 4 3 2 1

A C.I.P. record for this book is available from the Library of Congress.

Permissions for books published in Europe: *permissions@wkap.nl*
Permissions for books published in the United States of America: *permissions@wkap.com*

Printed in Great Britain by Biddles/IBT Global

Contributors

Ugo Ascoli • Department of Economic History and Sociology, University of Ancona, Ancona, Italy 60121

Jeffrey L. Brudney • School of Public and International Affairs, University of Georgia, Athens, Georgia USA 30602-1615

Jacqueline Butcher • MEMEFI, Mexican Center for Philanthropy, and Department of Education and Human Development, Universidad Iberoamericana, Mexico City, Mexico 53900

Ram A. Cnaan • Department of Social Work, University of Pennsylvania, Philadelphia, Pennsylvania USA 19104

Paul Dekker • Globus Institute, Tilburg University, Tilburg, 5000 LE and Social and Cultural Planning Office, The Hague, The Netherlands 2500 BD

Nina Eliasoph • Department of Sociology, University of Wisconsin, Madison, Wisconsin, USA 53706

Loek Halman • Faculty of Social Sciences, Tilburg University, Tilburg, The Netherlands 5000 LE

Femida Handy • Faculty of Environmental Studies, York University, Toronto, Ontario, Canada M3J 1P3

Virginia A. Hodgkinson • Center for the Study of Voluntary Organizations and Service Georgetown Public Policy Institute, Washington, D.C., USA 20007

Lesley Hustinx • Department of Sociology, Catholic University of Leuven, Leuven, Belgium 3000

Ronald Inglehart • Institute for Social Research, University of Michigan, Ann Arbor, Michigan, USA 48106-1248

Stanislovas Juknevicius • Lithuanian Institute of Philosophy, Culture and Arts, Vilnius, Lithuania 2001

Lucas C. P. M. Meijs • Faculty of Economics, Erasmus University, Rotterdam, The Netherlands 3000 DR

Shree Ranade • Institute For Women Entrepreneurial Development, Pune, India 411 004

Paul B. Reed • Carleton University and Statistics Canada, Ottawa, Canada K1A
0T6

Lester M. Salamon • Institute for Policy Studies, Johns Hopkins University,
Baltimore, Maryland, USA 21218

Aida Savicka • Lithuanian Institute of Philosophy, Culture and Arts, Vilnius,
Lithuania 2001

L. Kevin Selbee • Carleton University and Statistics Canada, Ottawa, Canada K1A
0T6

Per Selle • Department of Comparative Politics, University of Bergen and Rokkan
Center, Bergen, Norway 5015

S. Wojciech Sokolowski • Institute for Policy Studies, Johns Hopkins University,
Baltimore, Maryland, USA 21218

Bogdan Voicu • Research Institute for Quality of Life, Romanian Academy of
Sciences, Bucarest, Romania 76117

Mălina Voicu • Research Institute for Quality of Life, Romanian Academy of
Sciences, Bucarest, Romania 76117

Suzanne Weber • Institut für Erziehungswissenschaft der Philipps-Universität
Marburg, Germany 35035

Idit Weiss • School of Social Work, Tel Aviv University, Tel Aviv, Israel 69978

Dag Wollebæk • Department of Comparative Politics, University of Bergen, Bergen,
Norway 0464

Preface

Volunteering is one of those phenomena which, despite the limited number of people actually involved in it, is seen as highly important for the proper functioning of society. In fact, volunteering and active participation in voluntary associations are considered to be key components of civil society; it is felt that they generate social cohesion and societal self-regulation as well as strengthening political democracy by developing individual citizenship and organizing countervailing powers. Issues such as these have gained momentum in recent years, especially since Putnam's publications in the 1990s on civic community and democracy in Italy and on the decline of social capital in the United States. However, interest in these issues in fact dates back to the time of the Civic Culture project carried out in the 1950s and 1960s by Almond and Verba, and even much earlier to Tocqueville's famous study *Democracy in America* in the 1830s. All of these studies, and many more, stress the importance of voluntary civic engagement for the development and maintenance of civilized societal cohesion and political democracy. This research tradition addresses volunteering as just one form of voluntary social and political involvement that might well be linked with other forms, such as passive and active membership of voluntary associations, incidental political activism, or individual involvement in public discourse.

However, most studies on volunteering are written in another tradition that is more specifically directed toward direct helping behavior, service delivery, and unpaid work. Many articles, policy reports, and books have appeared on volunteering in diverse fields such as sports, faith-based organizations, human services, and schools; often they are quite practically oriented and focus on issues of recruitment and management. In general, they pay scant attention to the contributions made by volunteering to social cohesion and political democracy. Although those contributions are often gratefully acknowledged in introductory remarks, they are not the core issues of investigation in this tradition.

Thus, although volunteering as a topic of research is far from new, studies that specifically place volunteering in a civil society perspective are more rare. The aim of this book is precisely to explore further and dig deeper into this perspective, using empirical data garnered from various sources for countries all over the globe.

The contributions in this book deal with a broad spectrum of questions, ranging from the diversity, social and cultural determinants, and organizational settings of volunteering to its possible individual, social, and political effects. Some chapters give a general outline of the diversity of and developments in volunteering, and discuss future trends; others examine more closely the relationships between volunteers and clients and organizations.

In order to do justice to the collective—and still primarily national—notions of civil society, such as civic culture, trust as a trait of social relations, pluralism, and democracy, international comparative studies involving countries representing a broad spectrum of national characteristics, democratic histories, and cultural contexts are necessary. To achieve this, several chapters draw on data from large-scale surveys, notably the European Values Study (Halman, 2001), and World Values Surveys (*www.worldvaluessurvey.org*), or on data gathered within the framework of the Johns Hopkins Comparative Nonprofit Sector project (*http://www.jhu.edu/~cnp*). The availability of large-scale survey data that include details about volunteering and a number of indicators to reveal values enables interesting studies to be carried out to assess the impact of these values on volunteering at both the individual and macrolevels. The interrelationship of values or culture and volunteering at societal and individual levels is a recurring topic in the book.

However, this book deals not only with differences and similarities in volunteering between countries and the conditions that may be conducive to or hinder volunteering; other intriguing questions are also examined, such as why people volunteer, how they relate to each other and to the people they want to help, what ideals they wish to promote, and the life. Studies based on survey research may provide this kind of information, but a qualitative approach can produce better insights and provide a deeper understanding of people's drives, motives, and goals. Some of the chapters in this book discuss the results of in-depth interviews, group discussions, and participant observation.

We hope that the contributions in this volume will advance our understanding of the variety in volunteering, the differences between countries, the impact of the social settings and individual backgrounds of volunteering, and the social and political effects of volunteering. We also hope this book will contribute to the recognition of volunteering as an interesting topic for further social research. The idea of producing a book to raise the level of "academic" interest in volunteering developed in discussions with colleagues at the Netherlands Federation of Volunteer Organizations (NOV), during the preparations for the United Nations Year of Volunteers 2001. Another offshoot from these discussions, directed more toward practitioners and the general public, is Govaart, van Daal, Münz, & Keesom (2001), which contains a comprehensive summary of voluntary activities and projects in 21 countries.

We wish to thank all those who have prepared a contribution to this volume, as well as those who facilitated the production of the book. We as editors deliberately invited scholars from several disciplines to prepare contributions, in order to obtain the broadest possible overview of the current status of knowledge and research activities in the field of volunteering. We believe that the resulting variation is very properly reflected in the volume. This approach meant that our editorial aims were confined to eliminating repetition and incompatibilities and stressing the commonalities and bridging features. We hope that we have done this accurately. We thank the authors not only for their contributions but also for their patience in the final phases of preparing the book.

We also would like to thank the Social and Cultural Planning Office of the Netherlands (SCP) in The Hague, Globus, the Institute for Globalization and Sustainable Development, and the Department of Sociology of the Faculty of Social and Behavioral Sciences at Tilburg University, Netherlands, for making available the time for the editors to complete the book. Finally, we are grateful to Kluwer/Plenum for being so gracious when we failed to meet the various deadlines.

PAUL DEKKER
LOEK HALMAN

REFERENCES

Govaart, M., van Daal, H. J., Münz, A., & Keesom, J. (eds.), (2001). *Volunteering worldwide*. Utrecht, NL: NIZW.

Halman, L. (2001). *The European values study: A third wave*. Tilburg, NL: Tilburg University. *www.europeanvalues.nl*.

Contents

Chapter *1*

Volunteering and Values
An Introduction

PAUL DEKKER AND LOEK HALMAN

VOLUNTEERING

Volunteering has gained widespread public and political interest in recent years. Policy debates have taken place in many countries focusing on how to preserve and encourage volunteering, and various parliamentary and government commissions have studied ways to stimulate voluntary activities among diverse groups such as the young and the elderly, working parents and immigrants. 2001 was the United Nations Year of Volunteers, and this gave rise to all kinds of national and local manifestations, discussions and policy initiatives, often with a lot of media exposure. In the burgeoning social sciences literature on the (assumed) decline of civic community, the crumbling of civil society, and the erosion of social capital, volunteering is an indicator of the negative trends as well as a possible instrument for recovery. Volunteering is not just an expression of individual engagement and a spontaneous result of community life; it is often consciously organized and managed and it can be made an object of policymaking. This mixture of voluntariness and organization in the establishment of prosocial behavior makes volunteering a very interesting phenomenon.

But what exactly is volunteering? If we look at definitions of volunteering or of voluntary work around the world, we find three or four common elements: it is non-obligatory; it is carried out (among other things) for the benefit of others: society as a whole or a specific organization; it is unpaid; and, somewhat less common, it takes place in an organized context (cf. Dingle, 2001: 9; Govaart, van Daal, Münz, & Keesom, 2001: 16). Some definitions are more restricted as regards the beneficiaries and formulate the requirement that a "public good" is produced—thus excluding volunteers working for their own organization or their own group (Wilson,

2000: 216). Sometimes, there are other requirements, such as unconnectedness of the voluntary activities with the volunteer's paid work. The criterion of being non-obligatory is essential, but often not evident. There are situations requiring voluntary work that a rational person can hardly refuse, such as community service as an alternative for imprisonment or military service; voluntary work to enable students to obtain credits for their study or to gain the necessary experiences to find a job; or voluntary work to help reintegrate the long-term unemployed on the labor market, possibly with the added "incentive" of financial sanctions if they refuse. The transition from volunteering as "serious leisure" (Stebbins, 1996) to less and less voluntary activities in the occupational setting or perspective is a smooth one, and in general it is difficult to draw a line showing where coercive elements of an economic nature are so strong that activities are no longer voluntary. And what about voluntary activities performed to avoid social exclusion and isolation? Or feelings of moral or religious obligation? People we call volunteers sometimes refer to these feelings to reject the appellation: "It is not voluntary, I have no choice, I feel that I have to do this." Can we make a distinction here between a freely chosen sense of duty and a lack of freedom to resist subordination? State-ordered unpaid work is a much simpler case of coercion and is a reason to exclude it from volunteering. In the former communist countries where "obligatory voluntary work" existed, the voluntary element is now particularly emphasized (Govaart et al., 2001: 261), but the historical loading of the term still has a negative affect on willingness to get involved (see Chapters 8 and 9).

The criterion of being unpaid is also not entirely straightforward. From indisputable reimbursements of expenses and generally accepted small material tributes of appreciation, it is only a small step to the acceptance of payments below the market value and a reformulation of the criterion of the work being unpaid, to the work not being undertaken primarily for financial gain. The requirement of an organizational setting or link, finally, is probably the most controversial criterion. Many definitions do not include such a norm, and "unorganized" informal volunteering is sometimes explicitly acknowledged.

The terminology and connotations of volunteering differ between countries. The traditional German perspective of volunteering as "honorary work" (*Ehrenamt*), for instance, still lives on in the writings of a German parliamentary commission about "civic engagement." According to the Enquete-Kommission (2002: 99), voluntary activities are necessary for the political community, and this community is a precondition for involvement in associations, self-help groups, churches, enterprises and public facilities. This may sound strange for Anglo-Saxons who consider voluntary work primarily as unpaid work in the sphere of charity and services for the community, and see politics and advocacy as somewhat exceptional cases.

Countries also differ with regard to what people see as typical voluntary work (see Chapter 2) and what the main areas of activity are (see Chapters 3–5).

National research often mirrors the national traditions: in some countries people are asked about (economic) sectors, such as social services, health care and education, in which one might do unpaid work; in other countries people are presented with a list of membership organizations, and possibly some forms of political involvement, and are asked to state whether they are active as volunteers in any of those organizations. Cross-national comparative research is carried out in these different perspectives—cf. the "European" active membership questions in the European and World Values Studies (Chapters 4, 5, and 11) and the "American" unpaid work questions in the Johns Hopkins Comparative Nonprofit Sector Project (Chapter 5)—or incorporates lengthy explanations designed to focus the respondents of the surveys on the same broad set of activities (cf. Gaskin & Davis Smith, 1995; Lyons, Wijkström, & Glary, 1998).

BACKGROUND

Why do people volunteer? One explanation could be that volunteering reflects a person's personality: some people are by nature helpful, active and generous, and some people are less so. These are more or less stable differences, whether they are in people's genes or come from their upbringing or from some self-reinforcing experiences. We probably all know those people who always do something extra, are always willing to help, ready to take the initiative, whether in the workplace, in the neighborhood or at home. And we also know the other kind of people who remain passive most of the time, always have something else to do, are too tired, etc.[1]

An alternative explanation for prosocial behavior emphasizes the circumstances. The basic idea is that "people tend to do things because of where they are, not who they are." In subtly different circumstance people might behave in radically different ways.

> You stop on the highway to help someone ... and then the help you try to give doesn't prove to be enough, so you give the person a ride, and then you end up lending them money or letting them to stay in your house. It wasn't because that was the person in the world you cared about the most, it was just one thing led to another. Step by step. (Ross, quoted by Parker, 2000: 122–123)

Both explanations can be right and we often jump from one way of reasoning to the other to explain prosocial behavior. In daily life, we—victims of what cognitive psychologists call an "attribution fallacy"—are probably inclined to tell

---

[1] The personal readiness to engage in voluntary involvement is acknowledged in social science in various concepts, for instance in Bale's (1996) "volunteerism-activism attitude," a combination of feelings of efficacy with moral beliefs about voluntary work as a duty, altruism and a "feel good" factor.

a personality story to explain our own behavior, and a circumstantial story to explain the behavior of others. In social research, small-scale qualitative studies are generally probably more interested in how one thing leads to another, whereas large-scale survey research is more focused on differences between kinds of people and can say hardly anything about circumstances. Volunteering respondents in surveys are asked to rank or rate general statements to express the importance of the reasons for volunteering. Their answers are then analyzed to distinguish dimensions and clusters of motivations.[2] However, in discussions with volunteers it often proves difficult to distinguish different types of motivations. Volunteers themselves, for instance, do not distinguish systematically between egoistic and altruistic motives. They just could not say no when they were asked, wanted to make "a contribution," "a difference," or were looking for a "rewarding experience." And these words mean different things for different people. The impact of motives often remains unclear. People may volunteer for reasons that sound purely "selfish" without this in any way diminishing the level of commitment they show to the organization they volunteer for. That can be demonstrated by surveys, but for a better understanding of what drives people and what their arguments mean, we need more in-depth interviews, group discussions and also participant observations of how people actually discuss their motives in volunteer groups; Nina Eliasoph explores this in Chapter 12.

Motivations are also always simultaneously rationalizations: they impart volunteers" work with a purpose, confirm a desired identity, and reinforce commitment

---

[2] Respondents are presented with statements such as "Volunteering is an opportunity to change social injustices," "It is God's expectation that people will help each other," "Volunteering is an opportunity to return good fortune" or "This is an excellent educational experience," and "I was lonely" (cf. Cnaan & Goldberg-Glen, 1991), and are asked to indicate how important these reasons are for their own behavior. The researcher will try to construct more general motives from these responses, or to interpret the results in terms of different social and psychological functions being served by the activity, as personality traits that drive action, as values or general goals aimed for by the individual, or as benefits in a cost-benefit rational choice approach (cf. Wilson, 2000). The literature employs a variety of dichotomies or trichotomies to improve the insight into the motivation of volunteers—such as egotistic versus altruistic, intrinsic versus extrinsic, and altruistic, social, or material motives— and sometimes longer lists and occasionally a single dimension (Cnaan & Goldberg-Glen, 1991). A well-known classification into six categories of psychological functions by Clary et al. (1998) includes values (people act to express important beliefs, such as altruism and helping the less fortuned), understanding (people see voluntary work as an opportunity to learn, increase their knowledge or develop and practice new skills), social (people want to be accepted and "fit in" social groups they value or gain social approval), enhancement (people engage for personal development and to enhance their self esteem), protection (volunteering may help people cope with inner anxieties and conflicts, i.e. they want to help in order to avoid guilt), and career (people want to gain experiences useful for their job or career). Various classifications can readily be justified in empirical terms, depending on the reasons selected for submission to the interviewees. If there are ten instead of three moral reasons, morality will become a more important factor. If a reason such as "because it is fun" is included, this will probably change the understanding of the question, and make it harder for respondents to acknowledge more serious moral, religious and ideological reasons.

(Wilson, 2000). Volunteers invoke motives as an accepted vocabulary, because they are what their social group or organizational culture stimulates and because no other motives can be admitted to (or are even not asked for in closed-question surveys). It might be completely unacceptable for a "buddy" to terminal patients or a volunteer in a political organization to say they do the work for fun, just as it may be considered pretentious to suggest anything else when doing voluntary work for a local choir or sports club.

General motives are also very different from tangible reasons for participating. The way people have become involved in voluntary work is often not so much a consequence of a conscious search for involvement in a specific activity, but more a question of "being asked." They have been "drawn in" via their family, friends or neighbors who were already participating in voluntary work or who were in some way involved with an organization that needed volunteers (such as the school or sport club of one's children).

Moreover, motives relating to initiating an activity or proving something to others are seldom reasons for continuing to participate in voluntary work.[3] Within this context force of habit and obligations felt toward other volunteers or the organization play a larger role. It is then much more difficult for people to refuse an initial request. And once they have accepted a duty or duties and have entered into agreements with others, they will feel obliged to honor the obligations they have assumed. Moreover, people also derive pleasure from doing something that is needed by others, since being "needed" flatters their ego (cf. Pearce, 1993: 93–107).

"Being asked," the main reason why people get involved as volunteers according to surveys, diverts attention away from general motivations to social networks. People volunteer because they are asked to, and the chance of being asked is greater if they are involved in active social networks, if they go to church or are a member of a voluntary association. The decline of voluntary associations with intensive face-to-face contacts has negative consequences for volunteering, and it is unclear how much compensation other networks, such as friendship, workplace ties or the Internet, can offer (cf. Putnam, 2000; Wuthnow, 1998).

Apart from networks, it make sense to look at structural variables in a bid to discover factors that drive people to volunteer. Based on interviews with leaders of voluntary associations in Texas, Price (2002: 126) comes to the conclusion that ". . . civic engagement fluctuates mostly because opportunities and incentive structures fluctuate, not because notions about the intrinsic worth of participations do." Apart from restrictions on the availability of employees, students and welfare recipients caused by policy measures and economic circumstances, the leaders

---

[3] The study of what drives volunteers is preoccupied with initial motives. "Although research on job choice is a small component of research on employee motivation, interest in volunteer motivation is dominated by attempts to understand the volunteers" choice to join organizations—with a virtual absence of concern for what motivates volunteers" actions once they are working." (Pearce, 1993: 62).

interviewed mention the increasing time pressures in families and the growing numbers of retirees as most important factors. Lyons and Hocking (2000) speculate about "three, not necessarily exclusive, paths into volunteering" that would fit their empirical findings concerning sociodemographic differences in Australia: (1) people in their thirties and forties, when they have children, get involved because of the voluntary work that is attached to the services they want for their children; (2) people in rural areas tend to be more involved in voluntary activities and organizations because of the lack of professional services; here, services are more often provided by volunteers; and (3) people who are committed to working with others in the interests of some form of public good. Unlike the logic of necessity of the two first paths, we find a logic of public service, especially among the well-educated and older people. Speculations of this kind about why people volunteer can be more fruitful than the analysis of the motives volunteers choose to justify their involvement.

Most studies seeking to explain volunteering find only weak correlations with socio-demographic characteristics such as age, income, education and social class, and thus volunteering cannot be explained in toto from such attributes. Thus, it seems likely that explanations will be found in other individual features, such as values. Values can manifest themselves in motivations to volunteer, but they are more general and can be seen more as guidelines in people's lives than as clear directors of behavior. People are guided not only by their passions and self-interest, but also by their values, their norms and their belief systems. Values are considered to be deeply rooted dispositions guiding people to act and behave in a certain way (Halman & de Moor, 1994). It seems likely that the voluntary work people are engaged in depends to a considerable extent on values (Kearney, 2001 and Chapter 6). Altruism may be one of those values, but so may solidarity, reciprocity, beneficence, injustice, equality and inequality, and in the end religious values may also be mentioned in connection with voluntary work. Reciprocity indicates that people help others in the vague expectation that in the future the other person will help them in turn if it should become necessary; or else people help others in order to do something in return for the way others have helped them. Beneficence may be close to altruism in the sense that it is a moral view that connects duty and compassion which may be based, for example, on religious values. Feelings of solidarity as a reason for volunteering have to do with notions of identity and concern for others in society and it is reflected in an individual's willingness to contribute to the good of a person or social group. Volunteering may also result from feelings of injustice and inequality and ideas that inequalities should be eliminated from or sustained in society. Thus it can be argued that values, at the individual level, may be important attributes of volunteering.

However, from sociopsychological studies we know that there is not a one-to-one relationship between people's values and their actual behaviors. In their theory of "reasoned action," Fishbein and Ajzen (1975) have demonstrated rather convincingly that values are just one of the components that can explain human behavior. It is therefore no surprise that Wilson (2000: 219) concludes from a number of studies that "overall, the relation between values and volunteering is weak and inconsistent." Values are probably less important as predictors of whether somebody volunteers, but more of an aid to understanding what kind of reasons and motivations are appealing. Simple value questions and global correlations fail to capture the diversity of values that are relevant in different countries, for different groups in the population, and for different kinds of voluntary work. Depending on economic circumstances and traditions of state care and associational life, needs and opportunities to volunteer and the kind of work to be done differ, and thus relevant values will also be different. People with different values and norms will feel attracted to different organizations and activities, and a distinction of basic types of volunteering seems to be a first condition for a better understanding of the relevance of values at the individual level.[4]

But values may also be important at the aggregate, collective level in determining levels of volunteering in a society. As is becoming increasingly clear, culture matters. Of itself, such a statement does not reveal anything new: Weber has already demonstrated the close links between culture and society in his famous work on the *Protestant Ethic*. "Culture includes what we think, how we act and what we own" (Macionis & Plummer, 1998: 98), and because values are an important attribute of culture, it seems reasonable to assume that collective values are important for volunteering as well. Volunteering will be more common in societies whit a spirit of solidarity. Also, the kinds of organizations that are established may be attributed to a country's values: in more individualistic societies charitable organizations may be felt to be more a necessity for many people, while in more collectivistic societies the need may be considered less urgent. However, turning the relationships around, the level of volunteering may also have an impact on the values in a society. Salient examples are given in Putnam's work on democracy in Italian regions. In those parts of Italy where engagement is higher, democracy

---

[4] Apart from areas of activity or policy sectors (cf. Chapters 4 and 5), various basic types of volunteering are distinguished. Dingle (2001), for instance, suggests a global classification of mutual aid or self-help (ranging from jointly managing natural resources or providing health care and education in poor countries to support groups of people with the same illness or similar psychological problems in the rich countries); philanthropy or service (typically to deprived people not belonging to the group to which the volunteers belong, and often organized by nonprofit organizations); campaigning and advocacy (promotion of interests of own group, on behalf of others or some ideal, lobbying, activism); participation and self-governance (amateur politicians in municipal councils, members of public advisory bodies, members of the boards of nonprofit schools and other facilities, etc.). Arai (2001) distinguishes between citizen, techno and labor volunteers, depending on perceptions and valuations of the benefits and frustrations of volunteering. Dekker (2002) suggests unpaid work, active membership and active citizenship as different types of volunteering, with different meanings for the volunteers and probably different effects on social capital and political involvement.

performs better, but democratic values are also more widespread among the people. In voluntary organizations people get to know others, experience and learn the processes of negotiation and collaboration which are essential for a democracy to survive. Thus voluntary involvement and values may reinforce each other, as they will be mutually dependent on each other.

Value changes or culture shifts will have consequences for volunteering. Individualization is probably the most important value change currently affecting volunteering. In his "Acts of compassion" (1991), with the revealing subtitle "Caring for others and helping ourselves," Wuthnow concludes that ". . . being intensely committed to self-realization and material pleasure did not seem to be incompatible with doing volunteer work . . . People who were the most individualistic were also the most likely to value doing things to help others" (p. 22). A similar conclusion is also drawn in research on (post-)modernized and individualized "new volunteers" (Hustinx, 2001), who appear to be less interested in doing regular board work and prefer more specific goals and greater freedom. That can pose a serious management problem, and it is no coincidence that Dutch volunteer organizations today complain about growing numbers of "revolving-door volunteers," who move from one fashionable field of activity to another. However, decreasing organizational loyalty does not necessarily mean a decline in the commitment of volunteers toward their tasks, and with a little more flexibility organizations appear to be well able to attract new volunteers and to use their individualism as a resource. Individualization is not a trend with inevitable negative consequences for volunteering, or which unavoidably forces all volunteers" organizations to adapt to the same "new volunteers." Voluntary work does not have to react merely by assimilating; it has the autonomy to attract different groups and to attract the same group with different images, ideals and incentives.

OUTCOMES

What are the revenues of volunteering? First and foremost there are concrete results, ranging from the money collected for and the unpaid services delivered to those in need, via activities in local communities and public amenities that would not have been available without volunteers, to the maintenance of voluntary associations as such. In recent years, there has been a growing interest in the more general social and political effects of volunteering, often more in terms of unintended side-effects than goals as such. The notion of civil society has developed into an umbrella concept for reflections about the benefits of volunteering for community life and political democracy. Civil society is often seen as the exclusive societal sphere of voluntary involvement, at some distance from the economic activities of the market, the obligations of the state and the small-scale informal and intimate relations of private life. There are no clear-cut criteria for deciding where to place organizations in the twilight zone between civil society and the other realms. Few will dispute that local club life, voluntary associations and advocacy groups form part of civil society, but when it comes to organizations that lie closer to the community (such as informal neighborhood ties), the market (for example trade unions and professional organizations) or the state (e.g., state-subsidized agencies in the non-profit sector) it is less self-evident to regard these as part of civil society.

Social capital and *public discourse* can be considered as the largely unintended collective benefits of associating voluntarily. In the discussion on civil society, social capital refers to "social networks and the norms of reciprocity and trust-worthiness that arise from them" (Putnam, 2000: 19) while public discourse refers to the reflection on social problems, the articulation of collective values, and the development of political goals in a society.[5] Much research has been carried out in recent years on social capital, in particular measured as social trust, as a correlate of volunteering and other forms of voluntary involvement. In general, the strength of the statistical relationships appears to lag somewhat behind the theoretical and political expectations, and it remains unclear to what extent social capital or trust is a condition for voluntary involvement and how much it is its result (cf. contributions in Dekker & Uslaner, 2001). Tocqueville's ideas about the importance of voluntary social involvement for political democracy were a key issue in the study of political behavior long before the present discussions about civil society. Most research has confirmed the findings of Almond and Verba (1989 [1963]: 265), that involvement in voluntary associations stimulates political competence and involvement (cf. Chapter 11). For some years, however, a number of American authors have been suggesting significant deviations from the general pattern. Social participation might develop from being the basis for political participation into being its alternative. Galston and Levine (1997: 26) believe this is what is happening among American young people:

> Indeed, citizens, particularly the youngest, seem to be shifting their preferred civil involvement from official politics to the voluntary sector. If so, the classic Tocquevillian thesis would have to be modified: local civic life, far from acting as a school for wider political involvement, may increasingly serve as a refuge from (and alternative to) it.

However, most findings, including those for the large majority of the American population, still appear to be in harmony with the classical Tocquevillian wisdom:

---

[5] "Public discourse" is not a common focus to analyze and discuss the contribution of volunteering in a civil society perspective. By placing it next to and on an equal footing with "social capital," we draw attention to the political side of the civil society; we can highlight the fact that what is good for the formation of public opinion is not necessarily good for the formation of social capital (for example pressure groups with little membership participation); and we avoid social capital being blown up to become the source of everything which is good.

[V]olunteering is part of the syndrome of good citizenship and political involvement, not an alternative to it. Volunteers are more interested in politics
and less cynical about political leaders than non-volunteers are. Volunteering
is a sign of positive engagement with politics, not a sign of rejection with
politics. This is true for young adults as anyone else, and it is as true at the
turn of the century as it was twenty-five years earlier. (Putnam, 2000: 132)

Voluntary involvement might be the core of civil society, but that does not
make volunteering its main activity. There is more to voluntary involvement than
volunteering, and there are reasons for doubting the benign effects of volunteering compared to other forms of voluntary involvement. According to Wuthnow
(1998), the modern American volunteer is above all the unpaid helper of the
professional, and no longer the voluntarily associated active citizen who was the
carrier of community life and local democracy in the 1950s. Other American
scholars also show a certain dissatisfaction with modern volunteering. Putnam
and Etzioni greatly value people's voluntary activities, but are concerned about the
relationships within which and the attitude with which these activities take place.
Etzioni (2000: 19 ff.) stresses the importance of mutuality: "A good society relies
even more on mutuality than on voluntarism." In reciprocal relationships ranging from neighborly help through associational life up to Neighborhood Watch
(a growth sector of the American civic community, but born out of fear of crime),
a sense of community and morality are better able to develop than in one-sided
help relationships based on voluntary work. In order to limit this one-sidedness,
Etzioni also argues that voluntarism is best carried out in a "service learning mode"
that gives volunteers some benefit from their work in terms of their own education
or training, and that bestows some equality on the relationships. Putnam (2000:
127 ff.) wonders about the steadily declining participation by Americans in recent
decades in "community projects," whereas they report doing more voluntary work.
Evidently most people see their voluntary work "as providing personal rather than
community service." The growing amount of voluntary work is increasingly being
mobilized outside the contexts of clubs, churches and other associations. Volunteering, according to Wuthnow, Putnam and others, is more and more about
"getting things done" by individuals; the social aspects recede into the background
and cooperation comes to depend on the task to be carried out and is no longer
the core of the activity. However, it is not the efficiency of the performance of the
good deeds, but socializing and cooperation that form the breeding ground for
social capital and public discourse.

Voluntary work may well be the ideal medium for binding together a modern
society in which traditional integrating frameworks have disappeared and people
enter into relationships on the basis of common interests and shared aims. In an
age when usefulness is a dominant criterion, volunteering is a perfect activity for
people who still wish to do something unselfishly for other people but who feel

uncomfortable without common goals and things that have to be done. Some extra "social engineering" might however be necessary to lead these volunteers to the kind of voluntary associating that contributes to civil society (cf. Dekker, 2002).

STRUCTURE OF THE BOOK

The collection of chapters in this volume reflects the various aspects that can be distinguished with regard to volunteering in contemporary society. Some of the chapters focus on characteristics of volunteers, others on differences between countries. Some are more quantitative, using data drawn from large-scale survey projects, while others are more qualitative in the sense that they report on ethnographic studies with and in voluntary organizations.

A book on volunteering is not complete without a further exploration and clarification of its core concept. In Chapter 2, Lucas Meijs et al. address the issue of divergent perceptions among the public of eight countries as to what volunteering is. For a book such as this, with contributions from very different countries and containing several cross-cultural comparisons, it is essential to clarify how the definitions employed by social researchers relate to the common use of the same word. Previous studies by Cnaan et al. (1996) made clear that the definitions range from very broad (everyone who works without full financial compensation is a volunteer), to more narrow or strict (those who spend an extensive part of their time and effort without compensation are volunteers). According to these studies free will, rewards, formal organization, and proximity are the key components that are frequently used to define volunteering. However, the public perception of what is a volunteer is connected to the net costs incurred by the individual in the voluntary activity. The individual incurring higher net costs is likely to be perceived as "more" of a volunteer than someone with low net costs. Those net costs, which are defined as total costs minus total benefits to the volunteer, can include the time spent on volunteering, the effort involved and the loss of income incurred. Benefits or rewards, on the other hand, can be either material or immaterial, such as the improvement of social status, pleasure, new friendships, etc.. The chapter offers a framework to empirically assess public perceptions of volunteers, using a questionnaire with 50 questions describing an unpaid activity. Some items describe various acts of volunteering taking into account the four key dimensions of the definition of volunteering. Other items are developed to test the net cost approach. The instrument was applied in Belgium, Canada, Germany, India, Israel, Italy, the Netherlands, and the United States. The results show some remarkable similarities in top and bottom rankings of people's perceptions of volunteers across the different countries, but also some interesting differences and deviations. However, the main conclusion is that there is an urgent need for further conceptual and empirical work to clarify the ambiguity in the term "volunteering."

The next two chapters deal with the rate and scope of volunteering in various countries around the world, using data from the most recent surveys from the European Values Study and World Values Surveys. In Chapter 3, first, Virginia Hodgkinson reports on the rates of volunteering globally, demonstrating that patterns of volunteering vary widely from country to country. As others have done, she postulates that this variation is due to cultural differences, religious traditions, national histories and economic situation. In her analyses she focused on the relationship between the rates of volunteering in a country and that country's level of income and freedom ratings. She is unable to find much evidence for the idea that richer countries and countries that rank higher on the Freedom House index will have higher rates of volunteering. In the second part of her chapter, Virginia Hodgkinson further explores parts of what is called "social resource theory" (see also Wilson, 2000). Applying this theory, she predicts that people who are volunteers will also be more actively engaged in religious institutions, are more likely to be members of a voluntary organization, socialize more often with other members of the community beyond family and friends, and are more likely to be engaged in civic affairs than non-volunteers. Broadly speaking, these hypotheses can be confirmed in most of the countries around the world.

Ronald Inglehart (Chapter 4) also relies on the data from the most recent waves of the European Values Study and World Values Surveys. His chapter focuses on the impact of cultural change on volunteering. Contrary to the frequently voiced assertion that Americans are increasingly dropping out of the face-to-face organizations that build social capital, and that the "network society" gives rise to a multiplicity of weak social ties, weakening social institutions and the individual's sense of identity, the hypothesis put forward in this chapter is that while the established hierarchical organizations are breaking down, people are at least as interactive as ever. Not only are they interacting in new, more flexible, less permanent kinds of organizations, but they also participate more in these new settings than they did in the old ones. In Chapter 4 Inglehart examines patterns of organizational membership in different types of societies, comparing the types of participation that are most prevalent in agrarian, industrial and postindustrial societies. It is argued that the transition from agrarian to industrial societies has shifted the characteristic mode of participation from the church to the labor union. With the shift from industrial to post-industrial society, the characteristic form of participation takes place in charitable organizations and sports organizations. Though more loosely organized than the church or labor union, the new forms of participation may be as dynamic as ever. The evidence suggests that the popular claims that levels of volunteering are on the decline cannot be substantiated. On the contrary, levels of volunteering seem to be on the rise.

Data from the Johns Hopkins Comparative Nonprofit Sector Project in 24 countries are examined in Chapter 5. Lester Salamon and Wojciech Sokolowski use this data set to investigate and understand the cross-national variation in rates of volunteering *in toto* and the distribution of volunteering across service fields in advanced democracies. Like Inglehart in his chapter, they too find no evidence to support the popular view that levels of participation are declining. The main aim of the paper, however, is to explain differences between countries in terms of the size of and engagement in the voluntary sector. The arguments come from the "social origins theory" of the nonprofit sector, which posits that volunteering is dependent on social and institutional forces. Volunteering will be more common and widespread in countries with more developed non-profit organizational structures because such structures are instrumental in recruiting and maintaining volunteer participation. It is also argued that volunteering offers a means of achieving certain goals, ranging from self-actualization and enhancement of the quality of life, to the production and delivery of public goods. The importance of these different goals will depend on social policies, the political cultures and developmental paths of a country.

The reasons why people volunteer are explored further in Chapter 6. Paul Reed and Kevin Selbee investigate whether Canadian volunteers differ from nonvolunteers in Canada in terms of their values and ideals, and if so, whether the value patterns of the volunteers constitute a distinctive ethos. The question here is not whether volunteers display different behaviors compared with nonvolunteers—which was the main issue in Virginia Hodgkinson's chapter—but whether volunteers have distinctive value profiles. The authors rely on data from a national survey of 2,300 Canadians, covering almost 100 different values and ideals. While the findings show that volunteers do not differ much from nonvolunteers on most of the values and ideals included in the survey, remarkable differences are nevertheless found on certain values and ideas, and this applies not only for volunteers engaged in direct helping activities, but also for people who are charitable donors. The characteristic value profile that distinguishes volunteers from non-volunteers is described as "a syndrome of generosity mixed with civic engagement and concern for the common good" (p. 103). For the authors it is clear that values, perceptions, attitudes, and beliefs are among the key factors in a strong "helping and caring" syndrome.

Jacqueline Butcher questions the benefits of such a syndrome in Chapter 7. From a humanistic perspective, she focuses on the relationship between volunteers and the recipients of their voluntary efforts. She argues that it is the service attitude of the volunteer at the beginning and during the course of the relationship with the recipient that sets the tone and climate of the relationship, and that often determines the results. Here again, then, the importance of values is stressed; a service-oriented attitude on the part of the volunteer creates a climate of trust and results in a more satisfactory and productive relationship between volunteer and recipient. Since her analyses are confined to Mexico, she rightly asks whether the tradition of paternalism that appears to be a dominant cultural trait of Mexican people may have affected the volunteer-recipient relationship. In this respect,

Butcher is aware of the fact that in Mexico, as in other Latin American countries, volunteering is not considered to be part of the national culture and that it occurs mainly in informal settings, where it is seen not so much as a voluntary action but rather as part of a moral and/or religious obligation. However, as she argues, in contemporary Mexican society the situation with regard to voluntary organizations has changed. The government no longer mistrusts them and accepts them as part of society; moreover, globalization has led to an increase in the number of new groups and organizations. According to Butcher, the changing climate with regard to voluntary organizations is mainly due to the democratic changes that have taken place in Mexico.

Changes toward democracy have also taken place in the countries of Central and Eastern Europe. The collapse of communism and socialism and the rise of democracy have resulted in significant changes in voluntary activities in these countries. Although voluntarism existed in the socialist period, the character of volunteering has changed dramatically. This becomes clear from the contribution by Stanislovas Jucknevicius and Aida Savicka, who in Chapter 8 describe the transformation of volunteering in postcommunist countries in general and Lithuania in particular. They investigate the assumed decline of forced volunteering in communist organizations and the rise of voluntarism in new organizations and based on people's own free will. Using the survey data from the European Values Study for 1990–1991 and 1999–2000, they did indeed find evidence of this development, though the extent to which it is taking place is uneven across Central and Eastern Europe. They argue that the success or failure of the process of democratization and the establishment of civil society are crucial factors in this respect.

This also becomes clear in Chapter 9, in which Malina Voicu and Bogdan Voicu focus on volunteering in Romania. They are not very optimistic about the likelihood of an increase in voluntarism in Romanian society, precisely because of the reasons cited by Jucknevicius and Savicka in Chapter 8. Romania appears as a country where there is still a high degree of state control and where individual initiatives are not strongly encouraged and supported; this may explain why Romanian figures on volunteering appear so low within Europe. Romanians simply lack the conditions and opportunities to become engaged in voluntary work, and the structure of Romanian society appears to be not very conducive to the development of voluntary organizations. Romanian society does resemble that of other European countries as regards the individual determinants of volunteering. This means that the low level of education of most Romanians, coupled with high levels of poverty, are also not very conducive to the development of an active voluntary sector in Romania.

In the opposite corner of Europe, Norway shows a strongly developed voluntary sector. In Chapter 10, Dag Wollebæk and Per Selle argue that the Norwegian sector is undergoing fundamental changes; "idea-based" popular mass movements are gradually being replaced by leisure or interest oriented organizations.

The local and national levels of organizations are gradually becoming independent of each other. The chapter attempts to shed some light on the dynamics of these processes by examining the impact of generation, a concept subsequently applied both to organizations and individuals. The empirical results show that traditional values often associated with voluntary organizations, such as democracy and unpaid work, appeal to a much lesser degree to young people than to adults and the elderly. Instead, their outlook is more result and activity-oriented. This matches the trend in the new generation of local voluntary associations, which are more specialized, less ideological and demand less from their members than the movements that previously dominated the sector. These developments are linked to a general process of individualization, which manifests itself most strongly in those who are looking at the world in a new way.

The relationship between volunteering and politics and democracy is the main topic of the final two chapters. In Chapter 11, Loek Halman focuses on the attitudes of volunteers. Voluntary organizations are regarded as the bridges between citizens and the state and are considered as being of the utmost importance for a society to become and remain democratic. However, does this imply that people who are engaged in voluntary activities are more democratic than people who are not? This is one of the research questions investigated in this chapter. Another deals with differences and similarities in the degree to which the different European populations are involved in voluntary work. Explanatory factors may be the opportunities available and the number of voluntary organizations present in a society, economic development, religiosity, and democratic experiences in the recent past. A third issue concerns recent trends in volunteering in Europe. The chapter explores whether these trends could perhaps be due to an age effect. The analyses are based on survey data from the most recent European Values Study (EVS), while the longitudinal analyses also include data from the two previous waves of the Study. The general conclusion from the analyses is that volunteering and democracy are not necessarily mutually connected.

This is also the conclusion of Nina Eliasoph in Chapter 12, but this time based on ethnographic studies of the interaction in volunteers groups in the United State. The way in which people in these groups talk about social problems and approach politics raises serious doubts about the widely accepted idea that volunteering and involvement in voluntary associations naturally broadens citizens' horizons and strengthen their involvement in politics. Volunteers in the groups described in this chapter often avoid political discussions in public. In more private spheres, a lively discussion may occur, but once the scene turns public, silence prevails. The collective action context of "ordinary like-minded citizens who can make a difference" appears to be the main explanatory factor. In order to achieve something, volunteers believe they have to prevent overt disagreement, and to do so they prefer to avoid political discussions. This aversion to controversies and politics, however, undermines public spirit and public discourse.

Although the chapters in this book cover a wide spectrum of topics and issues related to volunteering in contemporary society, we believe they make clear that there is still much to do in order to gain a better understanding of volunteering, both as regards its variation across cultures and in terms of its diverse meanings and functions for the individual. Present research on volunteering is highly fragmented and often too one-sidedly focused on policy questions. The chapters in this book attempt to do justice to volunteering as a basic element of the organizing of voluntary social links and social capital in modern society, and place volunteering in a broader theoretical and empirical framework of value shifts, civil society, and political democracy.

REFERENCES

Almond, G.A., & Verba, S. ([1963] 1989). *The civic culture*. Newbury Park, CA: Sage.

Arai, S.M. (2000). Typology of volunteers for a changing sociopolitical context. *Loisir et Société / Society and Leisure*, 23, 2: 327–352.

Bales, K. (1996). Measuring the propensity to volunteer. *Social policy & Administration*, 30, 206–226.

Clary, E.G., Snyder, M., Ridge, R.D., Copeland, J., Stukas, A.A., Haugen, J., & Miene, P. (1998). Understanding and assessing the motivations of volunteers. *Journal of Personality and Social Psychology*, 74, 1516–1530.

Cnaan, R.A., & Goldberg-Glen, R.S. (1991). Measuring motivation to volunteer in human services. *Journal of Applied Behavioral Science*, 27, 3: 269–285.

Cnaan, R.A., Handy, F., & Wadsworth, M. (1996). Defining who is a volunteer. *Nonprofit and Voluntary Sector Quarterly*, 25, 364–383.

Dekker, P. (2002). On the prospects of volunteering in civil society. *Voluntary Action*, 4, 3: 31–48.

Dekker, P., & Uslaner, E.M. (Eds.) (2001). *Social capital and participation in everyday life*. London & New York: Routledge.

Dingle, A. (Ed.) (2001). *Measuring volunteering*. Washington, DC: Independent Sector and United Nations Volunteers.

Enquete-Kommission (2002). *Bürgerschaftliches Engagement* [civic engagement]. Opladen, (GE): Leske + Budrich.

Fishbein, M., & Ajzen, I. (1975). *Belief, attitude, intention and behavior*. Reading, MA.: Addison-Wesley Publishing Company.

Galston, W., & Levine, P. (1997). America's civic condition. *The Brookings Review*, Fall, 23–26.

Gaskin, K., & Davis Smith, J. (1995). *A new civic Europe?* London: Volunteer Centre UK.

Govaart, M., van Daal, H.J., Münz, A., & Keesom, J. (Eds.) (2001). *Volunteering worldwide*. Utrecht (NL): NIZW.

Halman, L., & De Moor, R. (1994). Comparative research on values. In: P. Ester, L. Halman & R. de Moor (Eds.), *The Individualizing Society*, pp. 21–36. Tilburg (NL): Tilburg University Press.

Hustinx, L. (2001). Individualism and new styles of youth volunteering. *Voluntary Action*, 3, 2, 57–76.

Kearney, J. (2001). The values and basic principles of volunteering. *Voluntary Action*, 3, 3, 63–86.

Lyons, M., & Hocking, S. (2000). Australia's highly committed volunteers. In: J. Warburton & M. Oppenheimer (Eds.), *Volunteers and volunteering*. Sydney: The Federation Press.

Lyons, M., Wijkstrom, P., & Clary, G. (1998). Comparative studies of volunteering. *Voluntary Action*, 1, 1, 45–54.

Macionis, J., & Plummer, K. (1998). *Sociology*. Upper Saddle River, NJ: Prentice-Hall.

Parker, I. (2000). Obedience. *Granta*, 71: 99–125.

Pearce, J.L. (1993). *Volunteers*. London & New York: Routledge.

Price, B. (2002) Social capital and factors affecting civic engagement as reported by leaders of voluntary associations. *The Social Science Journal*, 39, 119–127.

Putnam, R.D. (2000). *Bowling alone*. New York: Simon & Schuster.

Stebbins, R.A. (1996). Volunteering: A serious leisure perspective. *Nonprofit and Voluntary Sector Quarterly*, 25, 211–224.

Wilson, J. (2000). Volunteering. *Annual Review of Sociology*, 26: 215–240.

Wuthnow, R. (1991). *Acts of compassion*. Princeton, NJ: Princeton University Press.

Wuthnow, R. (1998). *Loose connections*. Cambridge, MA: Harvard University Press.

Chapter 2

All in the Eyes of the Beholder?
Perceptions of Volunteering Across
Eight Countries

LUCAS C. P. M. MEIJS, FEMIDA HANDY, RAM A. CNAAN,
JEFFREY L. BRUDNEY, UGO ASCOLI, SHREE RANADE,
LESLEY HUSTINX, SUZANNE WEBER, AND IDIT WEISS

INTRODUCTION

Volunteers are the cornerstone of the voluntary sector. While we are accustomed to this assumption, too little systematic work has been carried out to define the term "volunteer." Often too many different activities and situations are aggregated into this concept (Lyons, Wijkstrom, & Clary, 1998; Cnaan, Handy, & Wadsworth, 1996; Scheier, 1980; Smith, 1995; Tremper, Seidman & Tufts, 1994; Vineyard, 1993). People presented with seemingly similar examples of volunteering perceive them differently as volunteering, for unknown reasons. The same people may perceive volunteer activities differently depending on their own context or reference. Especially for international comparative studies, a better understanding of the definition and even more important perception of volunteering is needed.

Cnaan and his colleagues (Cnaan & Amrofell, 1995; Cnaan et al., 1996; Handy et al., 2000) have advanced the study of volunteering by documenting the scope and variability of the concept. Based on a comprehensive literature review, these authors showed that most definitions of volunteers are based on four key dimensions: free will, the availability of tangible rewards (remuneration), formal organization, and proximity to the beneficiaries. Furthermore, their conceptual and empirical analysis suggests that the public perception of the term volunteer is the outcome of people's conception of the net-cost of any given volunteer situation, which they define as total costs minus total benefits to the volunteer.

In this chapter we analyze cross-cultural differences in public perception of volunteering. Cultural and local attitudes toward volunteering likely differ across regions. Salamon and Sokolowski (see Chapter 5) analyze volunteering in a cross-national study in 24 countries. They make it clear that the amount of volunteering and the (organizational) context of volunteering is different between countries based upon the social origin of the nonprofit sector. This can lead to a different perception of who is a volunteer. Dekker (2002) describes a difference on the level of language and words. Dekker asserts that volunteering in the USA and UK context refers to mostly unpaid labor while "ideellt arbete" in Sweden means doing something extra for your association. The German "Ehrenamt" relates mostly to being a board member or being involved in the legal system. According to Dekker this leads to different kinds of volunteering style in the context of unpaid work or active membership.

To examine cross-cultural differences in the perception of volunteering, we use a questionnaire with 50 items depicting situations of unpaid work. This questionnaire was developed by Handy et al. (2000) to test the notion of net-cost as an explanation of the public perception of volunteering. The questionnaire now has been used in eight countries. Although the cross-cultural soundness of the questions may be challenged, the findings are interesting enough to recommend further research.

THE QUESTIONNAIRE

To test the variations in public perception of who is a volunteer, Handy et al. (2000) both adapted and extended the 23-item instrument used by Cnaan et al. (1996). The original 23-item survey was expanded with 27 new items deliberately and specifically developed to test a net-cost hypothesis regarding perceptions of volunteering (see Handy et al., 2000). The net-cost hypothesis means that the public perception of volunteering will be based primarily on the perception of the net-cost incurred by the individual—broadly defined as all costs minus all benefits associated with the volunteering activity. The individual incurring higher net-cost is likely to be perceived as "more" of a volunteer than someone with a lower net-cost. Handy et al. (2000) show that the higher the net-cost to the activity, the higher the individually perceived contribution, and consequently the higher the publicly perceived valuation of the volunteer.

Each item in the questionnaire uses a five-category Likert-type scale ranging from (1) not a volunteer to (5) definitely a volunteer. The questionnaires were self-administered and took 12–15 minutes to complete. To make the tables easier to read, the 1 to 5 scale has been transformed into a 0–100 scale.

In each region the questionnaire was transliterated to meet language requirements and social conventions for relevance to the volunteering scenarios presented. For example, in India the notion of volunteering "to impress a date" did not fit the cultural norms and was substituted with "to make personal connections." Another example that required attention was the notion of corporate volunteering, which was unknown in the Netherlands, Belgium, India, and Italy. Despite careful considerations of cultural nuances, we are not certain that the items developed are identical across countries. It should be acknowledged that the questionnaire was not developed specifically for cross-cultural comparison.

Our samples in each of the regions were samples of convenience. We attempt to compensate for the lack of randomness by having a large, heterogeneous sample (see Handy et al. 2000 regarding details of the data collection for the USA, Canada, India, and the Netherlands). Data for the USA (the two USA samples from Philadelphia and Georgia are merged in this chapter), Canada, India, the Netherlands, and India were collected in 1998. These data were used for testing the net-cost concept of volunteering. Additional data for Germany, Israel, and Belgium were collected in 1999 and 2000. These data are included in the present cross-cultural analysis.

A CROSS-CULTURAL ANALYSIS

In this chapter we analyze the data from eight countries in three steps. In the first step, we test the concept of volunteering as it is understood in the different regions by comparing the overall means. The second step is a more in-depth analysis of the rank order of the 50 items with respect to the perception of volunteering. We examine similarities and differences in the top and bottom ranks, corresponding to who is definitely perceived as a volunteer and who is not. The third step focuses on the largest differences between some regions in mean scores on items, an analysis that yields provocative differences by regions.

First we present the scores for the entire sample and the rank orderings for the different countries (Table 2.1). In this table the top five situations for every region appear in boldface, and the bottom five situations are in italics.

The Concept of Volunteering in the Regions

The first analysis simply looks at the overall mean of all of the volunteer scenarios (items) for each region (see the last row in Table 2.1). We present the mean for each of the fifty items in each region—an overall "volunteering perception score"—which provides a clue to the concept in these countries. The mean for the entire 50-item list hovers around 50 for all countries. The difference between the means across countries is not significant (0.05 level), except for the USA versus Italy. The means for the different items (the second column in Table 2.1) show

Table 2.1. Perceptions of Who Is a Volunteer Across Eight Countries

	Mean score[a]	Ranking[b]								
		All	CA	GE	IL	US	IN	IT	BE	NL
A teenager who volunteers to serve a meal at the soup kitchen for the homeless	94	1	1	2	2	3	3	1	3	4
A teacher who volunteers to serve a meal at the soup kitchen for the homeless	94	2	2	1	5	2	4	2	5	3
An adult who offer his/her time to be a Big Brother/Sister	93	3	4	5	1	1	2	7	1	2
An IBM executive who volunteers to serve a meal at the soup kitchen for the homeless	91	4	5	3	4	4	10	4	6	6
The medical doctor who volunteers to serve a meal at the soup kitchen for the homeless	90	5	6	4	6	5	9	5	7	7
A person who donates blood to a local hospital	90	6	8	11	8	9	1	3	4	15
An adult who volunteers to teach English as a second language to new immigrants	90	7	3	9	3	6	6	8	8	5
An unemployed person who volunteers to teach English as a second language to new immigrants	88	8	7	12	7	7	7	9	9	8
A childless adult who wants to engage with children offers his/her time to be a Big Brother/Sister	88	9	9	14	15	8	5	6	2	1
A member of Alcoholics Anonymous (AA) who leads an AA meeting every week	77	10	15	6	18	16	12	10	10	16
An IBM executive who serves on the board of a local library	77	11	11	16	9	10	18	12	14	11
A teenager who serves on the board of a local library as a student representative	76	12	10	13	14	11	17	16	12	13
The medical doctor who serves on the board of a local library	76	13	12	15	10	12	16	13	18	10
A teacher who serves on the board of a local library	72	14	16	17	11	13	19	14	17	9
The teenager who presents a program on youth leadership to an audience of peers at a religious youth conference	72	15	14	8	20	17	21	15	16	17

The home owner who helps create a crime watch group to safeguard his own neighborhood	71	16	13	18	16	14	32	21	11	14
The person who participates in a pharmaceutical study, to determine the effectiveness of a new drug	71	17	17	30	13	15	20	11	13	19
A member of a community sport club who leads a group of joggers every week	71	18	18	7	12	20	13	18	15	12
The person who is ill with Cystic Fibrosis, who participates in a pharmaceutical study, to determine the effectiveness of a new drug in treating the disease	60	19	19	31	23	19	14	17	19	28
An office manager who accompanies his wife to visit seniors in an nursing home	59	20	20	27	24	18	15	22	22	26
A parent who becomes a scout leader because of his/her child desires to be a scout. No one else will lead the troop so the parent agrees, but only as his/her child is involved	58	21	23	10	21	21	43	20	21	18
A child who assist in setting up booths at the volunteer fair because one of his parents is volunteer administrator and asks her/him to help	53	22	22	19	22	22	30	19	31	27
A teenager who offers to program the computer at a nonprofit agency, without pay, in order to establish "resume experience." After three months the teenager plans to quit and apply for a paying job	50	23	21	20	32	23	37	42	20	25
The hourly wage worker who, by his/her own choice. works overtime without pay	46	24	26	37	17	24	8	26	23	37
An office manager who, by his/her own choice. works overtime without pay	43	25	29	42	19	25	11	29	26	45
A teenager who volunteers to serve a meal at the soup kitchen for the homeless in order to impress his date	42	26	24	22	28	30	41	25	29	21
The assistant to the CEO of a local corporation who is volunteer chairperson of the United Way campaign who does the job for his boss	42	27	27	21	38	26	33	24	27	29
The teenager who presents a program on youth leadership to an audience of peers at a religious youth conference with hope to find a suitable date	40	28	33	23	27	36	46	28	25	24
The student who is helping Special Olympics as part of a high school graduation requirement	40	29	31	28	34	27	27	40	24	36

Continued

Table 2.1. (*Continued*)

	Mean score[a]	Ranking[b]								
		All	CA	GE	IL	US	IN	IT	BE	NL
An IBM executive who volunteers to serve a meal at the soup kitchen for the homeless in order to impress his date	40	30	28	24	29	32	49	33	35	20
A teacher who volunteers to serve a meal at the soup kitchen for the homeless in order to impress his date	40	31	25	25	33	31	48	35	34	22
The medical doctor who volunteers to serve a meal at the soup kitchen for the homeless in order to impress his date	39	32	30	26	30	33	44	36	39	23
The student who is doing a community service project as part of a high school graduation requirement	39	33	32	29	35	28	28	43	28	35
A lawyer who provides legal services to a nonprofit organization at half his/her regular time	35	34	38	32	25	35	26	27	44	46
The trainer who does a free workshop for the Breast Cancer Foundation as a marketing device	34	35	34	41	42	29	25	45	40	42
A college student enrolled in the National and Community Service program, who gives his time to Big Brother/Sister and receives a stipend and partial forgiveness of tuition	32	36	37	40	41	38	34	32	30	38
A college student who is enrolled in the National and Community Service program, and doing community service receives a stipend and partial forgiveness of tuition	32	37	40	39	39	39	35	37	36	39
A person who takes care of a spouse's children from a previous marriage (step-parenting)	32	38	43	45	40	46	22	38	32	40
The CEO of a local corporation who is volunteer chairperson of the United Way campaign ad who delegates all the work to the assistant	31	39	35	33	36	43	40	31	45	30
The paid staff person who serves on the board of United Way in a slot that is reserved for his/her agency	31	40	41	43	26	40	23	23	46	49

		CA	GE	IL	US	IN	IT	BE	NL
A teenager who agrees to offer his/her services as an usher at the symphony concert in exchange for a free ticket to the concert	30	41	42	45	41	45	39	38	33
The trainer who does a free workshop for an organization as a marketing device	30	42	36	44	34	29	47	42	43
An IBM executive who is granted a year of social service leave with pay, to become a temporary staff person with a nonprofit organization	29	43	39	31	37	31	44	47	47
The medical doctor who agrees to offer his/her services in case of an emergency at the symphony concert in exchange for a free ticket to the concert	29	44	46	47	44	47	41	37	32
A teacher who agrees to offer his/her services to the symphony orchestra (for three hours) in exchange for a free ticket to the concert	29	45	47	46	42	50	34	33	31
An IBM executive who agrees to offer his/her services on the fund raising of the symphony orchestra in exchange for free tickets	28	46	45	43	47	42	46	41	34
The medical doctor who delivers a research paper at a conference held by the American Medical Association (AMA)	26	47	44	48	48	24	48	43	41
The paid staff person who serves on the board of a nonprofit group in a slot that is reserved for his/her agency	24	48	48	37	45	36	30	49	48
A six-month old baby who accompanies her parents to visit seniors at a nursing home	15	49	49	49	49	39	49	50	44
An accountant charged wit embezzling, who accepts a sentence of 250 hours of community service in lieu of prosecution	11	50	50	55	50	38	50	48	50
Overall mean score per country[a]		55	50	55	56	50	46	54	55

[a] Scores between 0 (not a volunteer) and 100 (definitely a volunteer).
[b] Countries: CA = Canada, GE = Germany, IL = Israel, US = United States, IN = India, IT = Italy, BE = Belgium (the Dutch-speaking part), and NL = the Netherlands.

that the 50 items in the questionnaire seemed to have encompassed situations of clearly volunteering (with the highest score of 94) and a little less clearly situations of not volunteering (with a lowest score of 11). Analyzing the comments from respondents, especially the lower 20 items ("not a volunteer"), demonstrated that many items provoked a reaction. Respondents reacted with low scores to items such as the 6-month-old baby who accompanies her parents to visit seniors at a nursing home and the person who takes care of a spouse's children from a previous marriage (stepparenting).

Top and Bottom Rank Order Analysis

The second analysis examines the rank of the means given to each item within the sample of one region as compared to the samples of the other regions. We investigate whether there are any general trends inherent in the way respondents from all the regions ranked the items. More specifically, we examine whether there are similarities in who is perceived to be at the high end—"Definitely a Volunteer" (means close to 100), and at the low end—"Not a Volunteer" (means close to 0) for all the regions. We argue that if similarities exist, despite the cultural differences, it will enable us to claim that there exists a universal public perception of who is a volunteer.

Across the 50 items, we identify the five items ranked highest among all volunteer 5 scenarios for all regions (bold items in Table 2.1). The common items are:

- A teenager who volunteers to serve a meal at the soup kitchen for the homeless
- A teacher who volunteers to serve a meal at the soup kitchen for the home-less
- An adult who offers his/her time to be a Big Brother or Big Sister (with the exception of Italy)
- An IBM executive who volunteers to serve a meal at the soup kitchen for the homeless (with the exception of India, Belgium and The Netherlands)
- The medical doctor who volunteers to serve a meal at the soup kitchen for the homeless (with the exception of Canada, Israel, India, Belgium, and the Netherlands).

It must be noted that in the regions where these items did not rank among the first 5, they did rank in the first 10 statements. Another noteworthy point is the issue of providing food for homeless people as a clear volunteer activity. The plight of the homeless may be so gripping and understood by diverse peoples that it applies nearly universally across cultures and regions.

A closer look brings us to the first 9 items in the dataset for all regions combined that score more than 87,5, which are perceived as definitely a volunteer.

Analyzing these top 9 rankings for all regions shows that in Canada, the United States, Italy, and Belgium all 9 top items are within their own top 9 but in a different sequence. For three other countries, Israel, India, and the Netherlands, only one item is not the same in their top 9. For Germany the score is 6 out of 9. Thus, there appears to be a relatively large cross-cultural consensus in the public perception of who is considered "definitely a volunteer."

By contrast, some small differences in the top 9 deserve closer scrutiny. Rank order number 9, the childless adult who helps with Big Brother / Big Sister, scores higher in the Netherlands (1) and Belgium (2) but lower in Germany (14) and Israel (15). This probably has to do with the context of the question which in the Netherlands and Belgium was transliterated into "scouting," well known as an all-volunteer organization in these countries. Another difference is donating blood (7) which in the Netherlands (15) and Germany (11) scores lower while in India (1), Italy (3), and Belgium (4) it scores higher. Another exception is the hourly worker who works overtime without pay a situation that ranks 8th in India but is below rank 24 in all other regions.

At the other end of the scale, we examine the five items ranked lowest among all volunteer items for all regions. There is less consensus across the regions for this end of the scale, as shown by the list of exceptions. Overall the lowest five are (these items are underscored in Table 2.1):

- The IBM executive who agrees to offer services at the symphony concert in exchange for a free ticket to the concert (with the exception of Germany (rank order 36 in Table 2.1), Israel (43), India (42), Belgium (41) and The Netherlands (34)
- The doctor who presents a paper at the AMA (with the exception of Canada (44), India (24!), Belgium (43) and The Netherlands (41)
- The paid staff person who serves on the board of a nonprofit group in a slot that is reserved for his/her agency (with the exception of (Israel (37), India (36) and Italy (30)
- The six-month-old baby who accompanies her parents to visit seniors at a nursing home (with the exception of India (39) and the Netherlands (44)
- The accountant charged with embezzling, who accepts community service in lieu of prosecution (with the exception of India (38))

The six-month-old baby and the embezzling accountant were consistently ranked lowest in Canada, Germany, Israel, the United States, Italy, and Belgium (49/50 and 50/50). In addition, in the Netherlands, the embezzling accountant was ranked last, but the baby was ranked 44/50. In India the baby was ranked 39th. These findings indicate that respondents felt that "free-will" and "free choice" are important components in their decision-making concerning who is not a volunteer. The remaining choices indicate that those who receive overt remuneration (monetary or otherwise) are ranked lower as volunteers. With some modest exceptions, this pattern is consistent with the rankings found at the bottom third for all these regions.

In India, the five items ranked lowest include the individual serving at the soup kitchen to impress his/her date and those working at the symphony in exchange for tickets. As the concept of dating in India is not common for adults, "to impress his/her date" was replaced by "to make personal connections." This change may have elicited a lower rating for these individuals in India as "personal connections" is tantamount to volunteering to further oneself socially and economically. If items involving "personal connections" are excluded, the bottom five ranks include all four individuals who agree to offer services at the symphony concert in exchange for a free ticket. A parent who becomes a scout leader because of his/her child is also included in the bottom five rankings. It should be noted that, unlike the case in North America, in India scout leaders are schoolteachers who take on this obligation as part of their required extra-curricular duties for school. Furthermore, scouting meetings take place on school premises. Thus, teachers may be regarded as fulfilling their professional duties and therefore are not considered volunteers. The other three rankings include items ranked lowest in all other regions: the six-month old baby (39/50) and the accountant charged with embezzlement (38/50).

These findings from India suggest that although the cultural context does appear to affect the ranking of a volunteer scenario, it may be through artifacts and socially constructed images. Salamon and Sokolowski describe the social origins in their chapter. The tendency to rank an individual who receives explicit monetary or non-monetary remuneration less as a volunteer found in all other regions operates in India as well.

In the Netherlands, individuals receiving any paid remuneration were ranked least likely to be considered a volunteer. In the bottom five rankings are: the embezzling accountant; the paid staff on the boards of nonprofit organizations; the IBM executive on a year of social service leave with pay; and the lawyer receiving half his regular fee. This listing suggests that receiving any kind of monetary remuneration is the determining factor regarding who is least likely to be considered a volunteer in the Netherlands. This trend holds true for the bottom third of the rankings for the Netherlands.

In the items depicting a volunteer who receives an explicitly stated personal benefit for the volunteering activity, such as tickets to a symphony, differences can also be found. In Canada, Israel, the United States, India, and Italy, these items fall within the last ten (with the exception of the teacher in Italy). In Germany, Belgium and the Netherlands, getting a free ticket in return for volunteering is less problematic. This suggests that individuals who receive explicit personal benefits for their volunteering are considered less likely to be volunteers than those who do not. But there seems to be a cultural bias. In the Netherlands, the norm is that if an

Table 2.2. Comparing Big Brother/Big Sister and Scouting[a]

	Mean score	Ranking								
		All	CA	GE	IL	US	IN	IT	BE	NL
A childless adult who wants to engage with children offers his/her time to be a Big Brother/Sister	88	9	9	14	15	8	5	6	2	1
A parent who becomes a scout leader because of his/her child desires to be a scout. No one else will lead the troop so the parent agrees, but only as long as his/her child is involved	58	21	23	10	21	21	43	20	21	18

[a] Copy of two items from Table 2.1.

individual volunteers for any association, the services of that association should be freely available to that volunteer. In many cases membership dues are exempted. As a result, free symphony tickets are not considered exceptional private benefits to the Dutch volunteer. In the Dutch nonprofit sector there seems to be a much lower correlation between donating time and giving money than in the North American context.

Another example of the influence of receiving something in return for volunteering or the loss of free will can be seen by comparing the two questions on Big Brother/Big Sister and Scouting (Table 2.2). Especially in the Netherlands and Belgium, where "Big Brother/Big Sister" was transliterated into "scouting," the difference in rank order is remarkable. We believe that in the other regions the same reasoning influenced the perception.

Comparing Countries

The third analysis deals with the absolute differences between countries. To analyze the differences between countries we looked at the ten statements with the largest (absolute) difference. This means that these items are perceived as volunteering in one region, while in the other region they are not perceived as volunteering.

The first countries to be compared are the two Northern American regions. Table 2.3 (the comparison of Canada to the United States) shows that the highest difference in means is only 6 on a 0–100 scale. The sum of the (absolute) top-ten differences in means shows that the difference between Canada and the United

Table 2.3. Top Ten Differences between Canada and the United States

Volunteering situations	Difference
The CEO of al local corporation who is volunteer chairperson of the United Way campaign and who delegates all the work to his assistant	6
The paid staff person who serves on the board of a nonprofit group in a slot that is reserved for his/her agency	−6
A teenager who offers to program the computer at a nonprofit agency, without pay, in order to establish "resume experience." After three months the teenager plans to quit and apply for a paying job	6
The hourly wage worker who, by his/her own choice, works overtime without pay	5
A teacher who serves on the board of a local library	−5
A teacher who agrees to offer his/her services to the symphony orchestra (for three hours) in exchange for a free ticket to the concert	−5
An office manager who accompanies his wife to visit seniors in an nursing home	−4
A six-month old baby who accompanies her parents to visit seniors at a nursing home	−4
A childless adult who wants to engage with children offers his/her time to be a Big Brother/Sister	−4
An office manager who, by his/her own choice, works overtime without pay	−4

States is the smallest among all pairs of regions, just 48. Because those countries are considered to be quite similar, such a small difference was expected. The perceptions in the two regions are nearly same.

Comparisons between India and the other regions (Table 2.4) suggest a totally different picture. These differences emphasize sociocultural differences. In India working overtime without pay is seen as volunteering, while serving meals at a soup kitchen to impress a date ("to make personal connections") is not! As explained above, this perception has nothing to do with the act of serving meals but everything to do with impressing a date, because serving meals is considered to be volunteering in India too.

Table 2.4 shows the differences between the means of India and the other regions. A difference of −24.50 regarding the first case between the score of India and that of Canada, indicates that in India the teacher is perceived "less" of a volunteer in comparison to that same teacher in Canada. In India, especially the hourly wage worker and the office manager working overtime without pay, are perceived to be "more" of a volunteer in comparison to the persons in the other mentioned cases, except for Israel. Table 2.4 shows that in the other regions this is certainly not the case. The positive differences in all other regions indicate that in those regions a person working overtime without pay is perceived to be "less" a volunteer as she or he would be in India. This is especially the case for the

Table 2.4. Comparing India to the Other Regions on 8 Situations with Large Differences (mean India – mean other region)

Volunteering situations	CA	GE	IL	US	IT	BE	NL
A teacher who volunteers to serve a meal at the soup kitchen for the homeless in order to impress his date	-24	-31	-24	-22	-6	-17	-45
The medical doctor who volunteers to serve a meal at the soup kitchen for the homeless in order to impress his date	-21	-30	-24	-21	-5	-14	-41
The teenager who present a program on youth leadership to an audience of peers at a religious youth conference with the hope of finding a suitable date	-21	-31	-28	-18	-12	-22	-38
An IBM executive who volunteers to serve a meal at the soup kitchen for the homeless in order to impress his date	-24	-32	-28	-23	-7	-17	-46
An office manager who, by his/her own choice, works overtime without pay	30	48	10	27	41	32	57
The home owner who helps create a crime watch group to safeguard his own neighborhood	-38	-25	-34	-38	-11	-46	-49
A parent who becomes a scout leader because of his/her child desires to be a scout. No on else will lead the troop, so the parent agrees, but only as long as his/her child is involved	-38	-56	-40	-41	-30	-34	-56
The hourly wage worker who, by his/her own choice, works overtime without pay	36	52	14	31	45	35	56

Netherlands and Germany. It seems that they perceive overtime work as part of their paid job. In the United States, the hourly employee working overtime without pay is considered to be "more" of a volunteer than she or he would be in Canada. The opposite is true for the office manager working overtime without pay.

The statistics demonstrate that the differences are especially large with respect to the Netherlands. This would suggest that Dutch people who try to impress a date by volunteering are considered "more" of a volunteer than they would be in India. Apparently they perceive the personal benefit of finding a date not significant enough to consider the person in that situation "less" of a volunteer. This result corresponds to the situation described earlier in which a personal reward, such as symphony orchestra tickets, is included. As in India, the Italian sample view people impressing a date by volunteering "less" a volunteer.

The negative numbers suggest that in all other regions the home owner organizing a crime watch group and the parent becoming a scout leader are considered significantly "more" a volunteer than they are in India. One possible explanation is that such activities are more common in those regions than they are in India.

DISCUSSION AND IMPLICATIONS

The findings from the cultural analysis suggest that across all eight regions, a broad consensus exists regarding who is definitely a volunteer. Although some variation surfaced regarding who is least likely to be considered a volunteer, the findings show that remuneration and less free will have a definite negative impact on people's perception of who is a volunteer across all regions. But also contextual factors can play a role as well. Unfamiliarity with the volunteering option in Scouting in India or unfamiliarity with the concept of corporate volunteering outside the Northern American regions, leads to a low perception of volunteering in that sample.

An additional factor concerns expectations that are prevalent in one region yet manifested not at all in another. Doing something that is unexpected, such as accepting sentences of community service or working overtime without pay in India are seen as volunteering in that context. The issue of social origin of the perception of volunteering needs more research. There also seems to be social biases to the "perks" of volunteering that are acceptable. Especially in Germany, Belgium, and the Netherlands there are fewer problems with accepting free tickets. Perhaps this finding can be explained by the difference between perceiving volunteering as unpaid labor rather than as active membership, as described by Dekker (2002).

The presence of free choice and free will turn out to be important factors in the perception of volunteering. But there seems to be something more at play when these principles are violated. The ranking of a few activities that depict volunteer work when there is no free will is illustrative. For example, the assistant to the CEO and the high school students who were required to provide community service in order to graduate were ranked at the middle. Being forced to do the work indicates no free will in the choice of the activity and hence very little or no personal valuation of public benefits associated with the specific activity undertaken. However, ranking of these individuals in the middle indicates that these individuals are still indeed perceived as volunteers. Handy et al. (2000) state that this finding strongly supports the fact that the public assesses the individual's net-cost as a means to determine who is more or less a volunteer, and this may override free will or free choice.

Other examples of the absence of free will and free choice are respectively, the six-month-old baby and the accountant charged with embezzling. These examples are on the lower end of the item list.

By contrast, the clearly defined monetary and nonmonetary benefits received from the volunteering activity did play a crucial role in how the individual was perceived as a volunteer, suggesting a cultural theme. We are not able to say much about motives for volunteering that are not explicit. We assume that most volunteers are not purely altruistic, and acknowledge the fact that they benefit from the volunteering experience (or else they would cease the activity). However, for an individual to be perceived as a volunteer, the perceived costs should clearly outweigh the benefits, and the benefits should not be too explicit.

Despite such nuances, the net-cost concept as proposed by Handy et al. (2000) serves as the common denominator of all four dimensions of volunteering identified by Cnaan et al. (1996): free will, availability of rewards, formal organization, and proximity to the beneficiaries. It seems to us that this application of net-cost to understanding volunteering is helpful in defining who is not a volunteer and who is perceived as more of a volunteer. The evidence of this analysis shows that this concept applies in many countries and cultures.

This cross-cultural analysis makes clear that on the level of concrete situations of unpaid work the differences in perception can be large. A simple, culturally biased questionnaire to determine (and quantify) if people volunteer or not will not be very useful. There may also be a lesson in these findings for multinational nonprofit organizations. The way that they involve volunteers in their home country may not be the way they should involve volunteers in other countries. Meijs and Hoogstad (2001) describe the differences between a US/UK program management model of volunteering versus a European membership management model which treats volunteers in different ways. Membership management uses existing volunteers to deal with new challenges. By contrast, program management pursues specific goals and tasks, and in order to do this, recruits volunteers and puts them to work. In national organizations, membership management results in local branches that carry out the same activities as the national body, while program management leads to national organizations with local branches (if any) that are much more diverse and maybe not even linked. The membership management approach leads to a blurring the difference between members and volunteers even in service delivery organizations such as the Red Cross, while the program management only recognizes volunteers (not members).

REFERENCES

Adams, K. (1985). Investing in volunteers. *Conserve Neighborhoods, 47,* 1–15.
Brudney, J.L., & Stringer, G.E. (1998). Higher education in volunteer administration. In: M. O'Neill & K. Fletcher (Eds.), *Nonprofit Management Education: U.S. and World Perspectives* (pp. 95–109). Westport, CT: Greenwood/ Praeger.
Cnaan, R.A., & Amrofell, L.M. (1994). Mapping volunteer activity. *Nonprofit and Voluntary Sector Quarterly, 23,* 335–351.
Cnaan, R.A., Handy, F., & Wadsworth, M. (1996). Defining who is a volunteer. *Nonprofit and Voluntary Sector Quarterly, 25,* 364–383.
Dekker, P. (2002). On the prospects of volunteering in civil society. *Voluntary Action, 4,* 31–48.
Handy, F., Cnaan, R.A., Brudney, J.L., Ascoli, U., Meijs, L.C.P.M., & Ranade, S. (2000). Public perception of "Who is a volunteer?" *Voluntas, 11,* 45–65.
Lyons, M., Wijkstrom, P., & Clary, G. (1998). Comparative studies of volunteering. *Voluntary Action, 1,* 45–54.
McCurley, S.H., & Vesuvio, D. (1985). Brief response: Who is a volunteer. *Voluntary Action leadership,* Summer, 14–15.
Meijs, L.C.P.M., & Hoogstad, E. (2001). New ways of managing volunteers. *Voluntary Action, 3,* 41–61.
Scheier, I.H. (1980). *Exploring volunteer space.* Boulder, CO: Volunteer: The National Center for Citizen Involvement.
Shure, R. (1991). Volunteering: Continuing expansion of the definition and a practical application of altruistic motivation. *The Journal of Volunteer Administration, 9,* 36–41.
Smith, D.H. (1994). Determinants of voluntary association participation and volunteering. *Nonprofit and Voluntary Sector Quarterly, 23,* 243–263.
Stebbins, R.A. (1996). Volunteering: A serious leisure perspective. *Nonprofit and Voluntary Sector Quarterly, 25,* 211–224.
The President's task force on private sector initiatives (1982). *Volunteers: A valuable resource.* Washington, D.C.: Author.
Tremper, C., Seidman, A., & Tufts, S. (1994). *Legal barriers to volunteer service.* Washington, D.C.: Nonprofit Risk Management Center.
Van Til, J. (1988). *Mapping the third sector.* Washington, D.C.: The Foundation Center.
Vineyard, S. (1993). *Megatrends and volunteerism.* Downers Grove, IL: Heritage Hearts.

Chapter 3

Volunteering in Global Perspective

Virginia A. Hodgkinson

Volunteering time for a variety of purposes or caring and sharing has been a part of most societies throughout human history. The teachings of most major religions have supported care of the elderly, widows and orphans, and poor and otherwise dependent individuals. While most societies know these activities are ongoing along with other mutually supportive activities designed to build and support community, until recently, little attention has been paid to the role and contributions of volunteers. Data on volunteering is not regularly collected by governments, as is employment data. Although there is growing evidence of the contributions volunteers make to communities and society, there are few regular studies to document such assertions (Clotfelter, 1999). Practitioners assert that volunteers help to solve social and community problems, build social solidarity, and through organized citizens groups help to redress social wrongs, change public policy, and improve the quality of life of communities and nations. One of the purposes of the United Nations Year of Volunteers in 2001 was intended to address this information gap about volunteers and to encourage nations to conduct surveys of their volunteers and their activities.

Since the end of the Cold War, more attention is being paid to the development and preservation of democracy. Governments, including the United Nations, produce statistics on the roles and contributions of the government and market sectors to society, but until very recently, little has been known about the contributions of citizens to society. We are indebted to our eastern and central European colleagues for introducing the term "civil society" by which they meant that public space in societies, generally democratic societies, between government and the market where citizens could debate ideas, serve various causes, research, engage in political and social action, advocate and or protest, sing in choirs, associate in diverse kinds of organizations, serve others in need, educate, recreate, and generally participate and contribute to the life of their communities.

In its statement on the role of volunteering in social development, the Commission for Social Development of the United Nations Economic and Social Council stated:

> Volunteering constitutes an enormous reservoir of skills, energy and local knowledge which can assist Governments in carrying out more targeted, efficient, participatory and transparent public programs and policies. However, it is unusual for volunteering to be recognized as a strategic resource that can be positively influenced by public policy and even rarer for it to be factored into national and international development strategies. . . . The International Year of Volunteers (2001) offers a unique opportunity in bridging the gap between the acknowledgment of a long-standing tradition on the one hand, and a recognition of its potential as a major asset for promoting social development on the other.[1]

What do we know about volunteers in various nations? The first part of this chapter is devoted to an overview of volunteering globally using recent survey findings from the European Values Survey data and the World Values Survey data (EVS/WVS). This overview will address the rate and scope of volunteering in various countries and patterns of volunteering in those countries related to level of income and freedom ratings. Then the chapter will explore various characteristics of volunteers compared with non-volunteers in four categories: (1) religious activity, (2) membership, (3) social networks, and (4) political engagement.

THE RATE AND SCOPE OF VOLUNTEERING IN VARIOUS COUNTRIES

In an era of globalization and democratization taking place in many nations around the world, many governments have realized that they alone cannot provide all services and that citizen participation and initiative is important in the provision of many services, in maintaining community, and in building mutual trust and social solidarity. What once was invisible—volunteering or the voluntary gift of time to a variety of causes to serve public and social purposes—is rapidly being recognized as the glue that helps hold societies together and as an additional resource of use in solving social and community problems.

---

[1] Report of the Commission for Social Development, December 2000. United Nations publication, Sales No. E/CN.5/32001/6 Annex, p. 3–4.

There is growing evidence that nonprofit and voluntary organizations and activities are rapidly increasing around the world. Lester M. Salamon (1994), director of the Johns Hopkins Comparative Nonprofit Sector Project, has argued that we are in the midst of a "global associational revolution" that is one of the important characteristics of societies in the late twentieth century as the development of the powerful nation-state was in the late nineteenth century. He, along with colleagues in many countries is mapping this sector and more recently volunteers and their value in various economies. Such an effort was started early in the 1980s in the United States with the first publication of *Dimensions of the Independent Sector* (now the *Nonprofit Almanac*) in 1985 (see, for example, Hodgkinson & Weitzman, 1996b).

In another effort, scholars have collected data on membership and volunteering in the European Values Surveys (EVS) since the late 1970s under the auspices of a foundation, the European Value Systems Study Group which is composed of a group of academics from various European nations. The 1999–2000 EVS surveys are coordinated from Tilburg University. The World Values Surveys, which built upon the EVS, covered countries outside of Europe and are coordinated by the University of Michigan. The first global study was carried out in 1991 in coordination with the EVS survey. Since then, WVS waves were carried out in 1995–1997 and the most recent wave in 1999–2002. From a total of 26 countries in Europe and North and South America in 1981, the 1999–2002 waves of the EVS/WVS surveys will eventually have data from 73 nations covering over 80 percent of the world's population. In the current survey conducted by both EVS and WVS (circa 1999–2002), 23 new countries were added. The data in this overview are from those 47 countries whose data collection has been completed from the 1999–2002 surveys. The questionnaire in the EVS/WVS survey included a few questions on membership in organizations and volunteering. This is one of the few comparative survey efforts covering so many countries in different regions of the world. The questions in the survey related to membership and volunteering were quite limited. For example, no questions were asked related to the amount of time people spent volunteering; nor what they did when they volunteered. The list of types of organizations and activities for volunteers provided in these surveys were determined before there was a serious attempt to classify volunteer activity. As such, there is little comparability with more in depth studies on volunteering, such as those in the United States (see Hodgkinson & Weitzman, 1996a) and some surveys on giving and volunteering completed in the Johns Hopkins Comparative Nonprofit Sector Project (Salamon et al., 1999). However, the World Values surveys are a rich source of data for researchers on changing social and political values covering countries on all six continents, thus giving broad coverage on volunteer and membership rates. Furthermore, in the 1999–2002 wave, an additional question was added related to social capital.

DEFINING VOLUNTEERING

What is the definition of volunteering? Definitions are important, because in some countries, such as the United States, there are programs, such as the Peace Corps and AmeriCorps, in which a small stipend is paid during the volunteer period for living expenses. Additionally, in both programs a small grant is given at the end of service that can be put towards education. While these programs are very important, and results show that people who enter these programs do continue to actively volunteer after completing these programs, their service is not considered volunteering in the purest sense (Brown, 1999). Volunteering means conducting work for no pay. It is, however, acceptable for volunteers to have their out-of-pocket expenses, such as travel and meals, paid while doing this work. Paying for such expenses allows people with limited financial resources to participate. Another characteristic of volunteering is that individuals give their time freely; they are not required to volunteer. And finally, people who volunteer provide benefits to others, not simply to themselves or to their direct family members and/or relatives. In other words, volunteering can be done for friends, the community, the environment, the school, etc.

According to a new toolkit prepared for the United Nations, there are four types of volunteering: The first is mutual aid which includes self-help groups such as Alcoholics Anonymous, or community groups in countries like India that jointly manage resources such as water or forests. The second type is philanthropy or service to others or the community as a whole. This type of volunteering involves activities like tutoring or mentoring, teaching or caring for children. Much of this volunteering is done through voluntary organizations. The third type of volunteering is campaigning and advocacy. Examples of these volunteer activities include people who advocate for a variety of causes to save the environment, or to get legislation passed on a variety of issues such as to help people with disabilities or to increase public housing, or to ban land mines. And the fourth type of volunteering is participation, which includes such activities as serving on committees, as representatives to local governments, or as members of commissions trying to find options to solve community problems. So the range of volunteering is very broad (Dingle, 2001). The question related to volunteering in the EVS/WVS is also broad to reflect the various kinds of activities including grassroots local activities; in the EVS/WVS survey, volunteering is defined as doing work voluntarily for no pay. This definition is most commonly used by scholars (Wilson, 2000).

VOLUNTEER RATES BY NATION

In order to develop volunteering rates among the adult population in 47 countries, an unduplicated count of individuals who reported volunteering was calculated from the question asked about volunteering by various activities. Total volunteers were calculated by summing an unduplicated count of volunteers from each of the separate volunteer activities included in the questionnaire. Table 3.1 shows the percentage of volunteers by nations within geographical regions from weighted samples in the EVS/WVS 1999–2002. As can be seen, in Western Europe, the rate of volunteering ranged from 54 percent in Sweden to 12 percent in Portugal. The northern European countries and Great Britain had the highest rates of volunteer activity in Europe.

In the transitional democracies of Eastern Europe and Russia, the highest rates of volunteering were found in Slovakia (49 percent), the Czech Republic (30 percent), and Slovenia (25 percent). In countries where the transition to democracy has been difficult, volunteer rates were much lower: 7 percent in Russia and 10 percent in Serbia. There are a few explanations for the variation in rates of volunteering in Eastern and Central European countries. Firstly, these countries had different histories previous to their take over by the Soviet Union after World War II. In countries where there was more of an historical attachment to Europe, with its tradition of citizen involvement and philanthropy, such as Slovakia and the Czech Republic, there are have higher rates of volunteering, and these countries have moved more quickly to establish democracy and market economies. Second, when these countries were part of the Soviet Union, citizens were required to volunteer. Therefore, another reason for lower rates of volunteering in some Eastern European countries is that citizens feel free not to volunteer. For many of these citizens, volunteering is associated with required volunteering under communism (Kuti, 1996; Salamon et al., 1999).

In South America, Chile had the highest rate of volunteering, 43 percent, while Argentina has a much lower rate at 22 percent. In Asia, over 55 percent of the adult populations in Hong Kong and the Philippines volunteered. The rate in China was 77 percent, but this is because the population is expected to volunteer by the government. In another Asian nation, Japan, the volunteer rate was much lower at 16 percent. In North America, the United States had a volunteer rate of 66 percent, Canada 47 percent and, Mexico 36 percent. In Africa, both the Central African Republic and South Africa had high rates of volunteering at 75 percent and 59 percent respectively.

One can theorize that the wide variation in volunteer rates has to do with culture, national history, religious background, or economic situation, but the data are uneven. The volunteer rates of various nations cannot be fully explained by any one of these variables with much consistency (Salamon & Anheier, 1998). Volunteer rates are very high in the Philippines, a predominantly Catholic country with high participation rates even though it is a poor country. On the other hand, Japan, a very wealthy country, has a low level of volunteering, for, until recently, citizens depended on the state for most leadership in services and were restricted by the state to form voluntary associations. The United

Table 3.1. Volunteers as Percentage of the Adult Population by Country

	All volunteers[a]	Volunteers working in the field of			
		Social welfare[b]	Religion	Environment	Sports
North America					
United States	66	36	37	8	8
Canada	47	21	18	4	13
Mexico	36	12	20	3	7
South America					
Chile	43	12	17	2	12
Argentina	22	6	9	1	3
Western Europe					
Sweden	54	15	23	4	17
Britain	43	33	6	8	4
Finland	37	14	7	2	13
Denmark	33	9	3	2	14
Belgium	32	12	6	3	8
Iceland	32	13	5	1	11
Netherlands	31	12	11	n.a.	n.a.
Greece	31	13	6	5	9
Ireland	28	10	10	1	13
Austria	28	7	7	2	8
Italy	25	9	7	2	6
France	23	7	3	1	9
West Germany	21	4	4	1	6
Northern Ireland	20	7	9	1	3
East Germany	15				
Spain	15	4	4	1	4
Portugal	12	3	4	0	5
Eastern Europe					
Slovakia	49	14	13	2	14
Czech Republic	30	11	3	3	10
Slovenia	25	9	5	3	9
Croatia	23	5	6	2	7
Montenegro	19	6	2	3	5
Latvia	18	3	4	1	6
Belarus	18	4	4	2	1
Estonia	16	4	3	1	4
Bulgaria	15	4	2	1	4
Romania	14	2	4	1	1
Hungary	14	5	5	2	3
Poland	12	3	4	1	2
Lithuania	12	2	4	0	3
Ukraine	12	2	2	0	1

Continued

Table 3.1. Continued

	All volunteers[a]	Volunteers working in the field of			
		Social welfare[b]	Religion	Environment	Sports
Serbia	10	2	1	0	3
Russia	7	1	1	0	1
Asia					
China	77	62	4	28	13
Hong Kong	64	12	54	1	4
Philippines	57	19	30	9	12
South Korea	47	12	27	5	12
India	31	13	14	5	9
Singapore	30	13	6	4	9
Japan	16	7	3	1	3
Africa					
Central African Republic	75	32	39	8	20
South Africa	59	16	37	2	15

[a] The samples surveyed in each country ranged from 968 (Iceland) to 3,000 (South Africa) observations.
[b] Social welfare includes social services for the elderly, the handicapped, youth, and health.
Source: EVS/WVS 1999–2001; weighted results.

States has a high rate of volunteering, stemming from the historical legacy of a volunteer culture of addressing citizen needs. In general, Anglo countries have higher rates of volunteering. Governments in these countries encourage such citizen action. Furthermore the welfare state is more limited in most Anglo nations compared with most Western European and northern European nations. Across nations, however, there is no single predictor of volunteering that stands out.

THE FIELDS IN WHICH VOLUNTEERS ARE ACTIVE

Volunteers perform numerous functions in many areas of community life. They feed the homeless, visit the sick, tutor children, settle refugees, offer help at hospitals, counsel and care for abused women and children, provide care and activities for the elderly. They support the arts, and run recreational activities, advocate for causes, monitor government and business, serve as members of committees and boards, do office work, assist teachers, provide health care assistance, raise money for various organizations and causes, and found new organizations to address new needs.

Thus the areas in which volunteers are most active were analyzed in various countries. Volunteers perform different roles depending on the type of government. One theory is that in liberal democracies with more limited government, such as the United States and the United Kingdom, a substantial proportion of volunteer time is spent in social services. In some European countries, such as the Scandinavian countries and the Netherlands, where government provides funding for most social welfare, the majority of volunteering is in recreation and expressive volunteering related to civic issues and social movements. The situation is different in transitional democracies; under communism, the majority of associations that were permitted were in the areas of sports and recreation. These associations still remain the dominant type of nonprofit organization, although many new social welfare organizations have been formed under newly formed democratic governments (Salamon et al., 1999).

Table 3.1 also shows the patterns of volunteering for the adult population by selected areas of activity. The category of social welfare volunteering was created by combining volunteering in social care, health, youth activities, care for the elderly and care for people with disabilities. For example, it can quickly be seen that certain groupings of countries have definite patterns in volunteering. Countries of Anglo culture, such as Great Britain, Canada, and the Untied States, have much higher levels of volunteering in social welfare. Some countries are distinguished by the percentage of adults who volunteer to religious institutions: The United States, Mexico, and Canada in North America; Chile in South America; Sweden in Western Europe; Slovakia in Eastern Europe; the Philippines, Hong Kong, and South Korea in Asia; and South Africa and the Central African Republic in Africa. Several other countries have more than 10 percent of the adult population volunteering in sports: the United States, Canada, Chile, Sweden, Denmark, Iceland, Ireland, Slovakia, and the Czech Republic. Data by country confirm that patterns of volunteering vary by history, culture, and country. Salamon and Anheier (1998) tested differences in nonprofit sectors and volunteering by regime type and found that not all countries could be explained by either regime type or their social origins theory. We explored two comparisons at the country level: rates of volunteering by freedom ranking and rates of volunteering by economic ranking. First, we compared the rates of volunteering by comparing the nations in EVS/WVS with the Freedom House rankings to determine whether there were differences in the rates of volunteering based upon the level of freedom. The theory is that nations ranked as free will have higher rates of volunteering than those that were partly free or not free at all (Figure 3.1).

As can be seen in Figure 3.1, the relationship of rates of volunteering by nation compared to their Freedom House rankings is not clear. With the exception of China where volunteering is required, volunteering in several countries ranked as partially free exceed volunteer rates of many countries ranked as free. For example, the volunteer rates in Argentina, Hong Kong, and the Central African Republic

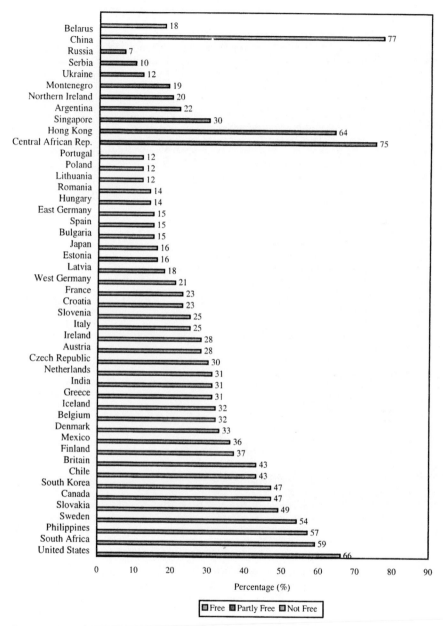

Figure 3.1. Volunteers as Percentage of Adult Population by Type of Country Regime (Measures of Freedom).

Source: EVS/WVS 1999–2001, *Freedom in the World 2001–2002.* Freedom House publication.

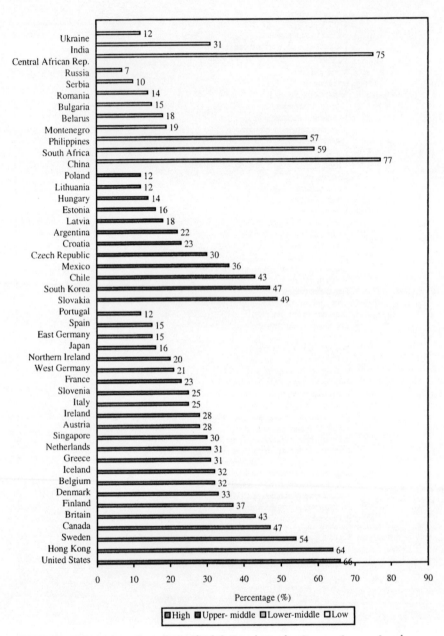

Figure 3.2. Volunteers as Percentage of Adult Population by Country Income Level.
Source: EVS/WVS 1999–2001, World Development Indicators July 2002 report. World
Bank publication.

exceed volunteer rates in most Central and Eastern European countries and some Western European countries. Other factors such as religious traditions and cultural histories obviously affect the propensity to volunteer. What this comparison does reveal is that the freedom ranking does not explain differences in the rates of volunteering among nations.

In our second comparison by country level, we compared rates of volunteering by economic ranking according to the World Bank. We theorized that richer countries would have a higher level of volunteering than poorer countries. Figure 3.2 arrays EVS/WVS countries by the World Bank rankings for country by low, lower-middle, upper middle, and high income. Again the theory that richer countries would have higher rates of volunteering is not proven in the data. Many lower middle-income countries, such as South Africa and the Philippines have among the highest rates of volunteering among all nations. Among upper-middle income nations, the Czech Republic, Mexico, Chile, and Slovakia have higher rates of volunteering than most western European Countries. These two measures-level of freedom by country and income by country—demonstrate that current theories related to level of economic development or level of freedom cannot explain the variation of volunteer rates within nations.

SOCIAL RESOURCES THEORY

Moving from country-level comparisons, we then focused on whether individual characteristics and behaviors could be used to explain various rates of volunteering among nations. Many surveys over the years have shown the relationship between human capital as demonstrated by income and level of education and the propensity to volunteer at higher rates (Verba et al., 1995; Wilson & Musick, 1998; Hodgkinson & Weitzman, 1996a; Brown, 1999). People with higher incomes, more education, and in professional or managerial positions volunteer at higher rates. These attributes are defined as human capital. Social resources theory as developed by Wilson and Musick (1998) includes both human capital and social capital, which they define as the number of networks people are in and the institutions with which they are associated. We chose to test the social capital element B religious activity, association membership, social networks and political engagement—to test whether there is a relationship among these variables across nations since Wilson and Musick's findings were limited to the United States.

Current theory predicts that individuals who possess certain characteristics will volunteer at higher rates: these characteristics include that volunteers will be active in religious organizations, voluntary associations, and/or other membership organizations, such as unions or professional associations. Furthermore, volunteers are more likely to have denser social networks and to be politically engaged (Putnam, 2000; Verba et al., 1995).

Table 3.2. Characteristics of Volunteers Versus Nonvolunteers

	Volunteers[a]	Attend religious services at least monthly[b]		Members of a voluntary organization[b]		High level of socialization[b,c]		Have signed/willing to sign a petition[b]		Discuss politics frequently[b,d]	
		Vol	Non-v	Vol	Non-v	Vol	Non-v	Vol	Non-v	Vol	Non-v
North America											
United States	66	64	43	99	81	83	69	98(.46)	96(.46)	78	61
Canada	47	53	26	98	53	85	57	95	88	66	55
Mexico	36	79	72	90	14	87	66	61	40	62	46
South America											
Chile	43	56	36	97	13	72	42	48	41	60	53
Argentina	22	61	38	94	28	82	58	63	48	64	46
Western Europe											
Sweden	54	13	5	100	91	71	47	98(.42)	97(.42)	83	76
Britain	43	31	9	64	12	81	43	94(.29)	92(.29)	58	29
Finland	37	23	9	99	69	80	57	86	79	78(.02)	71(.02)
Denmark	33	18	9	100	77	94	56	86	79	86	77
Belgium	32	37	23	99	50	82	41	93	86	76	59
Iceland	32	22	7	98	91	77	51	93(.02)	87(.02)	86	74
Netherlands	31	46	17	100	90	85	67	91(.15)	88(.15)	86	78
Greece	31	61	35	84	31	73	53	76(.96)	77(.96)	71(.36)	74(.36)
Ireland	28	77	63	95	41	92	71	89	81	68	56
Austria	28	55	37	100	54	88	55	87	77	83	70
Italy	25	64	50	98	23	85	51	88	79	78	64
France	23	21	10	97	22	81	43	90(.61)	89(.61)	71	62
West Germany	21	57	28	97	41	91	59	87	78	93	79
Northern Ireland	20	78	59	100	34	91	57	90	76	77	63
East Germany	15	20(.07)	11(.07)	91	36	89	47	92(.26)	86(.26)	95(.06)	86(.06)
Spain	15	45	34	94	15	80	66	64	54	69	54
Portugal	12	51(.89)	51(.89)	97	14	n.a.	n.a.	89	55	72	48
Eastern Europe											
Slovakia	49	57	43	97	34	82	52	84	74	87(.31)	85(.31)
Czech Republic	30	15	10	94	45	76	47	90	79	90(.03)	86(.03)

Slovenia	25	36(.02)	28(.02)	94	38	84	59	79	70	80	69
Croatia	23	56(.04)	48(.04)	97	27	90	56	95(.09)	92(.09)	85(.19)	82(.19)
Montenegro	19	15(.42)	18(.42)	93	33	87	65	74	62	76(.19)	71(.19)
Latvia	18	23	13	72	22	72	37	53(.12)	47(.12)	76(.88)	76(.88)
Belarus	18	22	13	83	38	72	60	39(.11)	33(.11)	87	77
Estonia	16	18	10	89	22	80	38	68	45	83(.35)	79(.35)
Bulgaria	15	34	18	88	8	81	43	63	36	78(.06)	71(.06)
Romania	14	47(.85)	46(.85)	100	8	60	43	56	36	78	58
Hungary	14	32	15	82	20	71	40	62	42	71	50
Poland	12	78(.95)	78(.95)	87	17	79	58	62	49	87	74
Lithuania	12	53	28	95	6	73	29	56(.62)	53(.62)	91	82
Ukraine	12	26	15	99	25	80	45	60	42	83	75
Serbia	10	28(.03)	19(.03)	87	25	92	70	76	60	84	74
Russia	7	14	9	100	27	61	37	54	39	84	73
Asia											
China	77	4(.08)	1(.08)	31	5	82	68	*n.a.*	*n.a.*	74	43
Hong Kong	64	89	68	100	64	96	85	35(.10)	40(.10)	49(.03)	43(.03)
Philippines	57	83	75	99	17	90	71	35(.02)	28(.02)	81	69
South Korea	47	57	21	96	50	84	64	85	77	78	71
India	31	57	49	93	14	89	77	63	40	75	45
Singapore	30	42	26	88	46	84	61	86(.04)	79(.04)	81	63
Japan	16	24	10	100	33	75	52	91	82	81	59
Africa											
Central African Republic	75	89(.15)	86(.15)	99	17	94	77	53	36	79(.02)	73(.02)
South Africa	59	76	57	100	49	91	75	68	52	65	56

a Percentage of adult population

b Data in parenthesis represents *p* level of statistical significance. Unless noted otherwise, data is significant at < .01 level.

c Individuals were considered to have a "high level of socialization" if they answered that they performed at least one of the following activities at least once a month: spend time socially with colleagues from work/profession, spend time with people at church, mosque, or synagogue, or spend time socially with people at sports clubs or voluntary/service organizations.

d Individuals were considered to "discuss politics frequently" if they answered that they frequently or occasionally discussed political matters with friends.

Note: Vol = volunteers; nonv = nonvolunteers

Source: EVS/WVS 1999–2001 weighted results.

We tested part of the social resource theory focused on social capital elements by comparing the characteristics of volunteers with nonvolunteers. The data are examined at the individual level to see what characteristics of an individual volunteer are present across countries. Four particular relationships are examined with respect to volunteering: religious activity, membership in voluntary organizations, socializing in various networks, and political engagement. For each, a hypothesis that has emerged from previous research is tested using the EVS/WVS data (Hodgkinson & Weitzman, 1996a; Wilson & Musick, 1998; Putnam, 2000; and Verba et al., 1995).

Hypothesis 1

Individuals who volunteer are more likely to be actively engaged in religious institutions than those who do not volunteer.

Previous literature has found that a consistent predictor of volunteering across regions has been active participation in religious institutions (Hodgkinson & Weitzman, 1996a; Hodgkinson & Weitzman, 1996b). Firstly, we tested the association between volunteering and participation in religious activities. We used monthly attendance at religious services to measure active engagement in religious institutions (Table 3.2).

Every country but two showed volunteers to be more actively engaged in religious institutions than nonvolunteers. In both of the exceptions, Poland and Portugal, volunteers and nonvolunteers were equally likely to be engaged in religious institutions and in volunteering. However, the findings for these two countries are not statistically significant. As can be seen in Table 3.2 most countries have significant differences in engagement levels.

Although neither volunteers nor nonvolunteers were very likely to be actively engaged in religious institutions in China, volunteers were far more likely to attend religious services frequently (4 percent) than nonvolunteers (1 percent). Larger percentage differences are more common, naturally, among the more religious societies, but the proportional difference of attendance in a religiously repressed society, such as China, speaks to the strong association between religious participation and volunteering. In the Netherlands, for example, volunteers are almost three times as likely as non- volunteers to be active in religious institutions.

Hypothesis 2

Individuals who volunteer are more likely to be members of a voluntary organization than those who do not volunteer.

Around the world, volunteers who are members of associations are overwhelmingly more likely to volunteer than nonmembers as shown in Table 3.2. These findings have been noted by others using EVS/WVS data and other databases.

(Dekker & Van den Broek, 1998; Hall, 1999; Hodgkinson & Weitzman, 1996a; Hodgkinson & Kirsch, 2000). Analysis has shown that members of associations are more likely to be asked to volunteer either for mutual benefit or public benefit while nonmembers are asked in greatly lower proportions (Brown, 1999; Hodgkinson & Weitzman, 1996a; Hodgkinson & Kirsch, 2000). As a result, it could be argued that the institutional or associational connection provides more direct opportunities for participation. A "member" in this analysis is someone who reported belonging to at least one voluntary association, which could include social welfare organizations, labor unions, religious congregations, political parties, sports and youth groups, gender, environmental, community groups, and other cause related groups, as well as cultural organizations.[2]

The results of this analysis reveal even more dramatic differences between volunteers and nonvolunteers. In Romania, volunteers are more than ten times more likely to be members of organizations than nonvolunteers. It appears that, consistent with theoretical predictions and the hypothesis, volunteering is highly associated with membership. In eight countries—Austria, the Netherlands, North Ireland, Sweden, Romania, Japan, Hong Kong, and South Africa—100 percent of volunteers were members of an organization. The lowest percentage of membership among volunteers was found in China with 31 percent, and the second lowest is Britain with 64 percent of volunteers being members. This is quite high compared to non-volunteer rates. Sweden has the highest rate of non-volunteer membership, at 91 percent, while China, in this category as well, has the lowest rate of nonvolunteer membership, 5 percent, closely followed by Lithuania, 6 percent and several other Eastern European countries. Eastern Europe probably offers the best contrast in the relationship between volunteering and membership, considering that membership in organizations (other than sports organizations) was not permitted under communist rule.

Hypothesis 3

Individuals who volunteer will socialize more frequently, often with other members of the community, beyond family and friends than those who do not volunteer.

A new question was added to the EVS/WVS survey this year as a measure of social capital: "I'm going to ask you how often you do various things. For each activity, would you say you do them every week or nearly every week; once or twice a month; only a few times a year; or not at all." The activities included spending

---

[2] A note of caution needs to be mentioned here related to the EVS/WVS surveys. Respondents in each country were asked whether they were members of a variety of types of organizations. Then they were asked if they volunteered at all and given the same list of organizations. Because these questions were so closely linked, there could be some bias in the responses. However, responses in the EVS/WVS do show great differences in the responses to each question and the findings of the EVS/WVS surveys are similar to other independent surveys noted in the text above.

time with your parents or other relatives, with friends, spending time socially with colleagues from work or profession, with people from your religious institution, or with people at sports clubs or other voluntary associations. A slight variation of this question was tried with promising results on the U.S. national survey of giving and volunteering (Hodgkinson & Weitzman, 1996a).

We used this question to examine whether there is an association between volunteering and socializing in networks. For this analysis, we defined high levels of socialization or dense social networks, as socializing with colleagues from work or profession, or from religious institutions, sports clubs, or other voluntary organizations more than once a month. We excluded the socializing with family and friends, as this is not an accurate proxy for social capital.

Results from the EVS/ WVS surveys indicate that individuals who volunteer are more likely to socialize at least monthly with members of sports or voluntary groups or with colleagues from work than are individuals who do not volunteer. Many of the same theoretical assertions explaining the association between volunteering and membership apply to socializing; individuals with more social contacts, for example, are more likely to be asked to volunteer; and more dense social networks facilitate volunteering (Putnam, 2000; Hodgkinson & Weitzman, 1996a; Wilson & Musick, 1998). Overall, volunteers are more likely to have more dense social networks than non-volunteers. In theory, a higher percentage of the population engaged in such networks will result in greater social capital (Putnam, 2000).

Hypothesis 4

Individuals who volunteer are more likely to be engaged in civic affairs than those who do not volunteer.

To test this hypothesis, the two variables we used as a proxy for civic engagement were: the frequency of discussing politics and signing or willingness to sign a petition. There are, of course, numerous country specific factors that greatly affect both of these measures of political engagement. In some countries petitions are too dangerous to sign, or too ineffective to be worthwhile; nonetheless, across countries these measures still offer statistically significant relationships that reveal that volunteers are more likely to be engaged in civic affairs and politics than nonvolunteers. Results from the EVS/WVS surveys were similar, although less comprehensive than findings of other analyses using these questions and other data (Dekker & Van den Broek, 1998; Stolle & Rochon, 1998). Volunteers are more likely to be politically engaged than non-volunteers in almost all countries. Generally, volunteers are more civically engaged than non-volunteers, but the differences between volunteers and non-volunteers are not as great in measures of civic engagement as in membership in organizations or active engagement in religion. Two exceptions do exist. In Hong Kong 35% of volunteers said they have or would sign a petition, compared with 40% of nonvolunteers. Even in Hong Kong, however, the relationship between volunteers and citizen engagement is ambiguous, for volunteers are still more likely to discuss politics more frequently than non-volunteers as hypothesized. Citizens may be less likely to sign a petition since their government is now under the control of China where free expression is restricted. For the discuss politics question, again one country deviated from the pattern; in Latvia, volunteers are slightly less likely to discuss politics frequently than non-volunteers.

DISCUSSION AND CONCLUSIONS

While theories at the country level do not fully explain differences in aggregate rates of volunteering, there are more consistent findings when individual characteristics of volunteers are compared across nations. This analysis finds that volunteers appear to be consistently more active members of society. When volunteers are compared with non-volunteers in active religious attendance, membership in organizations, dense social relationships beyond family and friends, and civic or political engagement, predictive relationships are revealed. In general, volunteers are likely to attend religious services more frequently, be members of associations, have more dense social networks and discuss politics more frequently than non-volunteers.

The patterns of each relationship differ slightly with the largest difference between volunteers and nonvolunteers evident in the membership category, and then religious activity. As predicted, individuals who are members of organizations or active in religious organizations are more likely to form social relationships and to be asked to volunteer (see Wilson, 2000, for a summary of this research). The differences in the proportion of volunteers and non-volunteers regarding political engagement (signing or being willing to sign a petition) are smaller than in other categories, but the findings are still consistent. Great Britain had the greatest difference in interest in politics between volunteers and nonvolunteers, with volunteers two times more likely to discuss politics frequently than nonvolunteers. In no country were volunteers less likely to discuss politics or even equally likely.

Overall, the results of this analysis are generally consistent and confirm the four stated hypotheses. The findings demonstrate that social resources in the form of religious organizations, membership organizations, and social networks are important for volunteering. These social resources are part of the building blocks leading to social capital. What they suggest is further analysis of resources at the country level. In other words, are individuals more likely to volunteer in countries where the density of voluntary and membership organizations is high? What is the relationship between the number of organizations and ease of networking and volunteer rates across nations?

Further analysis of EVS/WVS data to determine the role of human capital and its relationship to social resources is also needed (Wilson & Musick, 1998). Human capital includes education and income. Volunteering and its relationship to tolerance should also be explored. While it can be argued that volunteers are more likely to be civically active, these findings do not argue that volunteers are more tolerant. Findings might reveal that the characteristics of volunteers and the strength of social capital could lead to the social exclusion of other groups within a country. In other words social capital that is found only in particular groups in a society could have negative consequences (Foley et al., 2001; Putnam, 2000; Staub, 1989).

With the availability of the EVS/WVS surveys from transitional democracies in eastern and central Europe as well as new countries in Africa and the Middle East, it will be possible to compare values of western nations with the Middle East and Africa. Surveys in these countries will need to be repeated over time in order to examine changes in these societies and particularly in countries where there has been a major change in type of government. The EVS/WVS survey data provide scholars the opportunity to study social and political values in countries undergoing change. However, in relation at least to volunteering, future research would greatly benefit from a stronger theoretical base to explain the differences in rates of volunteering across nations. Questions about public policy related to volunteering might be helpful. In other words, do countries that encourage volunteering and/or citizen participation have higher rates of volunteering than nations whose public policy is neutral or which discourages volunteering? Answers to this question may afford another possibility to build theories of volunteering at the country level.

Finally, these EVS/WVS surveys need to be augmented with careful qualitative data about the range and scope of new volunteer activities. For example, older civic activities, such as membership in gender-related clubs are down, but membership in environmental organizations has continued to climb. In fact, between 1990 and 2000, such membership increased substantially in the United States and other European countries (Anheier et al., 2001; Hall, 1999; Ladd, 1999; and Skocpol, 1998). More careful analysis of such trends and the effect of changing values across and within nations on volunteering rates over time is needed in order to test theory and measures of change.

REFERENCES

Anheier, H.K., Glasius, M., & Kaldor, M. (2001). *Global civil society 2001,* Oxford, New York: Oxford University Press.
Anheier, H.K., & Salamon, L.M. (1999). Volunteering in cross-national perspective. *Law and Contemporary Problems, 62,* 4, 43–66.
Brown, E. (1999). The scope of volunteer activity and public service. *Law and Contemporary Problems, 62,* 4, 17–42.

Clotfelter, Ch.T. (1999). Why 'amateurs'? *Law and Contemporary Problems, 62*, 4, 1–16.

Dekker, P., & Van den Broek, A. (1998). Civil society in comparative perspective. *Voluntas, 9*, 1, 11–38.

Dingle, A. (Ed.) (2001). *Measuring volunteering*. Washington, D.C.: Independent Sector.

Hall, P.A. (1999). Social capital in Britain. *British Journal of Political Science, 29*, 417–61.

Hodgkinson, V.A., & Kirsch, A.D. (2000). The characteristics of citizen participation and generosity with implications for public policy. Paper presented at International Society of Third Sector Research, Dublin, Ireland.

Hodgkinson, V.A., & Weitzman, M.S., with Abrahams, J., Crutchfield, E., & Stevenson, D.R. (1996a). *Giving and volunteering in the United States*. Washington, D.C.: Independent Sector.

Hodgkinson, V.A., & Weitzman, M.S. (1996b). *The nonprofit almanac 1996–97*. San Francisco: Jossey-Bass Publishers.

Kuti, E. (1996). *The nonprofit sector in Hungary*. Manchester and New York: Manchester University Press.

Ladd, E.C. (1999). *The Ladd report*. New York: Free Press.

Putnam, R. (2000). *Bowling alone*. New York: Simon and Schuster.

Report of the Commission for Social Development (2000), Sales No: E/CN.5/32001/6 Annex, 3–4), New York: United Nations.

Salamon, L.M. (1994). The rise of the nonprofit sector. *Foreign Affairs, 73*, 3, 111–124.

Salamon, L.M., Anheier, H.K., List, R., Toepler, S., Sololowski, S.W., & Associates (1999). *Global civil society*. Baltimore: Johns Hopkins University Center for Civil Society Studies.

Salamon, L.M., & Anheier, H.K. (1998). Social origins of civil society. *Voluntas, 9*, 3, 213–248.

Skocpol, Th. (1998). How Americans became civic. In Th. Skocpol & M.P. Florina (Eds.), *Civic engagement in American democracy* (pp.27–80). Washington, D.C.: Brookings Institution Press.

Staub, E. (1989). *The roots of evil*. Cambridge and New York: Cambridge University Press.

Stolle, D., & Rochon, Th.R. (1998). Are all associations alike? *American Behavioral Scientist, 42*, 1, 47–65.

Verba, S., Schlozman, K.L., & Brady, H. (1995). *Voice and equality*. Cambridge: Harvard University Press.

Wilson, J. (2000). Volunteering. *Annual Review of Sociology, 26*, 215–240.

Wilson, J., & Musick, M. (1998). The contribution of social resources to volunteering, *Social Science Quarterly, 79*, 4, 799–814.

Chapter *4*

Modernization and Volunteering

RONALD INGLEHART

VOLUNTEERING IN KNOWLEDGE SOCIETIES

Does volunteering decline as a country becomes a knowledge society? Robert Putnam (1995; 2000) launched a spirited controversy with his claim that civic participation in the United States has undergone a severe long-term decline in recent decades. The possibility of such a decline has alarming implications for the functioning of civic life in general and democracy in particular, and his thesis gave rise to widespread debate and discussion. It has been linked with a general decline in trust in government and support for political institutions (Norris, 1999; Nye et al., 1997).

Evidence from the European Values Surveys and World Values Surveys (EVS/WVS) sheds new light on this debate, making it possible to examine it in a much broader perspective than ever before. Although these surveys do not provide time series evidence like the impressive database that Putnam assembled for the United States, they do provide cross-nationally comparable evidence concerning membership and volunteering in voluntary organizations across scores of countries spanning the range from low-income agrarian societies to rich postindustrial societies. The factors to which Putnam attributes the US decline in civic activism—from increased time spent in commuting and watching television, to increased female participation in the work force—are as applicable to most of these societies as they are to the United States. If Putnam's interpretation is correct, we should find lower rates of participation in advanced postindustrial societies, than in other societies. Conversely, if relatively low rates of membership and volunteering are unique to the United States, than they must be due to other causes than the ones Putnam suggests.

Moreover, the most important single driving force to which Putnam attributes the decline of civic participation in the United States is a generational shift, in which the younger birth cohorts show lower rates of civic engagement than older birth cohorts—and have done so for decades. If this phenomenon reflects factors linked with advanced industrial societies, rather than some unique and still unexplained fluke of American history, then we would expect to find a similar pattern in other advanced industrial societies, with younger cohorts showing lower rates of participation than their older compatriots. Furthermore, if these lower rates of participation among the young reflect an intergenerational decline specific to advanced industrial societies (rather than something inherent in the human life cycle), we would expect to find it in rich countries but not in poor ones. The EVS/WVS data enable us to test these hypotheses.

Why would we expect to find declining rates of civic activity among advanced industrial societies? The usual view is that economic development leads to a proliferation of voluntary associations, and consequently would be expected to bring *rising* levels of belonging and volunteering, rather than the opposite. Putnam's finding of declining participation in voluntary associations contradicts this expectation. He attributes the decline to a variety of factors, some of which (like the rise of the two-career family) are linked with advanced industrial society. But the causes of the most important single factor he identifies—a generational shift away from civic participation—remain unexplained. We are about to examine a global database. Let us consider the question of civic activism in a broad, long-term perspective, examining the impact of changes in the work force—and also the role of intergenerational cultural changes that tend to accompany economic development, but constitute a distinct and, thus far, largely overlooked aspect of changing levels of civic activism.

We suggest that the rise of industrial society tends to be linked with declining levels of direct participation. Although industrialization brings a proliferation of secondary associations, they tend to be bureaucratized organizations, dominated by a small number of leaders. They may have many members on paper, but in practice these members may actually engage in less first-hand civic activity than occurs in agrarian societies. Subsequently, the emergence of postindustrial society, bringing urban sprawl, longer commuting times, two-career families, electronic communications and such, may also cut into the time and energy available for first-hand interaction in civic activities. In short, economic development is not necessarily conducive to rising rates of civic participation—it may actually hinder it.

MODERNIZATION AND CULTURAL CHANGE: TWO DIMENSIONS OF CROSS-CULTURAL VARIATION

But this is only part of the story. Economic development also brings long-term intergenerational cultural changes that transform the basic values and motivations of the people involved. As will be demonstrated below, modernization gives rise to two distinct dimensions of cultural change. The first of these changes—a shift from Traditional to Secular-rational values linked with industrialization—tends to bring lower rates of civic activism (especially in certain types of associations); but a second major dimension of cultural change—a shift from Survival values to Self-expression values, linked with the emergence of the knowledge society—is conducive to *higher* levels of civic activism in general, and volunteering in particular. Again, it is important to specify the types of associations that are involved, for this second phase of cultural change also has a distinctive impact on participation in specific kinds types of associations. The nature of the shift from agrarian to industrial society, and the subsequent rise of a service (or postindustrial) society are well documented and widely understood; the two waves of cultural change that tend to go with them, much less so. Before examining the empirical evidence, let us review the theory and evidence underlying these two waves of cultural change.

Inglehart (1997; cf. Clark & Hoffman-Martinot, 1998) hypothesized that both the transition from agrarian society to industrial society, and the transition from industrial society to a knowledge-based economy, were linked with pervasive changes in beliefs and values that would be reflected in the contemporary value systems of the respective types of societies. In a factor analysis of national-level data from the 43 societies included in the 1990 World Values Survey, he found two major dimensions that accounted for more than half of the cross-national variance in more than a score of variables tapping basic values in a wide range of domains ranging from politics to economic life and sexual behavior. Each of the two dimensions taps a major axis of cross-cultural variation involving many different basic values; the first dimension taps a dimension referred to as "Traditional vs. Secular-rational values," while the second one taps "Survival vs. Self-expression values." As a society moves from an agrarian to an industrial basis, its value system tends to shift from Traditional to Secular-rational values; the transition from Industrial to Postindustrial or Knowledge society is linked with a shift from Survival to Self-expression values.

These two dimensions of cross-cultural variation seem robust. When the 1990–1991 factor analysis was replicated with the data from the 1995–1998 surveys, the same two dimensions of cross-cultural variation emerged as from the earlier surveys—even though the new analysis was based on surveys that covered 23 additional countries that were not surveyed earlier. Inglehart and Baker (2000) describe how these dimensions were measured, together with factor analyses at both the individual level and the national level, demonstrating that the same dimensional structure emerges at both levels.

The Traditional/Secular-rational values dimension reflects the contrast between societies in which religion is very important and those in which it is not, together with a wide range of other orientations. Societies near the traditional pole emphasize the importance of parent-child ties and deference to authority, along with absolute moral and sexual standards and traditional family values, and reject divorce, abortion, euthanasia, and suicide. These societies have high levels of national pride, and a nationalistic outlook. Societies with secular-rational values have the opposite preferences on all of these topics. Analysis of data from more than 70 societies demonstrates that societies with a high percentage of the work force employed in agriculture, tend to emphasize Traditional values; those with a high percentage engaged in industry, tend to emphasize Secular-rational values.

The second dimension emphasizes a different set of concerns, linked with the transition from industrial to postindustrial society. Societies that rank high on Survival values tend to emphasize Materialist values, show relatively low levels of subjective well-being and report relatively poor health, are relatively intolerant toward outgroups, low on interpersonal trust, and reject gender equality. They also emphasize hard work, rather than imagination or tolerance, as important things to teach a child and have low rates of participation in environmental protection. Societies high on self-expression values tend to have the opposite position on all of these topics. This dimension also has an extremely strong correlation with democracy: societies that rank high on Survival/Self-expression values show much higher scores on the Freedom House ratings of political rights and civil liberties, than societies that emphasize Survival values.

This chapter replicates the factor analyses just described, using the data from the 1999–2001 World Values Survey/European Values Survey. Although these surveys include 18 societies that were not previously surveyed, we obtain essentially the same structure that emerged from analysis of the 1990 surveys and the 1995 surveys. Figure 4.1 shows where 80 societies, containing most of the world's population, are located on these two dimensions.

We find large and pervasive differences between the worldviews of people in rich and poor societies; their basic values and beliefs differ on scores of key variables, in a coherent pattern. Richer societies tend to be high on both of these dimensions, while low-income societies tend to rank low on both of them. Does this mean that economic development brings predictable changes in prevailing values? The evidence suggests that it does: time series evidence shows that with economic development, societies tend to move from the lower left of Figure 4.1, toward the upper right—from the values prevailing in low-income societies, toward the values prevailing in high-income societies (Inglehart & Baker, 2000; Welzel et al., 2003).

But economic differences are not the whole story. Specific religious traditions seem to have an enduring impact on the contemporary value systems of these societies, as Weber, Huntington, and others have argued. The historically Protestant countries of Northern Europe form a distinctive cluster, reflecting the fact

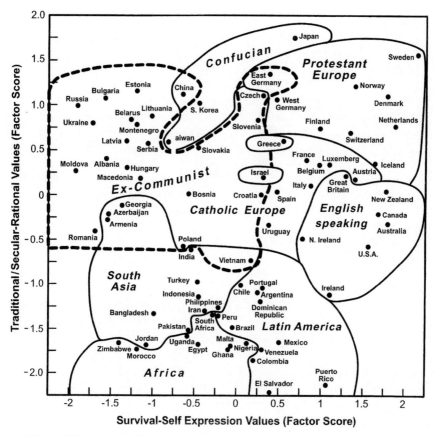

Figure 4.1. Positions of Societies on Two Dimensions of Cross-Cultural Variation.

that their publics have relatively similar values on political, religious, and economic questions, as well as on gender roles, child-rearing, and sexual behavior. The historically Roman Catholic European countries also have relatively similar values, forming another cluster—as do the publics of all eleven Latin American societies. The English-speaking countries constitute still another cluster of culturally similar societies, as do the seven African societies. Similarly, the publics of the four Confucian-influenced societies show relatively similar basic values and beliefs, despite large differences in their levels of economic development. The former communist societies also form a cluster (with the historically Orthodox ones falling nearer the "Survival" pole of the horizontal dimension, and the historically Catholic ones falling closer to the center). Finally, eight of the ten predominantly Islamic societies form a fairly compact cluster in the lower-left quadrant of Figure 4.1, straddling the border between Africa and South Asia. Almost half of the population of Nigeria is Islamic, and that country is also nearby on the cultural map.

A history of communist rule seems to leave a lasting impact on the value system of any society that has experienced it. Figure 4.1 includes 25 societies that experienced communist rule for periods ranging from 40 to 74 years. They all fall into an ex-communist cultural zone that ranks high on secularization and low on self-expression values, and occupies most of the upper left-hand quadrant of Figure 4.1. The core countries in this cluster have an Orthodox religious tradition, but it also includes a number of historically Roman Catholic countries (nearly all of which rank higher on self-expression values than do the historically Orthodox countries). The former communist zone also overlaps with the Protestant cultural zone (with the former East German region showing distinct values from those prevailing in the Western region, a decade after the Wall came down). The communist zone also overlaps with the Confucian zone (including China); with the South Asian zone (taking in Vietnam); and with the Islamic zone. Albania and Azerbaijan, the two Islamic societies that experienced communist rule, are substantially more secular than the other eight Islamic societies.

Societies that experience economic development tend to move from the lower left toward the upper right of the map. But cultural change is path dependent. The fact that a society was historically Protestant or Orthodox or Islamic or Confucian gives rise to cultural zones with distinctive value systems that persist when one controls for the effects of economic development (Inglehart & Baker, 2000). Religious heritage is not the only important variable; a society's value system reflects its entire historical heritage, including religious traditions, colonial ties, its level of economic development and the experience of communist rule. The following sections will examine how these two dimensions of cross-cultural variation interact with changes in the nature of the work force, to impact on participation in voluntary associations.

INTERGENERATIONAL DIFFERENCES IN MEMBERSHIP AND VOLUNTEERING

A major feature of the decline in civic activism found by Putnam is its intergenerational nature: he attributes roughly half of the total decline to a generational shift in which an enduring characteristic of the younger birth cohorts is the fact that they show lower rates of participation than older birth cohorts—and have done so for decades. Is this a uniquely American phenomenon, or something found across advanced industrial societies? Table 4.1 examines the correlations between age and (1) membership in various types of voluntary associations, and (2) volunteering (doing unpaid work) for these same types of associations. We analyze separately

Table 4.1. Correlations with Age in Rich Countries vs. Developing and
Former-Communist Countries

	17 rich countries[a]	31 developing and former-communist countries[b]
Membership		
Social welfare	.115	.040
Women's groups	.076	−.012
Religious, church organizations	.058	−.022
Political parties	.058	−.001
Other voluntary associations	.051	.017
Health related groups	.048	−.021
Local groups: poverty, unemployment, housing, racial equality	.026	−.007
Peace movement	.015	−.035
3rd World development, Human rights	.011	−.027
Environment, conservation	.005	−.041
Professional associations	−.010	−.022
Education, arts, music, cultural organizations	−.042	−.113
Labor unions	−.053	−.009
Youth work	−.095	−.135
Sports, recreational	−.138	−.168
Volunteer		
Social welfare	.085	−.004
Religious, church organizations	.056	−.033
Women's groups	.047	−.019
Health related	.037	−.041
Local groups: poverty, unemployment, housing, racial equality	.019	−.021
Peace movement	.002	−.052
Political parties	.000	−.143
3rd World Development, human rights	−.000	−.026
Labor unions	−.002	−.026
Environment, conservation	−.008	−.048
Professional Associations	−.009	−.017
Education, arts, music, cultural organizations	−.030	−.098
Sports, recreation	−.076	−.131
Youth work	−.080	−.121

[a] France, Britain, Ireland, Northern Ireland, Germany (W.), Austria, Italy, Spain, Belgium, Denmark, Sweden, Finland, Iceland, Luxemburg, U.S., Canada, Japan.
[b] India, China, Philippines, Vietnam, South Korea, Mexico, Argentina, Puerto Rico, Chile, Venezuela, South Africa, Uganda, Zimbabwe, Portugal, Greece, Hungary, Poland, Belarus, Czech Republic, Germany (E.), Slovenia, Bulgaria, Romania, Lithuania, Latvia, Estonia, Ukraine, Russia, Serbia, Croatia, Slovakia.
Source: EVS/WVS 1999–2001.

the data from 17 rich countries and 31 developing and ex-communist societies. Positive signs in Table 4.1 indicate that the young show lower rates of membership and participation than the old—in keeping with Putnam's findings; positive correlations appear in bold face type. Negative signs indicate that the young show *higher* rates of membership and volunteering than the old.

In the data from the 17 rich societies, we find the expected polarity in connection with membership in 10 of the 15 types of organizations. The two strongest negative correlations apply to membership in youth organizations and sports associations: it is scarcely surprising to find that the young are more active than the old in these types of associations. The young are *less* likely to be members of most other types of associations—at least in rich countries. But when we examine the relationship between membership and age in the 31 less developed societies, we find an interesting contrast: the correlations are negative in all but two cases: the young are *more* likely than the old to be members of everything except social welfare organizations and "other voluntary associations." The correlations are generally weak, but the pattern is consistent. The young are less likely than the old to be members of associations only in rich countries—which suggests that this phenomenon may be linked with economic development; it clearly does not reflect anything inherent in the human life cycle.

Though it does not apply to all types of associations, the evidence so far is consistent with the thesis that economically more developed societies are experiencing an intergenerational shift away from associational membership. But the evidence is is much weaker when we turn to volunteering: we find positive correlations between volunteering and age in connection with only half of the associations dealt with in the EVS/WVS surveys, and only four of the correlations are statistically significant. The young may be less likely than the old to be members of associations in rich countries, but they are not less likely to do unpaid work. Interestingly enough, however, *all* of the correlations between age and volunteering are negative in the 32 less wealthy countries—where younger people are *likelier* than the old to be members of almost all types of associations, and likelier to do volunteer work in *all* types of associations without exception. In contrast with this pattern, the young are *relatively* less active, in rich countries than in less developed ones. In this sense, the thesis of an intergenerational shift in rich countries still seems applicable.

Membership and volunteering show rather different characteristics—in keeping with the fact that volunteering to do unpaid work is a more selective activity, involved a smaller portion of the public than membership. Fully 21 percent of our combined cross-national sample considers themselves members of some religious association; only 12 percent report doing unpaid volunteer work for religious associations—and this is by far the most widespread form of volunteering. As Table 4.2 demonstrates, most forms of volunteering involve no more than 3 or 4 percent of the public.

Table 4.2. Participation in Voluntary Work in 50 Societies
(% Reporting Given Form)

Religious, church organizations	12
Sports, recreational	8
Social welfare for old, handicapped, deprived	7
Education, arts, music, cultural organizations	7
Youth work (boy scouts, girl guides, etc.)	5
Health related organizations	4
Local groups: poverty, unemployment, housing, racial equality	4
Political parties	4
Environment, conservation organizations	3
Women's groups	3
Labor unions	3
Professional Associations	3
Peace movement	2
Third World Development, human rights groups	2

Source: EVS/WVS 1999–2001.

THREE TYPES OF VOLUNTEERING

We cannot treat membership and volunteering as undifferentiated activities. As we have seen, membership and volunteering in various types of associations show contrasting relationships with age—and as we will see below, they are shaped by various background factors. Certain types of volunteering tend to go together, being relatively widespread in certain societies and among certain types of individuals. Table 4.3 illustrates this point, showing the result of a factor analysis of the national-level data. Three types of volunteering emerge, associated with three underlying dimensions.

The first dimension involves volunteering in environmental (or "Green") associations, peace movements, welfare activities for the old, the handicapped or the deprived, volunteering for health-related associations, and volunteer work for associations concerned with aiding the development of poor countries or with human rights. Certain countries tend to rank high in volunteering for all of these associations, while others rank low in all of them.

A second dimension involves volunteering for political parties, local organizations concerned with poverty and unemployment, women's groups, and labor unions. A third dimension reflects volunteering in religious or church-linked associations, youth work, sports groups, professional associations and educational and cultural associations. Certain societies tend to rank high on volunteering for this type of association, while others rank low on volunteering for all of them. We will analyze the background factors linked with high or low rates of participation in each of these three forms of volunteering, with particular interest in the effects

Table 4.3. Voluntary Work in Various Types of Organizations: National-Level
Factor Analysis (Varimax Rotation)

	1	2	3
	Green, peace, welfare health, 3rd world	Political parties, local, women, labor unions	Religion, youth, sports, professional, cultural
Conservation, environmental groups	.903		
Peace movement	.858		
Welfare services for old, handicapped, deprived	.775	.532	
Health related organizations	.757		
Third world development, human rights associations	.704		
Political parties		.866	
Local groups: poverty, employment, housing, racial equality		.842	
Women's groups		.775	
Labor unions		.689	
Religious, church organizations			.790
Youth (scouts)			.778
Sports or recreational groups			.725
Professional associations			.697
Education, arts, music or cultural organizations			.651

Source: EVS/WVS 1999–2001. Loadings below .5 not shown.

of variation in the structure of the work force, and that associated variations in prevailing motivations and value systems.

Table 4.4 shows the cross-national rankings in volunteering for Environmental and Conservation groups—an illustration of the type of associations linked with the first dimension. The results would be surprising to anyone who assumed that high rates of volunteering are found only in relatively rich countries. China and Vietnam rank high in the extent to which their publics do unpaid volunteer work for conservation groups—and they also rank high in participation in groups concerned with welfare services for the elderly, the handicapped and the deprived. By no coincidence, these are the only two societies in our sample that are still governed by communist parties. These societies have long traditions (and can employ powerful sanctions) in mobilizing large masses of people to do volunteer work for almost any goal that the leaders adopt. They seem to do so even today. We find exactly the opposite situation—very low rates of volunteering—in most of the countries formerly governed by communist regimes, especially in the Soviet successor states. The breakdown of communism ended the organizational

Table 4.4. Voluntary Work for Environmental or
Conservation Groups (%)

China	28	Malta	2
Greece	10	South Africa	2
Philippines	9	Bulgaria	2
Vietnam	8	Argentina	1
Uganda	7	Zimbabwe	1
India	5	Iceland	1
South Korea	5	Estonia	1
Sweden	4	France	1
Luxembourg	4	Britain	1
Canada	4	West Germany	1
Mexico	3	Spain	1
Czech	3	Ireland	1
Belgium	3	Northern Ireland	1
Slovenia	3	United States	1
Puerto Rico	3	Japan	1
Montenegro	2	East Germany	1
Austria	2	Poland	1
Belarus	2	Romania	1
Chile	2	Portugal	1
Finland	2	Lithuania	1
Croatia	2	Latvia	0
Slovakia	2	Russia	0
Italy	2	Serbia	0
Denmark	2	Ukraine	0
Hungary	2		

Source: EVS/WVS 1999–2001.

networks that once produced reportedly high rates of mass participation in these countries, leaving almost no infrastructure in its place. Communist rule seems to be an important influence on volunteering, but it is by no means the only on. Agrarian societies tend to rank high on this dimension, and we also find relatively high rates of volunteering in the Philippines and Uganda, two largely rural societies that have never experienced communist rule.

Table 4.5 shows the results of regression analyses that assesses the importance of social structure and cultural change on this type of volunteering. Having a relatively large percentage of workers employed in the agricultural sector is linked with relatively high rates of volunteering. As Model 1 indicates, the percentage employed in agriculture has a statistically significant positive linkage with high rates of volunteering in this type of association, explaining 9 percent of the variance by itself.

But when we add the society's score on the Survival/Self-expression, the percentage of explained variance rises from 9 percent to 31 percent. Societies that emphasize Self-expression values show relatively high rates of volunteering. The

Table 4.5. Regression Analysis of First Volunteering Factor: Greens, Peace Movement, Welfare, Health, Third World Development (Dependent Variable: Mean Score on This Dimension in Latest Survey Available for Each Society)

Independent variables	Model 1	Model 2	Model 3	Model 4
Percentage of labor force in agriculture (1990)	.016*	.024***	.026***	.020*
	(.007)	(.007)	(.007)	(.009)
Country's score on Survival/Self-expression	—	.867***	1.139***	1.09**
values dimension		(.236)	(.306)	(.386)
Experience under communist rule	—	—	.339	—
(1 = none, 1 = less than 45 years, 2 = 45 + years)			(.246)	
GDP/capita in thousands of U.S.$	—	—	—	−.028
(PPP estimates, 1995)				(.038)
Adjusted R^2	.09	.31	.32	.30
N	40	40	40	40

Cell entries are unstandardized regression coefficients (standard error in parentheses); $*p < .05$; $**p < .01$; $***p < .001$.
Source: EVS/WVS 1999–2001 for given country; GNP/capita (PPP estimates) and percentage of work force in agriculture from World Bank, World Development Report, 1997.

Table 4.6. Voluntary Work for a Political Party or Group (%)

Vietnam	24	Italy	2
China	10	South Korea	2
India	8	Ireland	2
United States	7	Croatia	2
Uganda	6	Chile	2
Greece	5	Lithuania	2
Slovakia	5	Romania	2
Malta	5	Estonia	1
Sweden	4	Britain	1
South Africa	4	Slovenia	1
Puerto Rico	4	Serbia	1
Mexico	4	Japan	1
Zimbabwe	4	Spain	1
Philippines	4	East Germany	1
Bulgaria	4	Ukraine	1
Austria	3	West Germany	1
Iceland	3	Portugal	1
Argentina	3	Northern Ireland	1
Belgium	3	Hungary	1
Montenegro	3	Latvia	1
Canada	3	Belarus	1
Denmark	3	France	1
Finland	3	Poland	1
Luxembourg		Russia	0
Czech	2		

percent employed in agriculture not only remains significant, its significance rises from the .05 level to the .001 level: societies with high proportions of the work force in agriculture tend *not* to rank high on self-expression values, but both factors are conducive to high rates of volunteering for environmental groups, peace movements, welfare groups and organizations concerned with developing countries.

A history of Communist rule also has a slight but statistically significant relationship on this type of volunteering, raising the percentage of explained variance from 31 percent to 32 percent (see Model 3). On the other hand, money per se does not seem to be a crucial factor: adding real per capita GDP to the regression (Model 4) does not explain any additional variance. The two variables with the most powerful impact on this type of volunteering are the percent employed in agriculture, and the society's score on the Survival/Self-expression dimension.

The second type of volunteering involves political parties, local groups, labor unions, and women's groups. Table 4.6 shows the rate of volunteering for political parties in each country for which we have data, as an example of the cross-national pattern found with this type of participation. Once again, both Vietnam and China show relatively high rates of volunteering—probably for the reasons discussed above. India, Uganda and the Philippines also show relatively high rates, further evidence that agrarian societies can produce high rates of volunteer work. But the advanced industrial societies such as the US and Sweden also rank relatively high.

The regression analysis shown in Table 4.7 indicates that having a high proportion of the labor force in the service sector is linked with relatively *low* rates of

Table 4.7. Regression Analysis, Second Volunteering Factor: Political Parties, Local Groups, Women's Groups, Labor Unions (Dependent Variable: Mean Score on This Dimension in Latest Survey Available for Each Society)

Independent variables	Model 1	Model 2	Model 3	Model 4
Percentage of labor force in service sector (1990)	−.032***	−.043***	−.045***	−.037*
	(.009)	(.011)	(.011)	(.015)
Country's score on Survival/Self-expression dimension	—	.485**	.860**	1.03*
		(.284)	(.330)	(.384)
Experience under communist rule (0 = none, 1 = less than 45 yrs, 2 = 45 or more yrs)	—	—	.480*	.419
			(.240)	(.250)
GDP/capita (in thousands) PPP estimates, 1995	—	—	—	−.036
				(.040)
Adjusted R2	.22	.26	.31	.31
N	40	40	40	40

Cell entries are unstandardized regression coefficients (standard error in parentheses); *p < .05; **p < .01; ***p < .001.
Source: EVS/WVS 1999–2001 for given country; GNP/capita and percentage of work force in agriculture, industry from World Bank, World Development Report, 1997.

volunteering for this type of activity—but high levels of Self-expression values are linked with relatively *high* rates of volunteering in this realm. These two variables tend to go together: "postindustrial" societies, with a majority of the work force employed in the service sector, tend to rank higher on Self-expression values than either agrarian or industrial societies. But one aspect of postindustrial society— employment in the service sector—tends to reduce volunteering for parties, unions, local groups and women's groups, while another aspect—the growing emphasis on Self-expression values—seems conducive to high rates of volunteering for such groups. Experience under communist rule plays a lesser role but is linked with high rates of volunteering—particularly for groups affiliated with political parties and labor unions.

The third type of volunteering involves work for religious or church-related groups, youth groups, sports groups and educational or cultural associations. Table 4.8 shows the cross-national rates of volunteering for religious or church-related associations, to illustrate the pattern found with this type of volunteering. China and Vietnam are no longer the leaders, in this type of volunteering—in fact,

Table 4.8. **Voluntary Work for Religious or Church Organizations** (%)

Zimbabwe	52	West Germany	6
Uganda	40	Luxembourg	6
United States	39	Hungary	5
South Africa	36	Iceland	5
Philippines	31	Slovenia	4
Puerto Rico	31	Spain	4
South Korea	27	China	4
Sweden	23	Belarus	4
Mexico	19	Latvia	4
Canada	19	Portugal	4
Chile	17	Romania	4
India	14	Poland	4
Malta	13	Lithuania	4
Slovakia	13	France	3
Ireland	10	Denmark	3
Vietnam	10	Japan	3
Argentina	9	Czech	3
North Ireland	9	Estonia	3
Austria	7	East Germany	2
Finland	7	Ukraine	2
Italy	7	Bulgaria	2
Britain	6	Montenegro	2
Greece	6	Serbia	1
Belgium	6	Russia	1
Croatia	6		

Table 4.9. Regression Analysis, Third Volunteering Factor: Church/Religious, Youth, Sports, Professional, Cultural (Dependent Variable: Mean Score on This Dimension in Latest Survey Available for Each Society)

Independent variables	Model 1	Model 2	Model 3	Model 4
Percentage of labor force in industry (1990)	−.055***	−.025*	—	−.025*
	(.014)	(.014)		(.015)
Country's score on Traditional/Secular-rational values	—	−.758**	−.834***	−.757**
		(.248)	(.189)	(.275)
Country's score on Survival/Self-expression values	—	.705***	.755***	.703**
	(.203)	(.183)	(.273)	
Experience under communist rule (0 = none, 1 = less than 45 yrs, 2 = 45 or more yrs)	—	—	—	−.003
				(.254)
Adjusted R^2	.27	.48	.41	.46
N	40	40	41	40

Cell entries are unstandardized regression coefficients (standard error in parentheses); *p < .05; **p < .01; ***p < .001.
Source: EVS/WVS 1999–2001 for given country; GNP/capita and percentage of work force in agriculture and industry from World Bank, World Development Report, 1997.

the US and three African countries (Zimbabwe, Uganda and South Africa) are the highest-ranking countries for this type of volunteering overall.

Table 4.9 shows the results of a multivariate analysis of the variables linked with this type of participation. The transition from agrarian to industrial society is linked with declining rates of participation in Religious associations, youth groups, sports, professional and cultural associations: as Model 1 demonstrates, the percentage of the labor force working in industry is negatively linked with this type of participation, and by itself it accounts for 27 percent of the cross-national variance. But cultural change has an even stronger impact on this type of participation—and we find indications of a curvilinear pattern: the cultural shift from Traditional to Secular-rational values is linked with *declining* rates of participation in these groups—but the shift from Survival to Self-expression values is associated with *rising* participation. When we add these two measures of cultural values to the regression, they almost double the amount of variance explained by the proportion of the labor force employed in industry (see Model 2). Moreover, when we drop the latter indicator from the regression, the two values indicators still explain fully 41 percent of the cross-national variance in participation in these groups—slightly more than was explained by the labor force variable alone (see Model 3). Model 4 tests the impact of communist rule on this type of participation. It does not explain any additional variance, controlling for the impact of the two cultural indicators and the percentage employed in industry.

CONCLUSIONS

Cultural change seems to play a major role in shaping participation in voluntary associations. Societies that place relatively strong emphasis on Self-expression values rank substantially higher on all three types of volunteering than other societies. Their publics not only give verbal endorsement to self-expression, they also seem to act on it. The shift from Traditional to Secular-rational values tends to depress participation in the third type of association, but the subsequent rise in Self-expression values, at a higher level of economic development, works in the opposite direction—with the result that development has a curvilinear impact on volunteering in religious, youth, sports, professional and cultural associations.

Overall, the evidence suggests that economic development tends to produce *rising* levels of volunteering, not falling levels as Putnam seems to have found in the United States. His evidence comes almost entirely from the United States, and one might argue that declining rates of volunteering are occurring in only in the United States and not in other post-industrial societies—in which case there would be no contradiction. But the explanations he provides for declining rates of participation in voluntary associations in the United States are largely applicable to other postindustrial societies as well. We will not attempt to reconcile our divergent findings here. We will simply note that evidence from other societies in general, and postindustrial societies in particular, does not point to declining rates of volunteering.

REFERENCES

Clark, T.N., & Hoffmann-Martinot, V. (1998). *The new political culture.* Boulder, CO: Westview Press.
Inglehart, R., & Baker, W. (2000). Modernization, cultural change and the persistence of traditional Values. *American Sociological Review, 65,* 19–51.
Inglehart, R. (1997). *Modernization and postmodernization.* Princeton: Princeton University Press.
Inglehart, R., Klingemann, H., & Welzel, Ch. (2003). *Modernization, cultural change and democracy.* Oxford: Oxford University Press.
Norris, P. (Ed.) (1999). *Critical citizens.* New York: Oxford University Press.
Nye, J.S., Zelikow, P.D., & King, D. (Eds.) (1997). *Why people don't trust government.* Cambridge: Harvard University Press.
Putnam, R. (1995). Bowling alone. *Journal of Democracy, 6,* 65–78.
Putnam, R. (2000). *Bowling Alone.* New York: Simon and Schuster.
Welzel, Ch., Inglehart, R., & Klingemann, H. (2003). Human development as a theory of social change. *European Journal of Political Research.*

Chapter 5

Institutional Roots of Volunteering

Toward a Macro-Structural Theory of Individual Voluntary Action

LESTER M. SALAMON AND S. WOJCIECH SOKOLOWSKI

INTRODUCTION

The "legitimation crisis" (Habermas, 1975) that has enveloped the state and large-scale corporate enterprise in recent years has prompted a search for alternatives among political leaders and community activists in many parts of the world. A useful byproduct of this search has been the discovery, or rediscovery, of an alternative social force (Touraine, 1988), the spontaneous self-organization of individuals in pursuit of collective goals, epitomized by the growth of nonprofit organizations and by the popular social movements that have characterized the 20th century, including the suffragists, Gandhism, Liberation Theology, the Civil Rights movement, the antiapartheid, antiwar, feminist, and environmental movements, "Solidarnnosc," and recently the protest movement against the negative aspects of globalization.

Unfortunately, the impulses toward self-organization and social participation often act like a Rorschach blot onto which people project their own expectations, hopes, or fears. In the process, a romantic mythology has grown up picturing spontaneous citizen action as both an alternative to social programs provided by the state, and the most effective vehicle for citizen participation in public affairs. If only the formal structures could be reduced, goes the argument, the natural forces of self-organization could reassert themselves and provide the needed solution to a vast array of social problems, including overcoming poverty, promoting economic development, protecting the environment, and enhancing the quality of life. Indeed, in some accounts a long-term decline of such spontaneous citizen action is under way, at least in the developed world, with profound implications for democratic practice (Putnam, 2000).

This paper takes a hard-nosed look at voluntary social participation in a cross-national perspective. Drawing on data gathered by the Johns Hopkins Comparative Nonprofit Sector Project (CNP), it maps volunteer participation in 24 countries and explains the observed patterns. It demonstrates that volunteering is augmented rather than inhibited by a formal organizational base, which in turn grows as a result of state support. It also shows how the social roles and functions of volunteering have been affected by social forces that have shaped the nonprofit sector throughout the 20th century: social class relations during industrialization, government social policies, and organized religion. This analysis suggests that volunteering, and more generally civic participation and self-organization of individuals to pursue common interests, are not acts of "spontaneous combustion" or "immaculate conception," but instruments and outcomes of social policies that are highly dependent on each country's institutional path of development.

To explore these points, the discussion here falls into three major sections. First, we outline the cross-national patterns in the scope and structure of volunteering as they emerge from empirical data. We then assess four alternative explanations for these patterns. A concluding section then pulls these strands of analysis together and assesses their implications for our broader understanding of volunteering internationally.

VOLUNTEERING IN 24 COUNTRIES: MAJOR FINDINGS

The data on volunteering examined here represent one product of a broader inquiry into the scope, structure, financing, and role of the nonprofit sector undertaken by a collaborative team of international researchers under the auspices of the Johns Hopkins Comparative Nonprofit Sector Project (CNP). Using

Table 5.1. Country Coverage of the Johns Hopkins Comparative Nonprofit Sector Project

Western Europe		Central and Eastern Europe	Other developed	Latin America
Austria	Ireland	Czech Republic	Australia	Argentina
Belgium	Netherlands	Hungary	Israel	Brazil
Finland	Spain	Romania	Japan	Colombia
France	Sweden	Slovakia	United States	Mexico
Germany	United Kingdom			Peru
Italy				

Table 5.2. Distribution of Volunteering, by Field, in 23 Countries

Field	Average share of FTE volunteers (%)	Standard deviation (%)
Social Services	31.1	18.9
Culture	26.7	16.1
Health	7.8	6.2
Development	7.2	9.7
Education	6.8	6.0
Professional	5.7	8.7
Civic/advocacy	5.3	5.4
Environment	3.6	3.7
Foundations	1.6	1.9
International	1.6	1.7

common definitions and a common methodology,[1] the CNP team has collected information on nonprofit employment, volunteering, and nonprofit revenue sources in 24 countries (Table 5.1), classified according to the principal activity (Table 5.2).

The CNP methodology, utilizing population and organizational surveys, captured most volunteer activity in the target countries.[2] What it showed is that the aggregate scale of this volunteering is huge, amounting to 11 million full-time equivalent (FTE) jobs in these 24 countries. Volunteering thus constitutes the lion's share of private philanthropy, on average outweighing private cash donations by a ratio of 2:1.

Perhaps the most striking finding, however, is the wide cross-national variation in the scale and distribution of volunteer activity. Figure 5.1 records the levels of volunteering in the 24 countries covered by the CNP project, expressed as a proportion of total nonagricultural employment. This method controls for differences

[1] For more details see Salamon et al., 1999.
[2] Volunteering for government agencies, informal volunteering, and religious worship volunteering is not included in this analysis. Since government volunteering often involves some form of official compulsion, it may not represent volunteering in a true sense. In any case, the amount of this volunteering is minuscule, and has a negligible effect on national totals. "Informal volunteering" denotes volunteer work performed mostly for family and relatives. It thus differs markedly from the public purpose volunteering that is our principal focus here. As far as religious-based service volunteering (e.g., running a church-sponsored soup kitchen) is concerned, we included it in the respective fields of activity together with secular volunteering. However, some countries also reported volunteering (relatively large in the US, the UK, Argentina and Brazil, but minuscule in other countries) in the field "religion," representing a difficult to disaggregate mixture of service-related volunteering and religious worship. We ran all analyses reported in this paper with and without this type of volunteering, and we found that this inclusion makes little difference to the obtained results. Since not all countries reported this type of volunteering, we excluded it from our final analyses to improve the cross-national comparability of the results.

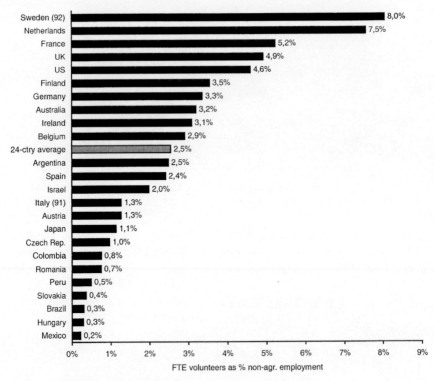

Sweden (92) — 8,0%
Netherlands — 7,5%
France — 5,2%
UK — 4,9%
US — 4,6%
Finland — 3,5%
Germany — 3,3%
Australia — 3,2%
Ireland — 3,1%
Belgium — 2,9%
24-ctry average — 2,5%
Argentina — 2,5%
Spain — 2,4%
Israel — 2,0%
Italy (91) — 1,3%
Austria — 1,3%
Japan — 1,1%
Czech Rep. — 1,0%
Colombia — 0,8%
Romania — 0,7%
Peru — 0,5%
Slovakia — 0,4%
Brazil — 0,3%
Hungary — 0,3%
Mexico — 0,2%

0%   1%   2%   3%   4%   5%   6%   7%   8%   9%

FTE volunteers as % non-agr. employment

Figure 5.1. Volunteering in 24 countries, ca. 1995, as percentage of National Employment. *Source:* Johns Hopkins Comparative Nonprofit Sector Project.

due to the different sizes of national economies, thus creating a cross-nationally comparable indicator.[3]

As this figure clearly indicates, the relative size of volunteer input varies greatly among the countries we studied. On average, it constitutes 2.5 percent of nonagricultural employment, but in Sweden and the Netherlands it exceeds that average by a ratio of 3:1. The less developed countries of Eastern Europe and Latin America have rather low levels of volunteering relative to the size of their economies-1 percent or less.[4]

---

[3] This methodology slightly overestimates the relative level of volunteering in less developed countries which tend to have larger agricultural employment than developed ones. This "overestimation" compensates for imperfect statistical data sources in less developed countries.

[4] Including religious worship volunteering (see footnote 2) does not substantially change this picture, because volunteering in most developed countries is so low that adding a fraction of it, no matter how large in relative terms, is insufficient to close the gap that separates them from the developed countries.

Even a cursory examination of Figure 5.1 reveals findings that are puzzling, however. Contrary to the perception of declining civic participation in the developed democracies (Putnam, 2000), the scale of volunteering in most of these countries (10 out of 15) is well above the 24-country average. What is more, volunteering varies considerably not just between the developed and the less developed countries, but also among the developed countries.

The extent of volunteering also varies across activity fields. Table 5.2 shows the shares of all FTE volunteering distributed across 10 fields of activity.[5] A convenient way of showing the cross-national variation is to calculate standard deviations for each field. The larger the standard deviation, the greater the diversity among countries with respect to the given type of volunteering.

The fields with the greatest average shares of volunteering are social services and culture and recreation. These two fields combined absorb nearly 60 percent of all volunteer input in the countries we studied. They also have the largest standard deviations (18.9 percent and 16.1 percent respectively), which means that the amount of volunteer input in these fields varies significantly from country to country.

While most volunteer input tends to concentrate in the areas of social services and culture and recreation, there are substantial differences among countries in the distribution of that input. In some countries (e.g., in Latin America) recreation attracts a negligible share of volunteer input, while in others (e.g., in Eastern and Western Europe) it attracts a much larger share. The same pertains to other fields of activity, especially social services, education, and health.

To analyze this rather complex picture of cross-national variation in the distribution of volunteering among fields, it is useful to group these fields according to the key social roles attributed to nonprofit and voluntary activism. Broadly speaking, these can be divided into two groups: *service* and *expression* (Kramer, 1981; Salamon, Hems & Chinnock, 2000). The service role is self-explanatory: it includes activities that have a use-value to society and its members, such as fulfilling people's needs, solving social problems, or emergency relief. This role is played by activities in the fields of social services, health, education, and economic development and housing.

The expressive role encompasses activities aimed mainly at the actualization of participants' aesthetic, cultural or political preferences, or social bonding. They may not have any clearly discernible economic value transferable to non-participants (as services do), but their main benefit is the enhancement of the quality of social, political, and cultural life. This role dominates activities in the fields of culture and recreation, environmental protection, civic activism and advocacy, and labor, business and professional associations.

[5] Unweighted averages of FTE volunteer shares in each in 23 countries. Austria is not included because we could not distribute volunteering to respective fields.

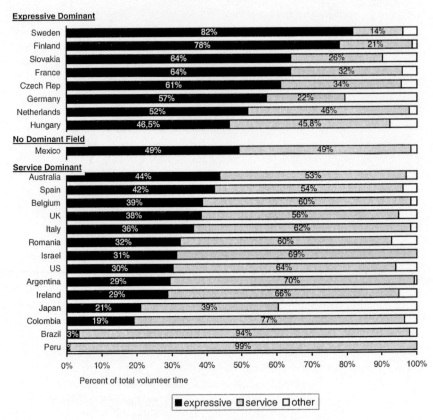

Figure 5.2. Types of Volunteering.

The distinction between service and expressive roles is a heuristic device signaling major tendencies rather than exclusive domains. Expressive activities such as culture or recreation may involve exchanges of economic value, but such exchanges are not their essential goals. For example, museums may sell souvenirs to popularize their collections or the arts in general. Similarly, educational institutions often embed expressive elements in their curricula, such as ethical values or political orientations, but their main function is to provide educational services that have a market value.

Figure 5.2 shows the shares of the expressive and service roles of volunteering in each of the 23 countries included in the CNP data set. These shares were computed by summing the shares of the respective fields that constitute each of the two roles.

As shown in Figure 5.2, most countries fall into one of two broad patterns in terms of the dominant type of volunteer involvement. For eight countries, the expressive type of volunteering is most common. For fourteen, it is the service type that dominates. These two patterns also differ in the relative importance of civic engagement activities (such as advocacy or political mobilization), which is much higher in the expressive-dominant than in the service-dominant pattern (on average 15 percent versus 6 percent of all volunteering, respectively).

How can we explain these differences in the amount and distribution of volunteering among nations?

EXPLAINING PATTERNS OF VOLUNTEERING

Overview

To answer this question, it is useful to examine the clues provided by existing theory and research. Broadly speaking, two such bodies of research are available. One of these focuses on essentially micro-structural factors, viewing volunteering primarily as an individual behavior, explainable by individual values, beliefs, preferences, interests, or social connections (Wilson, 2000). The central research question these explanations address is: what motivates people to volunteer? The two most frequently identified factors are social capital and personal value systems. "Social capital" denotes the strength of social ties that bind an individual to organizational activities (such as a social movement or nonprofit organizations or organized religion) and hence to volunteering: the stronger the ties, the greater the involvement in volunteer activity (McAdam, 1986, 1988; Snow et al., 1980; Sokolowski, 1966; Wilson & Musick, 1998; Zald & McCarthy, 1987). Personal value systems associated with propensity toward volunteering include altruism, self-understanding, and emotional gratification (Arrow, 1975; Howarth, 1976, 1975; Monroe, 1991; Piliavin, 1994). These two key factors are, in turn, associated with socio-demographic factors such as age, gender or ethnicity (Wilson, 2000).

The second group of studies focuses on macro-structural factors, viewing volunteering (and collective action in general) in the context of broader social forces and institutions. Unlike the micro-structural arguments, which look for individual motives, i.e. the propensity to volunteer, this approach concentrates on opportunity structures, i.e. social conditions that enable or impede voluntary action. These conditions are thought to include prevailing family structures such as excessive familialism, which is thought to undermine trust and thus inhibit voluntarism (Fukuyama, 1995); ethnic-cultural diversity, which is thought to serve as a catalyst for volunteering (James, 1987; Weisbrod, 1978); economic and political instability, which is thought to incite people to take various forms of collective action (Davies, 1969; Johnson, 1964; Skocpol, 1979; Tilly, 1978); and government policies that may compete with (Quadagno, 1987) or support (Salamon, 1995; Seibel, 1989) nonprofit institutions.

Although the micro-structural approach to volunteering clearly dominates the field, its utility in explaining variations in volunteering across countries, as opposed to within them, is open to question. This is so because it is difficult to ascribe national patterns to individual differences without explaining why these individual differences vary systematically from place to place. For this, however, a macro-level analysis is necessary, at least as a first step. Consequently, we focus our efforts here on macro-structural explanations. More specifically, we examine four possible explanations of the cross-national variations in volunteering that are evident in our data.

Four Possible Explanations

The Heterogeneity/Crowding-Out Thesis

The first possible explanation of the patterns of volunteering that we found grows out of the market failure/government failure theory of the nonprofit sector formulated by Burton Weisbrod (1978). This theory argues that voluntary action is necessary to offset the inability of both the market and the state to satisfy public demands for collective-type goods, particularly where considerable heterogeneity exists in a country. This is so, in the first instance, because free rider problems keep market producers from supplying collective-type goods; and in the second instance, because population heterogeneity makes it difficult to generate majority support for government to provide the full range of such goods. Voluntary action therefore emerges to satisfy the unsatisfied demand for collective goods on the part of particular components of the population. Voluntary action is thus a substitute for government action in supplying collective goods.[6] This leads to the following hypothesis:

> **Hypothesis 1:** The greater the government's involvement in providing social welfare and security, the smaller the scale of volunteering in a country.

Interdependence Theory

A much different conceptualization of the relationship between government and voluntarism has been proposed by researchers focusing on the evolution of social policy in market economies. Salamon (1987), for example, has argued that voluntary organizations are often a first line of defense in such situations, but because of certain inherent limitations (voluntary failure) look to the state for

---

[6] This "crowding-out" hypothesis echoes the "received wisdom" of the conservative discourse that portrays voluntary charity as an antidote to the "excesses" of government bureaucracy, and views the expansion of government as antithetical to more traditional institutions, such as the family and religion. (Quadagno, 1987).

assistance. In many cases, this leads to a cooperative relationship between state authorities and voluntary groups as considerations of effectiveness, legitimacy, and avoidance of unnecessary conflict or bureaucratization prompt government agencies to enlist voluntary organizations in the delivery of state-financed services (see also: DeLaat, 1987; Gronbjerg, 1987; Lune & Oberstein, 2001, Seibel, 1989; Salamon, 1995). Instead of a conflict between state and voluntary groups, this line of argument suggests a cooperative relationship instead. As such, it is consistent with a consensus or "corporatist" model of democracy that emphasizes the collaborative relationship between state and intermediary institutions (such as nonprofits and unions) (Lijphart, 1999).

Similar arguments have been advanced by some students of successful social movement mobilization (Gamson, 1990; Tilly, 1978; Skocpol, 1979). Although these writers do not deny the existence of certain adversity between government and grassroots activism, they also emphasize that the key to a grassroots movement's success is often the development of a collaborative relationship with the government.

These arguments suggest the following hypothesis about the relationship between the government and voluntary action:

Hypothesis 2: The greater the government support of social welfare activities, the greater the scale of volunteering.

Resource Mobilization Theory

The third macro-structural explanation of the scale of volunteering is essentially an extension of the social movement argument identified above. According to this "resource mobilization theory" of social movements the success of such movements hinges not only on the availability of governmental support, but more generally on the availability of social and organizational resources that can be used to mobilize participation (Smith, 1997; Wilson & Musick, 1998; Zald & McCarthy, 1987). In contrast to populist views that see formal organizations as antithetical to voluntarism, this line of thinking holds that formal organizational structures tend to encourage volunteer participation.

These arguments therefore lead to the following hypothesis:

Hypothesis 3: The greater the social and organizational capacity to mobilize volunteering, the greater the scale of volunteering.

Social Origins Explanation

The fourth explanation of cross-country variations in volunteering draws on the "social origins" theory of nonprofit sector development formulated by Salamon

Table 5.3. Institutional Traditions Affecting Nonprofit–State Relations

	Government social welfare spending	
Nonprofit sector size	Low	High
Small	Statist	Social-democratic
Large	Liberal	Corporatist

and Anheier (1998; see also Salamon, Sokolowski & Anheier, 2000). This theory views the evolution of the nonprofit sector as the product of a broader set of social relationships that shapes how societies cope with the tensions of industrialization. Of particular importance here are the relative influence of key social groupings—landed elites, commercial middle class elements, and workers—as well as the position and power of the state and religious authorities. Depending on the relative power of these social groupings, four more or less distinct patterns of development are possible, each characterized by a particular constellation of government social welfare spending and nonprofit sector role, as reflected in Table 5.3.

In the classic "liberal model," strong commercial middle class elements develop and are able to unseat conservative landed elites and fend off pressures from working class elements. The result, in the absence of a strong state apparatus or church, is limited state social welfare provision and heavy reliance on voluntary action instead.

At the opposite extreme from the "liberal model" is the "social democratic model." This pattern is likely where middle class elements, having unseated conservative landed elites, nevertheless encounter strong worker mobilization that cannot be easily resisted. Mobilized workers turn aside arguments about leaving social welfare protections to voluntary action and insist instead on the establishment of state-guaranteed, and state-provided, social welfare protections available as a matter of right. The upshot is extensive government social welfare protections. Although voluntary action may persist in such settings, it is likely to be largely expressive in form, with limited reliance on volunteers for service functions.

In between these two models are two others. In both of these models, conservative elements, including landed elites and religious authorities, retain significant power. Where industrialization has occurred, leading to significant worker mobilization, the result can be a "corporatist model" in which government social welfare protections are extended, but *through* voluntary organizations, many of them religiously affiliated. The result is a pattern characterized by substantial government social welfare spending coupled with sizable reliance on volunteers and charitable organizations, though mostly for service functions.

Table 5.4. Hypothesized Relationships Between Institutional Paths and the Scale and Roles of Volunteering

Institutional path	Volunteering scale	Dominant volunteering type
Social-democratic	High	Expressive
Liberal	High	Service
Corporatist	Moderate	Service
Statist	Low	Service

Where industrialization has not progressed and working class elements remain weak, the result is more likely to be a "statist model" characterized by limited growth in both government social welfare spending and voluntary activity.

These patterns of social development suggest two broad hypotheses about the scale and type of volunteering to expect:

Hypothesis 4a: Volunteering is likely to be relatively high in both the liberal and social democratic cases, but quite different in character. In the liberal regimes, volunteering can be expected to be primarily service oriented to fill in for an absent state, whereas in the social democratic case it can be expected to be primarily expressive, ensuring that pressure is put on the state to protect social welfare protections it has taken on.

Hypothesis 4b: Volunteering is likely to be moderately high in the corporatist case and low in the statist case. In both cases, moreover, it is likely to be oriented chiefly toward service provision.

Table 5.4 summarizes these relationships between institutional paths and the scale and composition of volunteering stipulated by the social origins theory.

Testing the Theories

How well do these theories account for the variations in the scale and composition of volunteering found in the countries we studied? To answer these questions, we operationalized each of the theories and tested them against our data.

The Heterogeneity/Crowding-Out Theory

To test the heterogeneity/crowding-out hypothesis, we examined the relationship between the share of each nation's Gross Domestic Product (GDP)

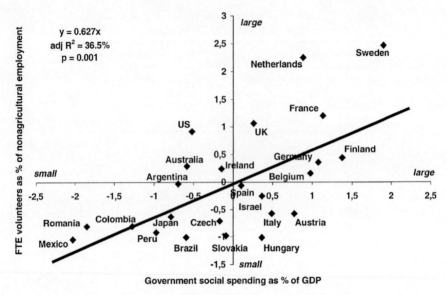

Figure 5.3. Volunteering and Government Social Spending.

devoted to social welfare spending and the scale of its volunteering measured as the share of non-agricultural employment.[7] The results, reported in Figure 5.3, show that contrary to what this hypothesis stipulates, low levels of government social welfare spending are not associated with high levels of volunteering. To the contrary, the opposite seems to be the case: instead of decreasing, the amount of volunteering *increases* as government social welfare spending increases, a result more consistent with the interdependence theory than the heterogeneity/crowding out theory. What is more, this alternative relationship is quite strong, explaining 36.5 percent of the cross-national variance[8] in the amount of volunteering. These results thus lend credence to the interdependence theory identified above.

---

[7] We used linear regression, standardizing both variables to facilitate presentation of the observed relationship in a graphic form.

[8] Since the 24 countries includes in the CNP data set do not represent a "sample" in a statistical sense, but can be more accurately thought of as a "population," it would be inappropriate to use the probability of sampling error (the statistical significance or p) in hypothesis testing. Instead, we rely only on the adjusted R-squared statistic that indicates the percentage of explained variance on the dependent variable, and adjusted by the number of independent variables and the number of observations on which the relationship is based. For the sake of completeness, we also report the p-significance statistic, but this statistic is meaningful only if the reader insists on viewing the 24 countries as a sample rather than a population.

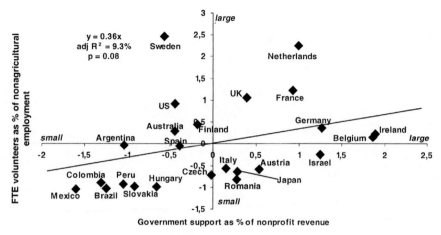

Figure 5.4. Volunteering and Government Support for the Nonprofit Sector.

Interdependence Theory

To test the interdependence theory further, we examined the relationship between the level of volunteering and the extent of government support to voluntary initiatives, as measured by government financial support for the nonprofit sector as a share of total nonprofit income. As Figure 5.4 shows, the results are in the expected direction: the higher the share of nonprofit revenue accounted for by government in a country, the greater the level of voluntary activity. However, this relationship explains only 9 percent of the observed cross-national variance in volunteering.

Resource Mobilization Theory

To test the "resource mobilization" explanation, we measured the organizational resources available to stimulate volunteer mobilization as the overall size of the formal nonprofit sector in a country, as reflected in the number of paid nonprofit FTE jobs as a share of the nation's nonagricultural employment. The results, reported in Figure 5.5, indicate that the relationship hypothesized in the "resource mobilization" theory is in the direction hypothesized: the scale of volunteering in a country increases as the size of the formal nonprofit sector increases. What is more, this relationship accounts for a significant 27 percent of the cross-national variation in the amount of volunteering.

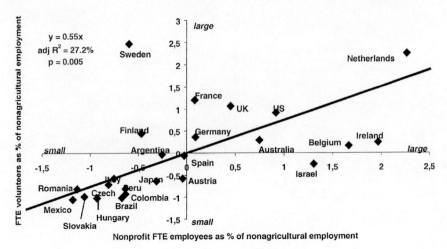

Figure 5.5. Volunteering and Paid Nonprofit Staff.

Social Origins Theory

Finally, to understand what might lie behind these findings, we tested the social origins set of theories. To do so, we calculated the proportion of predictions flowing from this theory with regard to both the amount and type of volunteering proved correct.[9] For this purpose we assigned each of the 24 countries to one of the four "ideal-type" patterns.

In most cases, the size of the nonprofit sector and the amount of government social spending alone provided sufficient criteria for this classification. But some countries experienced significant regime changes, which affected their level of social welfare spending. In such cases, we also considered social and political history as additional criteria. Both Italy and the U.K., for example, have relatively high levels of government social welfare spending like Western European welfare states. However, in Italy, the strong, if ambiguous, position of the Church in the social welfare system argues for treating this country as a "corporatist" rather than a "social democratic" case. By contrast, in the U.K. the long history of limited government social welfare spending prior to the post-World War II Beveridge reforms in health care argues for assigning this country to the "liberal" pattern rather than the "social democratic" one. Similarly, Spain falls close to the average levels on both of our variables, making it difficult to assign it to one of the four institutional paths. Given the powerful role of religion and the limited success

[9] Since the independent variable in this test is categorical rather than metric, and hypothesized relationship is not expected to be linear, we did not use regression. We used the percent of correct predictions as a substitute for the explained percent of variance (adjusted R-squared) statistic.

Table 5.5. Summary Results of Testing Volunteering Amount and the Dominant Type of
Volunteering Predicted by the Social Origins Theory

Institutional tradition	Number of cases	Average volunteering as percent of labor force	Dominant volunteering type and percent of total
Social democratic	2	5.8	Expressive–80
Liberal	3	4.2	Service–58
Corporatist	9	3.4	Service–53
Statist	6	0.6	Service–70
Hybrid (statist/soc-dem)	3	0.5	Expressive–57

of working class mobilization, however,Spain seems to fit most closely into the "corporatist" model.[10]

Once this classification of countries in terms of the four basic "models" was completed, we then assessed their relative level and type of volunteering against the hypotheses outlined in Table 5.4. Table 5.5 reports the results of this analysis.[11] What it shows is that the predictions derived from the social origins theory find significant confirmation in our data. Thus, in the first place, as predicted, the countries reflecting the liberal and social-democratic patterns have decidedly higher levels of volunteering than those in the corporatist and statist patterns, with hybrid countries not far behind.

Similarly, the predicted dominant type of volunteering in each of the groups of countries finds support in the data. Thus, as predicted, the extensive volunteering in the social democratic countries is overwhelmingly expressive in character, whereas the volunteering in the liberal and statist countries is much more heavily service oriented. Similarly, service volunteering is more prominent as well in the corporatist countries, as our theory also predicted.

A closer look at individual countries (see Table 5.6) reveals that the predictions of the social origins theory in regard to the volunteering amount were confirmed in 20 out of 23 of the cases (87 percent), and that the predictions

[10] Similar classification problems arose with regard to the Central European countries. The mixture of relatively high government social welfare spending and historically restricted avenues for nonprofit development in the Czech Republic, Hungary, and Slovakia make it necessary to treat these countries as a hybrid of statism and social democracy. In this case, we predict low levels of volunteering and the dominance of the expressive role in volunteering. The former is the result of constraints imposed on civil society under the Communist regime, the latter has its roots in the Communist social policy.

[11] For the purposes of Table 5, Volunteering amount was considered moderate if it fell within $+/- 1$ percent of the 24-country mean, which is 2.5 percent. All values below 1.5 percent were considered "small," and all values above 3.5 percent were considered "large." The role was considered "dominant" if it included the largest percentage-share of all volunteering. The classification of individual countries into institutional paths, predicted and observed amounts of volunteering, and role are shown in Appendix Table.

Table 5.6. Volunteering Amount and the Dominant Type of Volunteering Predicted by the Social Theory, by Country

Country	Regime type	Volunteering amount			Dominant role			
		Predicted*	Observed (%)	Confirmed	Predicted	Observed	Value	Confirmed
Argentina	Corporatist	Moderate	2.5	+	service	service	70	+
Australia	Liberal	High	3.2	+	service	service	53	+
Belgium	Corporatist	Moderate	2.9	+	service	service	60	+
Brazil	Statist	Low	0.3	+	service	service	94	+
Colombia	Statist	Low	0.8	+	service	service	77	+
Czech R.	Statist/social democratic	Low	1.0	+	expressive	expressive	61	+
Finland	Social democratic	High	3.53	+	expressive	expressive	78	+
France	Corporatist	Moderate	5.2	–	service	expressive	64	–
Germany	Corporatist	Moderate	3.3	+	service	expressive	57	–
Hungary[1]	Statist/social democratic	Low	0.3	+	expressive	expressive	46,5	+
Ireland	Corporatist	High	3.1	+	service	service	66	+
Israel	Corporatist	Moderate	2.0	–	service	service	69	+
Italy	Corporatist	Moderate	1.3	–	service	service	62	+
Japan[2]	Statist	Low	1.1	+	service	service	39	+
Mexico	Statist	Low	0.2	+	service	none	both 49	–
Netherlands	Corporatist	Moderate	7.5	–	expressive	expressive	52	–
Peru	Statist	Low	0.5	+	service	service	99	+
Romania	Statist	Low	0.7	+	service	service	60	+
Slovakia	Statist/social democratic	Low	0.4	+	expressive	expressive	64	+
Spain	Corporatist	Moderate	2.4	+	service	service	54	+
Sweden	Social democratic	High	8.0	+	expressive	expressive	82	+
UK	Liberal	High	4.9	+	service	service	56	+
US	Liberal	High	4.6	+	service	service	64	+
Average			2.5				65	
Number of observations that support the theory				20				19
as % of 23 observations				87				83

* low = <1.5%; high = >3.5%; moderate = >1.5% and <3.5%
+ = Prediction confirmed; – = Prediction not confirmed.
[1] Service role share is 45.8%.
[2] Expressive role share is 21%.

regarding the dominant type of volunteering were correct in 19 out of the 23 cases (83 percent).

While these findings provide substantial support for the social origins theory, however, we should not ignore the handful of cases that are inconsistent with the predictions. The amount of volunteering was incorrectly predicted in three out of 23 (13 percent) of the cases, including some rather significant cases: France, Italy, and the Netherlands. The dominant type of volunteering was incorrectly predicted in four cases (17 percent of all cases): France, Germany, Mexico, and the Netherlands. How can we explain these deviations and to what extent does our theory help with the explanations? Let us look at several of the cases.

Mexico is an example of a "statist" society where volunteering nevertheless takes a mainly expressive form according to our data, contrary to what the social origins theory would predict. The reason for this, however, is that 40 percent of all volunteering in Mexico is for trade unions, which have been an extension of the state bureaucracy and the former ruling party (PRI). Because of this, it is probably appropriate to exclude such volunteering as not wholly voluntary. Once this is done, the remaining expressive component of volunteering is quite small, only 20 percent of the total, which is much more in line with the statist pattern predicted by the social origins theory.

Similarly, France, Germany, and the Netherlands have more volunteering, and a more expressive form of volunteering, than our theory would be predict. However, this may be a product of the growth of progressive political activism in these countries in relatively recent years (the 1960s and 1970s), disrupting the historic pattern (Archambault, 1997). In addition, the growing popularity of sports and leisure activities in France and the Netherlands has worked in the same direction, boosting expressive volunteering above where it would otherwise be (Veldheer & Burger, 1999). In short, the problem with these predictions is not that the theory is fundamentally unsound but that the classification of countries into particular groupings may need to be adjusted to take account of recent developments.

SUMMARY AND CONCLUSIONS

In short, contrary to the concerns of some, citizen participation in the form of volunteering seems to be alive and well, at least in the 24 countries studied as part of the Johns Hopkins Comparative Nonprofit Sector Project. Particularly striking is the extent of such volunteering in advanced, industrial societies, moreover. Volunteering represents the equivalent of 4.5 million FTE jobs in Western Europe and nearly 5 million FTE jobs in the U.S.

At the same time, considerable variation exists in the total amount of volunteering and in the distribution of that volunteering across service fields and countries. From the evidence available, it appears that this variation is related to the extent of government social welfare activity, but in the positive direction predicted by the interdependence theory not the negative direction predicted by the heterogeneity/crowding out theory. That this is so seems to be due to the contribution that government support makes to the expansion of organized nonprofit activity. In short, contrary to some prevalent beliefs, it is not the absence of formal nonprofit organizations, but their presence, that seems to encourage volunteering. This is consistent with the assertion embodied in "resource mobilization" theory that volunteering, like social movement activity, requires resources, including particularly organizational resources.

These relationships are not simply linear, however. Rather, they are related in rather complex ways to a broader set of social relationships. Although it is difficult to characterize these relationships and group countries precisely in terms of them, there seem to be distinctive styles of social problem solving, with corresponding styles of reliance on volunteering, in different societies. Thus, for example, there appears to be a distinctive "social democratic pattern" of volunteering, characterized by high levels of volunteering, but mostly of an expressive rather than service type. This pattern is associated, moreover, with the distinctive set of relationships thought to produce this pattern. By contrast, the quite different social relationships characteristic of the liberal and corporatist regimes produce a much more service oriented pattern of volunteering, whereas in statist regimes, for reasons predicted by the social origins theory, volunteering is more stunted. Although some developed corporatist countries (France, Germany, and the Netherlands) have a larger than expected concentration of volunteering in the expressive fields, these exceptions can be explained by social-political changes that have taken place in those countries during the 1960s and 1970s.

Our study thus suggests that volunteering is not just an individual choice or a spontaneous outburst of altruism. Rather, it is affected by larger social and institutional forces. Especially telling is the challenge our data seem to pose to the conservative political theory that government social welfare involvement crowds out private voluntary initiative. If anything, the opposite seems closer to the truth.

The results here therefore seem to confirm the usefulness of a macro-structural approach to volunteer participation. Social and political structures do seem to affect the likelihood that volunteering will occur and that it will take a particular form. At the same time, to generate a full explanation of volunteering, there is still a need to bridge this macro-structural approach to an analysis of the micro-structural factors that affect whether individuals take advantage of these opportunities. Hopefully, the analysis here will provide a useful foundation for this broader investigation.

REFERENCES

Archambault, E. (1997). *The nonprofit sector in France*. Manchester and New York: Manchester University Press.

Arrow, K. (1975). Gifts and exchanges. In: E.S. Phelps (Ed.), *Altruism, money and economic theory*. New York: Russell Sage.

Davies, J. (1969). The J-curve of rising and declining satisfactions as a cause of some great revolutions and a contained rebellion. In: H.D. Graham & T.R. Gurr (Eds.), *Violence in America*. New York: Signet Books.

DeLaat, J. (1987). Volunteering as linkage in three sectors. *Journal of Voluntary Action Research, 16*, 97–111.

Fukuyama, F. (1995). *Trust*. New York: The Free Press.

Gamson, W. (1990). *The strategy of social protest*. Belmont, CA: Wadsworth.

Gronbjerg, K. (1987). Patterns of institutional relations in the welfare State. *Journal of Voluntary Action Research, 16*, 64–80.

Haberman, J. (1975). *Legitimation crisis*. Boston: Beacon Press.

James, E. (1987). The independent sector in comparative perspective. In W. Powell (Ed.), *The independent sector* (pp. 27–42). New Haven: Yale University Press.

Johnson, Ch. (1964). *Revolution and the social system*. Stanford, CA: The Hoover Institution.

Kramer, R.M. (1981). *Voluntary agencies in the welfare state*. Berkeley: University of California Press.

Lijphart, A. (1999). *Patterns of democracy*. New Haven: Yale University Press.

Lune, H., & Oberstein, H. (2001). Embedded systems. *Voluntas, 12*, 17–33.

McAdam, D. (1986). Recruitment to high-risk activism. *American Journal of Sociology, 92*, 64–90.

McAdam, D. (1988). Micromobilization contexts and recruitment to activism. *International Social Movement Research, 1*, 125–154.

Monroe, P.B. (1991). John Donne's people. *Journal of Politics, 53*, 2, 394–533).

Piliavin, J.A. (1994). Feeling good by doing good. *American Sociological Association paper*.

Putnam, R.D. (2000). *Bowling alone*. New York: Simon and Schuster.

Quadagno, J. (1987). Theories of the welfare state. *Annual Review of Sociology, 13*, 109–128.

Salamon, L.M. (1987). Partners in public service. In W.W. Powell (Ed.), *The nonprofit sector* (pp. 99–117). New Haven: Yale University Press.

Salamon, L.M. (1995). *Partners in public service*. Baltimore: Johns Hopkins University Press.

Salamon, L.M., & Anheier, H.K. (1998). Social origins of civil society. *Voluntas, 9*, 3, 213–248.

Salamon, L.M., Anheier, H.K., List, R., Toepler, S., Sokolowski, S.W., and Associates (1999). Global Civil Society. Baltimore, MD: The Johns Hopkins Comparative Nonprofit Sector Project.

Salamon, L.M., Hems, L., & Chinnock, K. (2000). The nonprofit sector (Working papers of the Johns Hopkins Comparative Nonprofit Sector project, no. 37). Baltimore: The Johns Hopkins Center for Civil Society Studies.

Salamon, L.M., Sokolowski, S.W., & Anheier, H.K. (2000). *Social origins of the nonprofit sector*. Paper presented at the 29th Annual Conference of ARNOVA, New Orleans, November 16–18.

Schervish, P.G. (1999). The citizenship of care. *American Sociological Association paper*.

Seibel, W. (1989). The function of mellow weakness. In E. James (Ed.), *The nonprofit sector in international perspective*. Oxford: Oxford University Press.

Skocpol, Th. (1979). *States and social revolutions*. Cambridge: Cambridge University Press.

Smith, D.H. (1997). Grassroots associations are important. *Nonprofit and Voluntary Sector Quarterly, 26*, 3, 269–306.

Snow, D.A., Zurcher, L.A., & Ekland-Olson, S. (1980). Social networks and social movements. *American Sociological Review, 45*, 787–801.

Sokolowski, S.W. (1996). Show me the way to the next worthy deed. *Voluntas,* 7, 3, 259–278.

Tilly, Ch. (1978). *From mobilization to revolution.* Reading, MA: Addison-Wesley.

Touraine, A. (1988). *Return of the actor.* Minneapolis: University of Minnesota Press.

Veldheer, V., & Burger, A. (1999). History of the nonprofit sector in the Netherlands (Working papers of the Johns Hopkins Comparative Nonprofit Sector project, no. 35). Baltimore: The Johns Hopkins Center for Civil Society Studies.

Weisbrod, B. (1978). *The voluntary independent sector.* Lexington, MA: Lexington Books.

Wilson, J. (2000). Volunteering. *Annual Review of Sociology,* 26, 215–240.

Wilson, J., & Musick, M. (1998). The contribution of social resources to volunteering. *Social Science Quarterly,* 79, 4, 799–814.

Zald, M.N., & McCarthy, J.D. (Eds.) (1987). *Social movements in an organizational society.* New Brunswick, NJ: Transaction Books.

Chapter **6**

Do People Who Volunteer Have a Distinctive Ethos?
A Canadian Study

PAUL B. REED AND L. KEVIN SELBEE

PROLOGUE AND GUIDING QUESTIONS

In the mid-1940s, Le Chambon was an unremarkable village of 3000 souls in the mountains of south-east France, midway between Geneva and Marseille. During the four years of World War II when much of France was under the control of its German occupiers, a handful of Le Chambon's residents performed an exceptional act: they secretly sheltered and provided safe passage for nearly five thousand Jews who would otherwise have been rounded up and sent to the camps in Germany and Poland, most to their deaths. The residents of Le Chambon who participated in this sustained act of courage did so at great risk to their own lives and without thought for personal advantage. This historical event prompts for many the question, why did they do it? What was it about these few people, and not the many others around them, and visibily no different from them, that energized such behavior? As Philip Hallie has recounted it in *Lest Innocent Blood Be Shed* (1979), a significant part of the answer can be found in the particular set of moral precepts and values they held in common as members of a small Protestant church congregation.

There is no direct modern-day equivalent of Le Chambon, but there is a modest parallel in a much more mundane form: the corps of individuals in numerous contemporary societies who contribute significant, ongoing effort to charitable and community organizations with no expectation of benefit for themselves.

Volunteering in Canada cannot be considered extensive; the general participation rate of 27 percent (in 2000) belies the fact that about half of all volunteer time is contributed by fewer than 10 percent of Canada's adults, and the majority of individuals who volunteer contribute only a handful of hours over the span of a year. This means that active volunteering is the practice of a very modest subpopulation of Canadians. So while active volunteers differ from their fellow citizens by virtue of engaging in contributory behavior, do they differ in other ways as well, ways that help understand why they contribute through cooperative effort to a collective good in a cultural context that strongly favors competitive individualism and maximizing the private good?

We have shown (Reed & Selbee, 2000) that the subpopulation of active volunteers in Canada—those whose annual time volunteered is above the median—displays a small but consistently dominant set of social and demographic characteristics that are different from those of non-volunteers. Active volunteers differ by being much more involved in civic activities generally, having had more exposure to volunteer experiences during their youth, having a university education, having higher-status and -income occupations, having certain religious characteristics, and having dependent children living at home. A significant lacuna is the lack of information on the values and beliefs, especially the distinctive ones, that characterize volunteers. (By values and beliefs we mean the enduring principles, ideals, and assumptions adopted by individuals which underlie their preferences and guide their decision-making and behavior.)

The literature on values and beliefs prevalent among volunteers is both scarce and limited in scope. None gives a general picture of the broad set of values or the worldview of volunteers. David Horton Smith's 1994 review of the literature on determinants of voluntary association participation and volunteering identified only two studies in which values were explicit variables. The study by Hougland and Christenson (1982) in North Carolina in 1973, for example, found that fourteen "dominant American values" were "never very strong" in their overall association with volunteering, and not one value was associated with all types of volunteer organization. Sundeen and Roskoff (1995) studied the link between selected goals and values, and involvement in volunteer activity by teenagers 12–17 years old; they found no clear pattern of values characterizing youth volunteers, although they concluded their research "confirm(ed) that values comprise an important set of determinants of participation in voluntary association participation and volunteering" (1995: 354).

Beyond the several studies pertaining specifically to the possible presence of certain values among people who volunteer, there is a handful of observers who have remarked in a more diffuse way on the distribution of prosocial values in American society. Bellah et al. (1985), suggest that American mores fall into two quite different categories that constitute two different worldviews or frameworks of meaning and interpretation, which they label the "culture of separation" and the "culture of coherence". In the former, the individual is viewed as a social atom, free or separated from the social, political and civic institutions of society and energized largely by self-interest. In contrast, the culture of coherence acknowledges the intimate connection of the individual to others in society, precisely because they are part of the institutions that make up a society. This worldview has its roots in the biblical and republican traditions that typify a significant portion of US history.

Among the primary distinguishing elements of the culture of coherence are values and beliefs that embrace: a genuinely integrated societal community rather than separation and individualism; a language of mutual responsibility and practices of commitment to the public good; the explicit acknowledgement of interconnectedness and a broader conception of what one's "community" is, i.e., more than just one's geographic locale; the maintenance of public institutions that are more tolerant of diversity and that nurture common standards of justice and civility.

Others have similarly identified the link between a particular set of values and beliefs and general contributory or prosocial behaviors. Wuthnow (1995) speaks of frameworks of understanding that entail a positive view of "caring." Wilson and Musick (1997) refer to a "culture of benevolence" that generates attitudes and values which are supportive of helping behavior. And Schervish and Havens (1997) speak of "frameworks of consciousness," or patterned ways of thinking, that contain "mobilizing beliefs" (an admixture of fundamental orientations, general values, and specific concerns) and induce commitment to a cause. None of these observers suggests directly that people who are volunteers will have values distinct from those of non-volunteers, but their commentaries imply the likelihood of systematic difference.

An important unresolved issue is the form that value differences take. While some prior research has suggested that volunteers differ from non-volunteers less in the substantive *content* of values and beliefs than in the *strength* of values held in common, Janoski et al. (1998), found large volunteer-nonvolunteer differences in terms of values concerning prosociality.

So whether there is a distinctive set of values associated with volunteering clearly stands as a matter for empirical probing. Values and beliefs, whether narrowly or broadly conceived, that are embraced by individuals who engage in volunteer activity constitute an unmapped area in our understanding of volunteering and contributory behaviors.

The present study has several particular features: it examines a large number of values along with perceptions and beliefs; it utilizes data from a nation-wide survey in Canada; it seeks to identify the set of values, perceptions and beliefs that are distinctively associated with volunteering rather than those that are determinants of this behavior; and it addresses the question of whether such a constellation of values constitutes an ethos, i.e., has consistency and coherence.

DATA AND ANALYSIS STRATEGY

The data on which this study is based were created in 1997 in face-to-face, in-home interviews with a nationally representative sample of more than 2000 individuals across Canada. The questionnaire contained 144 questions in 9 sections, of which eight were concerned with a wide range of values, perceptions, and beliefs pertaining to selected aspects of Canadian society and the requirements for a good society, with a subset of questions addressing selected respondent behaviors including volunteering and charitable giving, and one section contained a range of standard sociodemographic variables such as occupation, education, income, place of birth, etc. This national survey was conducted under the auspices of the project, "Individuals, Institutions, and the Social Contract in Canada," directed by one of the present authors (Reed).

Data from 92 of the questions concerned with values, perceptions and beliefs have been used in this study, the responses to many of which took the form of 4-point ordinal (i.e., Likert) scales. There were three dimensions to the dependent variable in the analysis: the first was the respondent having volunteered during the 12 months preceding the interview, i.e., "helping some organization or group by doing such things as canvassing, organizing activities, coaching, providing care, delivering food, doing clerical or administrative work, or other kinds of activities." The second was the frequency of formal volunteering, varying from "more than once a week" to "less frequently than once or twice a month". The third dimension was the respondent having helped others outside their household directly "on their own, not through an organization or group . . . . in the past twelve months . . . . [in such ways] as cooking, shopping, babysitting, writing letters, shoveling snow, mowing the lawn," etc. Together, these three questions permit comparisons in pairwise combinations between people in the categories of formal volunteering, direct or informal helping, volunteering of different magnitudes (frequency), and non-volunteering. This set of categories, in comparisons, permits considerable choice, without a priori judgment, as to which measure of contributing to the well-being of others is maximal or optimal.

The sample of 2014 respondents had the following composition: individuals involved only in formal volunteering: 99 (4.9%); in direct personal helping only: 577 (28.6%); in both formal and direct helping: 948 (47.1%); involved in neither: 346 (17.2); and 44 (2.2%) cases with data missing.

A suite of questions guided our analysis. While the primary question was, is there a distinctive set of values, beliefs and perceptions that distinguish volunteers from non-volunteers?, there were subordinate questions about the form or category of volunteer: high-time volunteers or moderate-time volunteers? Formal volunteers only or formal and/or informal volunteers (helping others directly, not through an organization)?

Our analytical strategy consisted of two stages: the first was to compare a variety of these categories in terms of the 92 values, perceptions, and beliefs to ascertain the extent and content of differences between various pairs of categories. The second stage involved logistic regression modeling to identify the extent to which values, perceptions, and beliefs were influential, alone and in combination with a set of sociodemographic factors, in differentiating (1) all volunteers from nonvolunteers, (2) active (i.e., weekly or more frequent) volunteers from nonvolunteers, and (3) both formal and direct helping volunteers from individuals who were neither.

ANALYSIS

We undertook a series of types of volunteers pair-wise comparisons of categories involving the 92 values, perceptions and beliefs. For each comparison of two categories of individuals, the degree of association between categories and responses to each of the 92 value and belief items was measured using a X^2 test. A significant level of association (at the 5% level of alpha) indicates that the two groups under consideration were statistically different in their response patterns. Typically this means that one group more strongly agreed or disagreed with a particular statement than did the other. Examination of each item where there was a significant difference revealed that in most cases the difference in response patterns was a matter of degree, rather than indicative of opposing views. For example, for Question 38n: "I don't see how my taxes benefit me, or society," 53% of volunteers agree or strongly agree with the statement while 62% of nonvolunteers agree or strongly agree. The difference between these two groups was a matter of degree; nonvolunteers were statistically more likely to agree with this item although the majority of both groups did agree with the item. On some items, in contrast, not only was the response pattern different, it reflected an *opposition* of views between the two groups. For example, for Question 38m: "These days I am so hard pressed to take care of my own needs that I worry less about the needs of others," the majority of volunteers (62%) disagreed with the item while the majority of non-volunteers (55%) agreed. We have designated the items where two groups generally express *opposing* views as the *principal differentiating questions*.

The results for the seven pairings showing the largest and smallest differences are presented in Table 6.1. Not surprisingly, the largest number of differences occurred between (1) individuals who were both formal volunteers and informal direct helpers, and individuals who were neither (different on 69 of 92 value variables); (2) all formal volunteers versus non-volunteers (different on 66 of 92); and followed closely by (3) direct helping individuals and non-volunteers (63 of 92). At the other end of the spectrum, comparisons within overall categories yielded small differences: formal-only volunteers versus direct helping: only 19 of 92, and individuals volunteering weekly or more versus less than weekly: only 16 of 92.

The results support several conclusions. First, the differences in values, perceptions and beliefs lie fundamentally between individuals who volunteer or

Table 6.1. Result of Pairwise Comparisons on 92 Values and Beliefs

Groups being compared	Number of significantly different values[a]
1a. All formal volunteers vs. all nonvolunteers	66/92
1b. More than weekly volunteers vs. nonvolunteers	49/92
1c. Weekly or more volunteers vs. nonvolunteers	53/92
1d. Weekly or more volunteers vs. less than weekly volunteers	16/92
2. Formal plus direct helping volunteers vs. neither	69/92
3. Direct helping individuals only vs. nonvolunteers	63/92
4. Formal-only volunteers vs. direct helping only individuals	19/92

[a]Chi^2 is significant at the .05 level or better.

help in some way, regardless of whether it is done through an organization or directly and personally (or if the former, done weekly or less frequently) and individuals who do not volunteer. Second, the statistically significant differences are extensive, occurring on 68 to 75 percent of the measured values. Third, while the differences are generally moderate for the majority of questions, they are especially strong for a small subset of eight. These strong, principal differentiating questions are the following:

- Q.8 a) The best way to be a good member of the community is to mind your own business and not bother other people. (Volunteers disagreed, non-volunteers agreed.)
- Q.8 b) Individuals cannot be expected to join or support organizations that promote interests other than their own. (Volunteers disagreed, non-volunteers agreed.)
- Q.8 h) There is nothing wrong with giving advantages to people from the same ethnic, cultural or racial group as yourself. (Volunteers disagreed, non-volunteers agreed.)
- Q.8 n) Immigrants cannot expect to be considered as fully Canadian as those who were born and raised here. (Volunteers disagreed, non-volunteers agreed.)
- Q.30 d) How much do you trust businessmen *not* to take advantage of you? (Volunteers were trusting, non-volunteers were not.)
- Q.38 j) The needs of individuals are the responsibility of themselves and their families and not of the community. (Volunteers disagreed, non-volunteers agreed.)
- Q.38 l) As long as one pays one's taxes, it is not necessary to support community organizations and activities. (Volunteers disagreed, non-volunteers agreed.)

- Q.38 m) These days I am so hard-pressed to take care of my own needs that I worry less about the needs of others. (Volunteers disagreed, non-volunteers agreed.)

We have, then, evidence in these bi-variate relationships that volunteers, however specified, exhibit a set of values, perceptions, and beliefs that are different from those of non-volunteers. These eight questions point to a number of factors which we would argue are consistent and coherent and thus constitute an ethos that is distinctive to volunteers. The elements in this ethos are:

1. Recognition of the existence and importance of a civic or communal good.
2. Belief that individuals have a responsibility to support and contribute to the common good, regardless of the responsibilities for supporting the common good that may be delegated to organizations or institutions such as churches or governments.
3. Belief in the necessity of active personal involvement in contributing to the common good over and above the standard obligations of citizenship such as paying taxes.
4. A worldview that is notably (a) rather more universalistic or cosmopolitan than particularistic, (b) inclusive, (c) trusting, and (d) more prosocial than individualistic.
5. A worldview that sees individuals and their social milieu as interconnected rather than separated.

We turn now to multivariate analysis of the full set of values and beliefs that differentiate volunteers from non-volunteers, in concert with socio-demographic variables.

The questions on values, perceptions, and beliefs were designed in thematic clusters dealing with related issues. As a result, the responses tend to be modestly correlated but not enough to form reliable additive scales. The questions comprising section 8, for example, all refer to broad norms of behavior. Among the 120 pair-wise combinations of these sixteen questions, there are 81 significant correlations, but only six are greater than 0.3 and none are greater than 0.4. Although these questions are related, they are not merely indicators of a single underlying construct. (This is also evident in a reliability (alpha) of only 0.65 for a simple additive scale of these questions, and in the fact that the first component of a principal components analysis accounts for only 20% of total variance.)

Because the items are correlated, the bivariate results may mislead in a way that suggests that a question distinguishes between two groups to some extent when in fact it is simply acting as a proxy for a related question that more strongly differentiates the two groups. To identify which values, perceptions, and beliefs most clearly distinguish between the pairs of groups we have already examined,

Table 6.2. Logistic Regression Models Comparing All Volunteers with Nonvolunteers

	Model 1 values only	Model 2 values + background
	effect[a]	effect[a]
Values (for question number see Appendix)[b]		
Should mind own business (Q8a)	−14.6*	ns
Laws should always be respected (Q8i)	25.8**	26.9**
People should stay attached to ethnic group (Q8o)	−17.3*	−17.7**
Standard of living is declining (Q9b)	−18.7**	−18.7**
Fewer job opportunities for my gender (Q14)	24.1**	23.2**
Should be careful trusting others (Q29)	−21.6**	−19.8**
Have much control over your life (Q31)	20.9*	18.4*
Canada better off if less government (Q38h)	19.2**	18.9**
If pay taxes, that's enough community support (Q38l)	−18.6**	−19.1**
So hard-pressed I don't worry about others (Q38m)	−29.6**	−31.7**
Very concerned about my city (Q52)	33.5**	33.7**
Sociodemographics		
Lives in a rural community		38.9**
Education in years of schooling		9.4**
Constant	−2.12**	−3.03**
% R^2	11.0	12.1

[a] % Change in the odds of being a volunteer; significance: *$p < .05$; **$p < .01$; ns: not significant.
[b] All values variables are coded in such a way that high scores reflect strong agreement with the statement.

we estimated logistic regression models. Table 2 presents the models that compare all formal volunteers with nonvolunteers, Table 3 presents a comparison of active formal volunteers with nonvolunteers, and Table 4 presents a comparison of formal and direct helping volunteers with those who did neither formal volunteering nor direct helping. Our strategy in developing the models for each comparison was to take all the variables (questions) that were found to be significantly associated with being a volunteer in the first section of the analysis above, and estimate a logistic regression model predicting membership in either the volunteer or nonvolunteer categories. The variables with the highest probability of having no effect on the dependent variable were progressively eliminated from the model until only those that had a statistically significant effect remained. These are presented as model 1 in each of Tables 6.2, 6.3 and 6.4. The next step was to enter a set of social and demographic variables and then progressively eliminate those that had no influence on the likelihood of being a volunteer, along any of the values variables from model 1 that were no longer significant, once socio-demographic variables were controlled for. The results of this procedure are found in model 2 in Tables 6.2, 6.3 and 6.4.

The logistic regression coefficients in these tables are presented as the percentage change in the odds of being a volunteer. This is a straightforward way

Table 6.3. Logistic Regression Models Comparing Active Volunteers with Nonvolunteers

	Model 1 values only	Model 2 values and background
	effect[a]	effect[a]
Values (for question number see Appendix)[b]		
Laws should always be respected (Q8i)	21.2*	22.8*
People should stay attached to ethnic group (Q8o)	−23.0*	−20.8*
Fewer job opportunities for my gender (Q14)	33.9*	28.5**
Should be careful trusting others (Q29)	−16.9*	ns
Feel very at home in my community (Q34)	42.8**	33.6*
Needs are responsibility of individual/family, not society (Q38j)	−21.8**	−20.6*
If pay taxes, that's enough community support (Q38l)	−22.9*	ns
So hard-pressed I don't worry about others (Q38m)	−37.4**	−42.2**
Very concerned about my city (Q52)	44.7**	44.9**
Sociodemographics		
Lives in a rural community		53.1**
Lives in the Prairies		77.3**
Lives in British Columbia		126.4**
Religiosity		36.5**
Education in years of schooling		14.4**
Constant	−3.81**	−5.62**
% R^2	18.2	23.7

[a] % Change in the odds of being a volunteer; significance: *$p < .05$; **$p < .01$; ns: not significant.
[b] All values variables are coded in such a way that high scores reflect strong agreement with the statement.

of presenting the effect of an independent variable on the likelihood of being a volunteer, and allows for a direct comparison of the relative strength of the various value and belief variables. These coefficients indicate the percent change in the odds of being a volunteer that would occur given a one-unit change (from agree to strongly agree, for example) in the relevant independent variable (Menard, 1995: 49). The interpretation of the R^2 for each model is analogous to its use in ordinary regression analysis: it shows the proportion of total variability in the dependent variable that is accounted for by the model. The larger the R^2, the better the model was able to discriminate between the two groups being compared.

All Volunteers versus Nonvolunteers

Model 1 in Table 6.2 shows the eleven questions that significantly differentiate between volunteers and nonvolunteers. This model accounts for 11% ($R^2 = 0.11$) of the variation in the probability of being a volunteer. In model 2,

Table 6.4. Logistic Regression Models Comparing Respondents Who Were Both Formal and Direct Helping Volunteers with Those Who Were Neither

	Model 1 Values only	Model 2 Values and background
	effect[a]	effect[a]
Values (for question number see Appendix)[b]		
Feel strong obligation to my ethnic group Q6d	−20.4**	ns
Children should learn to cooperate Q7c	64.0**	ns
Children should learn loyalty to ethnic group Q7d	−25.4**	−22.0**
Children should learn to work hard Q7e	53.2**	46.7*
Immigrants are not as Canadian as native-born Q8n	−19.9**	−20.5**
Equal chances at education and jobs Q37	67.3**	56.4**
If pay taxes, that's enough community support Q38l	−25.6**	−28.6**
So hard-pressed I don't worry about others Q38m	−45.0**	−42.1**
Very concerned about my city Q52	32.1**	28.3*
Sociodemographics		
Lives in midsize town		341.5**
Lives in small town		219.7**
Lives in a rural community		307.0**
Education in years of schooling		16.6**
Lives in British Columbia		142.7**
Constant	−1.15**	−2.52*
R^2	22.5	31.1

[a] % Change in the odds of being a volunteer; significance: *p < .05; **p < .01; ns: not significant.
[b] All values variables are coded in such a way that high scores reflect strong agreement with the statement.

two (from a total of ten) sociodemographic factors are sufficiently influential to be added to the first model containing only values; education and living in a rural area. The effect of one value question (Q.8a) drops out of the model when education is controlled. The second model accounts for 12% of the variation in volunteering. In both models, the explained variation is small, indicating that the value factors, even with the sociodemographic variables taken into account, are not very effective in predicting who will be volunteers and nonvolunteers. In other words, when comparing individuals who had been, with those who had not been, volunteers at any time at all over the 12 months preceding the survey, there is very little difference in their values and beliefs. On this basis, the value set of volunteers as a whole is shown to differ little from that of non-volunteers. However, comparing all volunteers to non-volunteers may not be the most appropriate way to determine whether or not there is a distinctive set of values associated with being a volunteer because of the heterogeneity known to exist in the full population of volunteers, so we move on to another pair-wise comparison which reduces that heterogeneity.

Active Volunteers versus Nonvolunteers

As a group, volunteers include individuals who give several hundred hours of their time during the year, and others who give only a few hours. Thirty-six percent of volunteers in our sample reported doing volunteer work less frequently than once a month, while 35% reported volunteering once a week or more often. For the first group, volunteering may be incidental to their values and beliefs while for the second group, whom we have labeled as active volunteers, the substantially greater commitment of time and effort may be a direct expression of their values, perceptions and beliefs. In order to identify a distinctive set of values among volunteers, it may be more appropriate to compare only significantly *active* volunteers with nonvolunteers.

Model 1 in Table 6.3 estimates the probability of being an active volunteer versus being a non-volunteer on the basis of the value questions alone. This model accounts for 18% of the variation in the data, a clear improvement over the previous two models that compared all volunteers with nonvolunteers. When the sociodemographic factors are added, the regression (model 2) rises further to one quarter ($R^2 = 0.24$) of the variation in volunteering. While these are still modest levels of variation accounted for, it is significant that just seven attitude questions and four sociodemographic factors actually do so well in predicting who will be an active volunteer.

Seven of the nine value variables in model 2 are coded on a 4-point scale in such a way that strong agreement with each statement receives the highest score. The two exceptions are a question about how concerned one is with what is happening in one's city where the higher score reflects being very concerned, and the question on job opportunities for one's gender where the high score indicates that the respondent believes there are fewer opportunities for their gender.

Model 2 shows that active volunteers have a stronger sense of belonging to their community (Q.34) and are more concerned about conditions in their city (Q.52). They care more about others (Q.38m) and are less ethnocentric (Q.8o). They believe that society has some responsibility to help the needy (Q.38j) and that laws (i.e., legitimate authority) should be respected (Q.8i). And finally, active volunteers are more likely to believe that individuals of their gender have fewer opportunities for jobs and promotions than do their opposites. Together, these views suggest that active volunteers manifest a heightened sense of social responsibility and involvement. This finding fits with previous research indicating that volunteers tend to be more "other-directed" than nonvolunteers. But beyond this, the fact that most of the value questions are not present in the models suggests that broad contrasts representing liberal-conservative, or left-right political and social philosophies in general, are *not* dimensions of significant difference between volunteers and nonvolunteers.

Both Formal and Direct Helping Volunteers versus Those Who Were Neither

The final part of the multivariate analysis compares individuals who were both formal volunteers and direct helpers, with individuals who were neither. Not surprisingly, these groups stand in sharp contrast. On one side are people who have helped others in the preceding 12 months, *both* through an organization as a formal volunteer *and* by lending assistance directly to strangers, friends, neighbors, or non-household relatives. On the other side are those who were neither formal volunteers nor direct helpers. The first group is actively involved in their community in various ways while the second is not involved at all. If there is a generalized ethos of prosociality or benevolence that underpins helping behaviors, it should be most clearly evident in the comparison of these two extremely different types of individuals.

Model 1 in Table 6.4 supports this contention. Nine value and belief questions by themselves account for 23% of the variation in being a helper. With controls for sociodemographic background factors (Model 2), this rises to 31%. In both models, there are marked differences between these groups in their values, perceptions and beliefs.

From Model 2 in Table 6.4, it is evident that those who help others show more concern about others (Q.38m) and about their community (Q.52). They believe in equality of opportunity (Q.37) and the value of hard work (Q.7e), and have a less narrowly circumscribed sense of community (Q.7d and Q.8n). They also believe that individuals must do more for others in society than simply being responsible taxpayers (Q.38l). Together, these items show that a basic level of helping behavior is underpinned by a broader concern for one's community, coupled with a basic sense of fairness as an organizing principle in society.

CONCLUDING COMMENTARY

The combination of several key elements in this study—the large number of questions on values, perceptions, and beliefs; the measures of both formal volunteering and direct personal helping; and the measure of frequency of volunteering—have enabled us to respond affirmatively to the question, Do people who volunteer have a distinctive ethos? Yes, some but not all do. Our analysis indicates that (1) the full ethos consists of both *a limited set* of *strongly* differentiating values and beliefs *and* a *large number* of *mildly* differentiating values, but that (2) this ethos characterized principally by people who manifest a higher or more generalized level of prosociality. While little difference in values was found between volunteers and non-volunteers, substantial differences were found between active (i.e., frequent) volunteers and nonvolunteers, and between formal and direct helping volunteers, and people who were neither. In addition, even when sociodemographic variables were accounted for in the logit models, values continued to have clear and significant effects in differentiating volunteers from non-volunteers. Arguably, the presence of this ethos among individuals who are higher-frequency (i.e., more strongly committed) volunteers and who also engage in direct personal acts of caring and helping is indicative of something more than just prosociality—of a syndrome of generosity mixed with civic engagement and concern for the common good.

These unambiguous findings may be to some degree a product of the 92 particular values, perceptions and beliefs on which we compared volunteers of various kinds with non-volunteers. Perhaps a different or larger set of questions would have yielded different results; this will only be ascertained by further empirical probing. What is clear, though, is that values, perceptions and beliefs, broadly identified, occupy a significant, perhaps key place in the panoply of factors that distinguish people who manifest a strong "helping and caring" syndrome.

Active volunteering is distinctive—we might even say anomalous—in several ways in Canadian society. It has a relatively low incidence as a general social phenomenon but an elevated incidence in some social environments and among individuals with certain characteristics. Being cooperative action toward providing a collective good of some kind, it runs counter to such dominant elements of contemporary North American culture as possessive individualism and the competitive maximizing of self-advantage. As with all anomalies, it begs for explanation. Efforts to construct a better understanding of the correlates of, and the social dynamics that give rise to, active volunteering will have to take account not only of contextual (macrosocial) and personality (microsocial) factors but the presence of a distinctive set of values and beliefs, perhaps even a worldview, among volunteers. That a particular ethos characterizes active volunteers coincides with our finding from other research (Reed & Selbee, 2000) that three of the most strongly correlated characteristics of such individuals are particular family background and early life experience, religious belief (which is often transmitted from parents to children), and the presence or absence of a university education. These three factors all entail social learning and social reproduction and likely play influential roles in creating the ethos that underlies volunteering. There will be significant payoff for theory-building when we are able to understand the influence of the ethos factor relative to other categories of variables, and even more so when we understand the societal processes by which the distinctive ethos of active volunteers is selectively generated and transmitted.

APPENDIX

The 92 value, perception, and belief items used in the analysis are taken from the questions below. Each item is identified by its question number and by a lower case letter identifying the subsection of the question involved. The section headings in the questionnaire are included here in order to clarify the intent and grouping of related questions. For illustrative purposes, we indicate with an asterisk the 53 questions where active volunteers (weekly or more often) were significantly different from nonvolunteers.

I. Conception of the "good" society

1. Which of the following do you think is the most important for a society to function well?
    a) That people give up some of their personal advantages for the common good
    b) That all people put aside their different backgrounds and become a common people
    c) That there is a widespread commitment to a set of common values*
    d) That individuals independently pursue their own goals
2. Which of them do you consider the least important?
    a) That people give up some of their personal advantages for the common good
    b) That all people put aside their different backgrounds and become a common people
    c) That there is a widespread commitment to a set of common values*
    d) That individuals independently pursue their own goals
3. Whom do you admire more?
    a) People who go their own way without worrying about what others think; or
    b) People who learn to fit in and get along with others?

II. Requirements of membership

Nature of Obligations

4. People have different ideas about their main obligations as a member of society. Which of the following do you consider your most important obligation
    a) To pursue your own goals and aspirations to the best of your abilities
    b) To always consider the common good in your decisions and actions
    c) To uphold basic human and moral values in all circumstances*
    d) To maintain the distinctive identity and heritage of our society
5. And which do you consider your least important obligation?
    a) To pursue your own goals and aspirations to the best of your abilities*
    b) To always consider the common good in your decisions and actions
    c) To uphold basic human and moral values in all circumstances
    d) To maintain the distinctive identity and heritage of our society

Social Boundaries of Obligation

6. How strong an obligation do you feel towards helping the following kinds of people: Very strong, moderately strong, not too strong, or not strong at all?
    a) Family
    b) Close friends*
    c) People in the same boat as I am in life
    d) People from my ethnic, cultural or racial group*
    e) Any person in society who needs help*

III. Required individual qualities and principles of behavior

Individual Qualities

7. Please tell me how important you think it is that children be encouraged to learn each of the following at home: very important, somewhat important, not very important, or not at all important?
   a) To be concerned for the needs of others*
   b) To stick to your principles even if it is not easy or popular*
   c) The ability to cooperate with others*
   d) Loyalty to the traditions of your ethnic, cultural or racial group
   e) Motivation to work hard
   f) The desire to get ahead in life

Principles of Behavior

8. Do you strongly agree, agree, disagree or strongly disagree with each of the following statements
   a) The best way to be a good member of the community is to mind your own business and not bother other people*
   b) Individuals cannot be expected to join or support organizations that promote interests other than their own
   c) Everyone owes something to society and should try to give something back*
   d) Only agreements that are written and signed need to be honored; verbal agreements don't matter*
   e) It's OK to try to get out of paying tax any way we can because everyone else is doing it*
   f) Being honest makes it more likely that you will not come out ahead*
   g) Promises are just made to get people to do things for you and don't always have to be kept*
   h) There is nothing wrong with giving advantages to people from the same ethnic, cultural or racial group as yourself*
   i) Laws should be respected and obeyed regardless of your opinions about them*
   j) Everything is relative, and there just aren't any definite rules to live by*
   k) Each person can make real progress only when the groups to which they belong make progress

IV. Entitlements

   l) People have a right to be able to do what they want to do with their lives
   m) Everyone is entitled to help from others when they are in serious need or face difficult situations*
   n) Immigrants cannot expect to be considered as fully Canadian as those who were born and raised here*
   o) People have to stay attached to their own ethnic, cultural or racial group because it is only there that they can count on being fully accepted*
   p) A child molester is entitled to the same treatment by the police and the courts as any other individual*

V. Threats to the "good" society

9. People have different views about the problems faced by our society today. Do you strongly agree, agree, disagree, or strongly disagree that the trouble with our society is:
   a) that there are too many people who expect to get something for nothing?
   b) that the standard of living is declining?*
   c) that there are too many people preoccupied with what they can get out of the system rather than with what they can contribute to the common good?
   d) that there is less willingness to help those in need?
   e) that we encourage too much ethnic, cultural or racial diversity in the country?
   f) that too many people will sacrifice their principles in order to get ahead economically
10. Do you strongly agree, agree, disagree or strongly disagree with the following statements:
    a) Tolerance for people who are different from ourselves is declining in our society
    b) Public trust is being weakened by the behavior of people in positions of public responsibility and leadership
    c) Public trust is being weakened by the behavior of people who manage business corporations
    d) There is too much concern for every group's fair share and not enough for the needs of the society as a whole
    e) People today are less concerned with fairness and social justice than they were a few years ago*
    f) In our society, there are two sets of rules: one for those who have money and one for everyone else

VI. Experiential variables

Sense of Fairness

12. What about you personally: how fairly do you feel you are being treated in this society: very fairly, somewhat fairly, not too fairly, or not at all fairly?*
13. Let me ask you about opportunities for jobs and promotions. Do you think that people of your own ethnic, cultural or racial background have more, the same, or fewer opportunities for jobs and promotions as people of other ethnic, cultural or racial backgrounds?
14. What about men and women: do you think that [men/women: gender of respondent] have more, the same, or fewer opportunities for jobs and promotions than [women/men]?*
16. How fairly would you say that the class you belong to is treated in our society today: very fairly, somewhat fairly, not too fairly, or not at all fairly?*
17. I would like to ask you about federal government programs: Is the province you live in getting more than its fair share of these programs, about its fair share or less than its fair share?

Assessment of Economic Situation and Degree of Security

We are also interested in finding out how people are getting along financially these days.

18. As far as you and your family are concerned, would you say you are very satisfied, somewhat satisfied, somewhat dissatisfied, or very dissatisfied about the way you are getting along financially?*

20. Do you think that a year from now you and your family will be better off, worse off, or about the same financially as you are now?
21. How would you assess the economic prospects for young people today? Do you think they are very good, good, poor, or very poor?
22. What about your own children or grandchildren? Do you think their prospects are very good, good, poor, or very poor?*

Assessment of Status, Recognition and Status Security

This country is made up of many different kinds of people. Although each one makes a contribution to our society, that contribution may not be recognized to the same degree.

23. I would like to ask you about the contribution to society of people of your own ethnic, cultural or racial background. How satisfied are you with the recognition people of your background are receiving for their contribution to society: very satisfied, somewhat satisfied, somewhat dissatisfied, or very dissatisfied?
24. Would you say that people of your background are receiving more, less or about the same recognition for their contribution to society as they did a few years ago?
25. What about people with your level of education or training? How satisfied are you with the recognition that they are receiving for their contribution to society: very satisfied, somewhat satisfied, somewhat dissatisfied, or very dissatisfied?*
26. Do you feel that people with your level of education and training are receiving more, less or about the same recognition for their contribution to society as they were a few years ago?
27. And what about [men/women: gender of respondent] How satisfied are you with the recognition that [men/women] are receiving for their contribution to society: very satisfied, somewhat satisfied, somewhat dissatisfied, or very dissatisfied?
28. Do you feel that [men/women: gender of respondent] are receiving more, less or about the same recognition for their contribution to society as they were a few years ago?*

Trust

29. Do you strongly agree, agree, disagree or strongly disagree with the following statement: Individuals should be careful about trusting others since there are too many people who only seek to benefit themselves.*
30. Some people place different amounts of trust in others; they may be concerned that others may take advantage of them. How much do you trust the following people to not take advantage of you: a lot, some, not very much or not at all?*
    b) your friends*
    c) people who have different political beliefs
    d) politicians in the federal
    e) businessmen*
    f) members of your ethnic, cultural or racial background
    g) people who have different moral values
    h) politicians in your province
    j) your family
    k) people who have different religious beliefs

Sense of Control

31. Some people feel they have control over the way their lives turn out, and other people feel that what they themselves do has no real effect on what happens to them. What about you: do you feel you have a great deal of control, some, not very much or none at all over the way your life turns out?*

Degree of Social Integration

32. How satisfied are you with the number of good friends you have? Are you very satisfied, somewhat satisfied, somewhat dissatisfied, or very dissatisfied?*
34. How much do you feel at home in the community where you live: very much, somewhat, a little, or not at all?*
35. How much do you feel at home in this society as a whole: very much, somewhat, a little, or not at all?*

VII. Consequence Variables

Position on Social Justice Issues

36. In our society, various sorts of programmes exist to help people in need. Do you think that such programmes should be funded mainly through voluntary contributions or mainly through taxes?
37. In your view, how important is it that everyone has the same chances at a good education and a good job as anyone else? Very important, somewhat important, not very important, or not at all important?*
38. Do you strongly agree, agree, disagree or strongly disagree with the following statements:
    a) Places should be reserved for ethnic and racial minorities to ensure their adequate representation in the work place
    b) There should be programmes for people disadvantaged in one way or another to make sure that they have the same chances as everyone else
    c) Everyone in society has a right to a minimum income

Position on Alternative Life Styles: Inclusion or Exclusion

    d) I do not approve of people with ideas and lifestyles that differ significantly from what is generally accepted
    e) I find that to be gay or lesbian is acceptable*

Position on Cultural Diversity

    f) Ethnic, cultural and racial groups should try as much as possible to blend into Canadian society
    g) The ideal society is one in which people are sufficiently similar to feel at home with one another*

Importance/Responsibility of Public and Private Sectors

    h) The country would be better off if there were less government.
    i) Canada would be a better place to live if there were fewer laws and regulations*

g) The needs of individuals are the responsibility of themselves and their families and not of the community*

k) Helping people in need should be the responsibility of volunteer and charitable organizations; governments should become involved only as a last resort

l) As long as one pays one's taxes, it is not necessary to support community organizations and activities*

m) These days, I am so hard-pressed to take care of my own needs that I worry less about the needs of others*

n) I have trouble seeing how the taxes I pay benefit me or society*

Social Participation

People are mostly concerned about their families, their jobs and the demands of day-to-day living, but they may also be concerned about what happens in the community where they live and in the larger society.

50. How much are you concerned—a lot, a fair amount, not too much, or not at all with what happens in Canadian society as a whole?*

51. How much are you concerned with what happens in your province?

52. And what about the city or town you live in?*

REFERENCES

Bellah, R.N., Madsen, R., Sullivan, W.M., Swidler, & Tipton, S.N. (1985). *Habits of the heart*. Berkeley: University of California Press.

Hallie, P. (1979). *Lest innocent blood be shed*. New York: HarperCollins.

Hougland, J.S., & Christenson, J.A. (1982). Voluntary organizations and dominant American values. *Journal of Voluntary Action Research, 11*, 4.

Janoski, T., Musick, M., & Wilson, J. (1998). Being Volunteered? *Sociological Forum, 13*, 495–519.

Menard, S. (1995). *Applied logistic regression analysis*. New York: Wiley.

Reed, P.B., & Selbee, K. (2000). Distinguishing characteristics of active volunteers in Canada. *Nonprofit and Voluntary Sector Quarterly, 29*, 4, 571–592.

Schervish, P.G., & Havens, J.J. (1997). Social participation and charitable giving: a multivariate analysis. *Voluntas, 8*, 3, 235–260.

Smith, D. (1994). Determinants of voluntary association participation and volunteering: A literature review. *Nonprofit and Voluntary Sector Quarterly, 23*, 3, 243–263.

Sundeen, R., & Roskoff, S.A. (1995). Teenage volunteers and their values. *Nonprofit and Voluntary Sector Quarterly, 24*, 4, 337–357.

Sundeen, R A., & Raskoff, S.A. (1995). Teenage volunteers and their values. *Nonprofit and Voluntary Sector Quarterly, 24*, 337–357.

Wilson, J., & Musick, M. (1997a). Who cares? Toward an integrated theory of volunteer work. *American Sociological Review, 62*, 694–713.

Wuthnow, R. (1991). *Acts of compassion*. Princeton, NJ: Princeton University Press.

Wuthnow, R. (1995). *Learning to care*. New York: Oxford University Press.

Chapter 7

A Humanistic Perspective on the Volunteer-Recipient Relationship
A Mexican study

JACQUELINE BUTCHER

INTRODUCTION

The definition of a volunteer is both ample and distinctive, denoting an individual who, out of free will, acts for the benefit of others without receiving remuneration for that action. As the American Red Cross (1989) defines them: "Volunteers are individuals who reach out beyond the confines of their paid employment and of their normal responsibilities to contribute time and service to a non-for-profit cause in the belief that their activity is beneficial to others as well as satisfying to themselves," basically coinciding with other recent definitions, such as the one employed by the United Nations, drawn by experts on Volunteering and Social Development (1999). They suggest that volunteering takes different forms and meanings in different settings, and "what may be seen as volunteering in one country may be dismissed as low pay or labor intensive work in another." An increasing number of cross-cultural and cross-country studies suggest that this statement could be regarded as the general understanding of volunteering. The benefits that volunteers appreciate through this type of activity have been studied from interdisciplinary angles and are widely recognized. This chapter draws attention to existing ideas of satisfaction and benefits in voluntarism extending the analysis to discuss and examine, not only what volunteers receive through their actions, but also the perceptions and reactions of the recipients of voluntary action, with a primary focus on the quality of the exchange and the kinds of relationships that the participants establish.

Our main observations in this chapter are based on a humanistic analysis of an empirical study on volunteer and recipient perceptions and benefits, including a look into the relationships resulting from face to face interactions. This study was designed to answer the questions: How do individuals establish a volunteer-recipient relationship? What kind of relationship is productive for both sides and what benefits do both individuals perceive, if any? How are attitudes important? How is the element of service important in these interactions? Is there a difference between giving, helping and serving others? And finally, how does culture affect the relationships between volunteers and recipients?

The study was undertaken with Mexican volunteers. This setting introduced the possibility of traditional paternalistic practices contained within the culture influencing the relationships between volunteers and recipients as they evolved. Consequently, there was specific research interest in seeing if traditional dependency permeated into the one-on-one interactions between volunteers and recipients, as well as finding out if these relationships strived for either autonomy or dependency, thus reinforcing paternalistic patterns of behavior.

It is known that history has a strong influence in how nongovernmental organizations (NGOs) are formed in a society, implying that attitudes within voluntarism may vary in different cultures. Therefore, understanding the context in which voluntary action exists can illuminate the way civil society, civic participation, and attitudes toward volunteering have been shaped.

It could be said that in Mexico, a mentality of dependency historically stems from structures that were imposed during the Spanish conquest (1524) when the Catholic Church destroyed the problem solving capacity, the reciprocity and solidarity customs that the indigenous population had established to sustain and address community problems. Such traditional systems were replaced by the concept of social assistance or welfare, based on an idea of Christian charity. After the Independence and the laws of Reform (1860), authority changed and most social institutions were taken over by the State. Even after the Mexican Revolution (1910), social welfare was considered a social right. The more recent neoliberal trends began transferring more welfare functions onto civil society, but without the necessary resources or appropriate laws in place that would enable this shift to succeed.

In the 1960s, as NGOs proliferated around the globe, civic participation began to become important in public affairs. Some authors propose that an impulse to greater civilian involvement can be traced to the 1985 earthquake in Mexico City (Schmelkes, 1997). This is not to say that voluntary action has not been present in Mexican civil society, but that voluntarism in more formal settings and through NGOs is a more recent phenomenon (Butcher, 2001).

Volunteering in Mexico and in Latin America, does not take after the Tocquevillean tradition and is not considered part of the formal culture. Although volunteer action is present, it occurs many times in informal settings and remains unaccounted for. It takes the form of communitarian participation, especially among the indigenous population. Similar actions by other social groups are still considered a part of a moral and religious obligation, not expressed as membership in an established voluntary organization (Butcher, 2003).

Globalization has brought change in the last three decades and new groups have recently appeared in the national scenario. According to Centro Mexicano para la Filantropia (CEMEFI) (Mexican Center for Philanthropy), in a period of ten years, 1984 to 1994, as many NGOs were created as in the previous 100 years and their numbers are increasing. As in most of Latin America, NGOs in Mexico were seen with distrust by the government. However, the relationships between these organizations and government are experiencing a new facet due to a democratic vote that, in 2002, ended the 70-year rule of one political party. Today the climate for participation now seems more encouraging.

A HUMANISTIC APPROACH TO VOLUNTEERING

How man/woman is conceptually understood is the basis for the construction of theory around his attitudes and underlying motivations for taking action. Psychology encompasses various trends and perspectives in the pursuit of a better understanding of human behavior based on distinctive anthropological and philosophical differences. It could be said that contemporary psychology is divided into two major groupings. The first would be Positivist Psychology, based on the scientific method and natural sciences. Its main purpose is to study human behavior by applying the same laws and methodology employed in biology, mathematics, and physics: testing, experiments, quantification, and measurements of tangible results. Psychoanalysis and Behaviorism are in this group. The second would be Humanistic Psychology, which presents a holistic approach on the understanding of man. Transpersonal Psychology is part of this group since it includes transcendence within human potential. In general terms, the humanistic proposal differs from the psychoanalytic vision that considers the forces of the unconscious as the main explanation and source of the human conduct. It also differs from the behaviorist approach that considers human behavior as a product of external stimuli. The humanistic viewpoint is inclusive, encompassing different human dimensions, also taking into account values, purpose, meaning, and transcendence.

In the case study presented in this chapter, the humanistic perspective is the theoretical lens through which the relationships between volunteers and recipients are analyzed. Adoption of this psychological view is pertinent and distinctive since most previous inquiries on volunteerism, motivation and voluntary action employ positivist assumptions and mindset. However, such earlier research has been extremely useful for understanding volunteer participation and motivation for giving, thus presenting a strong basis for further studies in economy, sociology and social and clinical psychology. One of many such studies, reported by Luks (1980), included more than 3200 women. It investigated the relationship between volunteers' experiences and their health. The results were revealing. The great majority described a stimulant physical sensation during volunteering and the majority reported experiencing enhanced self-worth, a feeling of calm and well-being. This effect of what is now known as *Helper's High* or *Helper's Calm*, as Luks named it, is due to the biochemical effect of the secretion and release of endorphins into the body, which are known for their stress-reducing effect. These same substances are also released after a strong physical exercise or workout. However, altruism has advantages over exercise in terms of creating a positive state because, although the feel-good sensation is most intense when actually touching or listening to someone, it can apparently be recalled. The conclusion of this study is that voluntary action is not only physically good for the human body to counterattack stress, but it also has a double effect: when it happens and when it is brought back to memory. In most cases, when people remembered the volunteer episode, endorphins were released again. Two final observations: one, is that to receive this benefit, the action must be voluntary, if forced to help, for whatever reason, you may not benefit; and two, this effect only occurred when the voluntary action involved a face to face interaction. It did not arise when money was donated, no matter how important the cause, nor from volunteering without close personal contact.

Studying human nature in all its dimensions and unifying objective and subjective theories is useful to grasp a greater understanding of human beings. Years ago Weber spoke to this point when he combined comprehension (*Verstehen*) and explanation (*Erklären*), thus looking into both essence and existence. Humanism is interested in the subjective and qualitative aspects of human life, centering its study on the *self*, as well as on human phenomena such as: self-awareness, self-actualization, liberty, interpersonal relationships, personal values and the attitudes that flow from them. The person, in becoming aware of him/her self, becomes responsible for his/her existence and is able to recognize that even though there are limiting external environmental conditions, physical limitations and experiences that may be in the way of development, we all possess a positive potential that is inclined to self realization. So that life lived in the here and now, becomes a continuous process of learning and looking for meaning in one's own existence. Within these concepts, psychological disorders are viewed as blocking this process and several therapeutic systems are in place to facilitate individuals into developing their own potential (Gonzalez, 1995).

This perspective also recognizes that as we develop physically, the mind is subject to external factors such as social forces and heredity conditions that influence the development of individuals, but do not necessarily fully determine personality and conduct. This view goes deep into the understanding of human interpersonal relationships and how we learn about ourselves as we evolve into mature individuals. Through relationships we are able to create an ambience where growth is possible. Expressing these views in his Client Centered Therapy, Rogers (1961) considered that therapeutic relationships are established though an honest acceptance of the other person, empathy and congruency on the part of the therapist. These three conditions, in turn, are able to create a climate that facilitates self-discovery and at the same time is conducive to growth and personal development of self.

Relationships can be influential as to how we choose to enact what we consider important, in other words, on how we live our values. Relationships also open the possibility of a dialogue that may promote a setting of trust, understanding and shared participation. Rogers (1959) further explains his idea of how people relate to each other in formulating his General Law of Interpersonal Relationships. Buber (1970) presents the concept of relationships as "encounters." In his book, *I and Thou,* he speaks of the risks that are involved in our interactions with others. The relationships he considers worthwhile are those that involve the whole being, thus transforming the relationship into a true commitment "whoever commits himself may not hold back part of himself" (Buber, 1970: 60). But what he values most of all is going through the experience of the encounter: "what counts is not these products of analysis and reflection but the genuine original unity, the lived relationship" (Buber, 1970: 70).

Voluntary action and volunteer-recipient relationships are such lived experiences where a climate for personal growth can be established. This is not to say that every human exchange becomes an encounter, but, with a certain disposition, the chances are there. The attitude that a volunteer presents through the course of this relationship could further enhance these possibilities, in this case the attitude of service. Buber (1970) relates this to transformation "service transforms the It-world into a You-world: it humanizes things and bring them into the sphere of Being." In other words, things received through "service" and "encounter" are being transformed into resources that dignify human existence. Many other humanistic authors support the belief in an innate human potential as the basis for self-development and transformation. In a relationship, this potential is true for both participants of any given interaction and this principle can serve to study volunteers and the recipients of their actions as well. The volunteer-recipient relationship is a result of the one-on-one interaction of two individuals that become involved in a chosen activity or from working together towards a common purpose. Circumstances around the relationship are numerous: It could occur while acquiring or happen during the process of creating something collectively: a garden, a community center, a library. It may also flourish from a simple presence: a volunteer reading to the blind, attending an HIV patient or lecturing a child on a museum piece. Finally, Frankl in his *Logotherapy* (1970) lays out the importance of adding meaning to the purpose of human existence. Voluntarism is often said to provide meaning to the lives and the existence of those who engage in it. How true would it be if we could say that both participants in a relationship discover meaning in their lives because of voluntary activity?

VOLUNTEERING AS "SERVING" AND AS "HELPING"

While studying volunteering and voluntary action, the terms "helping" or "serving" others are frequently used indiscriminately or interchangeably. Many researchers utilize the term of "helping behavior" when they refer to voluntarism. For this study, a qualitative distinction was made to separate both actions. In "helping," there is an exchange of goods and/or services. There is a giver and a receiver, but not necessarily an opportunity for reciprocity. In "serving," the quality of the exchange is different. It goes beyond helping by presenting an opportunity for both reciprocity and equality. Helping implies a form of a gift to someone else, sharing a part of what is owned. Serving amplifies the spectrum of the gift into sharing and offering not only what we have, but as part of what we are.

In the American Red Cross definition of a volunteer, the word "service" is mentioned. In humanistic terms, the meaning of "service," as in "service to others," acquires a distinctive importance as a part of volunteer activity and voluntary action. Serving, in volunteering, becomes a way of giving freely of oneself. It is a preamble and a path to giving because it implies being at the disposition of another to simply offer a gift to participate and share on equal terms in a relationship. Sharing or giving what? Fromm (1956) asks himself, "What does one person give another?" And in answering his own question, he says "He gives of himself. Of the most precious he has, he gives of his life . . . [H]e enriches the other person, he enhances the sense of aliveness by enhancing his own sense of aliveness. In the act of giving something is born, and both persons involved are grateful for the life that is born for both of them" (Fromm, 1956: 23). For some authors, giving of oneself offers a means into human transcendence. "Man is *transcendence*. Only in the surpassing of himself . . . he is fulfilled. The more he transcends himself, the more he actualizes his own essence" (Coreth, 1985: 178).

Giving becomes the expression of an offering, but in the end, what supplies meaning to the offer is love. In the act of love, giving is a means, not an end. If we give without love, we only offer what we have, not what we are. Strictly speaking, this would be considered charity in the Judeo-Christian tradition. Spiritual traditions from both the East and the West include service and giving to the "other" as key pieces within their philosophies. In Christianity, it is through the "other," that salvation is granted. In the Buddhist tradition, the path of service and compassionate action (*nish kam karma yoga*) (Dass & Bush, 1992) is one of the conduits to illumination. In the *Bavagahad Gita,* sacred book of Hinduism, there are a series of instructions on practices for the transformation of the heart and the mind through selflessness. In the act of volunteering, it is at the level of charity that altruism appears. But not all volunteer actions reach this level of selfless devotion. If we created at a continuum of voluntary action, we could think of placing altruism at one end of the continuum and helping at the other. Voluntary action takes place within the whole continuum, the degrees of commitment, participation and action fluctuating constantly, beginning voluntary activity at any given place and changing our position as the action flows.

As we live through the experience of volunteering, our feelings, emotions, and values change and evolve. It is the action itself that makes people become aware of the possibilities of their own development. In enacting what we consider valuable and important, we also become able to develop our own "self-actualizing" potential (Maslow, 1988) to experience personal growth. These actions must begin from an existing free will. An act of "service" begins with a decision and an attitude toward others, "the act of will and intention, implies a decision of accepting or not accepting an impulse." (Assagioli, 1989).

In a way, all of us have had many opportunities to serve others. Some become conscious efforts to do so. Then all encounters with other human beings have the possibility of becoming "service relationships" (Butcher, 1997). In voluntarism, there is a decision to take advantage of that opportunity. Ideally, voluntarism creates the proper environment and provides a space for interpersonal relationships to flourish. These relationships seem to be beneficial for both those who engage in them: for the volunteers themselves and for those who receive the volunteers' "service."

AN EMPIRICAL STUDY WITH MEXICAN VOLUNTEERS

The methodology for this study was established under Qualitative Research parameters following strict procedures and based on a set of assumptions for twenty unstructured open ended ethnographic (in-depth) interviews. Qualitative Research includes tools used for research in this field such as heuristic research (Moustakas, 1990), phenomenology (Ritzer, 1995), symbolic interactionism (Swartz, Howard & Jacobs, 1979), and anthropology (Geertz, 1973). Among forms of inquiry, the constructivist paradigm (Guba & Lincoln, 1994) was chosen to establish a methodological pathway. Interpersonal relationships are immersed in the "way" things are done and this is why diverse perspectives of the participants were taken into consideration: culture, significance and feelings of the individuals during the interaction and the personal meaning for both partakers of the relationship. These were studied under a set of assumptions:

A. Service is understood from a humanistic point of view, respecting individual freedom of choice and of action.
B. Volunteers present different attitudes as they engage in their work that may vary as the volunteer-recipient interaction develops. The voluntary

action itself, when committed and continuous, can lead to the discovery of service.

C. Because there are many different possibilities of establishing relationships in a voluntary-recipient exchange, two distinctive kinds were considered:

   1. "Service relationships" are horizontal in nature and not exclusive of voluntary action. These relationships provide dialogue and an opportunity for encounter, while promoting openness and respect of the choices of others. Usually, both participants benefit from the experience. They occur whenever an attitude or spirit of service is present, leading to autonomy. Service is viewed as facilitating a process, creating autonomy and independence, thus providing a possibility for change on both sides of the relationship and producing longer lasting-results. If a volunteer that initiates a relationship exhibits a "service" attitude, a climate of trust is created and both individuals can establish a more productive relationship for both of them.

   2. "Help relationships" are unequal, even hierarchical in nature. This relationship occurs in a climate of control or mere exchange. Possibly, only one side of the volunteer-recipient relationship perceives some form of personal benefit. These relationships inhibit growth and encounter. A "helping" attitude would be considered paternalistic, creating dependency and basically, producing short lived results, since the individuals that are "helped" regress to their habitual patterns once the "help" is no longer there.

We are well aware that any interaction or relationship between two individuals is extremely complex and that there are many factors that can determine the outcome. To study the volunteer-recipient relationship, one hypothesis was built around the attitudes of the volunteer as he/she initiated voluntary action. It was thought that some volunteer attitudes were more "productive" or conducive to personal development and autonomy than others. This applied to both participants in the relationship. The second hypothesis was built around cultural issues of paternalism and the known historical background previously presented in this chapter.

Figure 7.1 portrays the processes and types of the relationships and outcomes that can be derived from the assumptions listed above. Volunteer attitudes of serving or helping and recipient behavior of acceptance or rejection provide combinations of interactions. Each combination can establish a climate leading to outcomes of either mutual growth allied to increased autonomy, or unilateral benefit with greater dependency. This analytic framework assists in understanding the results of the study.

The table offers a graphic interpretation of three methodological moments which do not relate to a specific time frame, although the one-on-one interaction between the volunteer and the recipient had to be effective for at least one year

	1. Initial conditions	2. Climate of relationship	3. Outcome	
Volunteer	a. Serving attitude	a. Unconditional climate: • facilitates processes • establishes "service relationship" • seeks independence	a. Reciprocal benefit: (possibility of personal growth) Both sides benefit	Promotional mode Autonomy
	b. Helping attitude	b. Conditional climate: • controls processes • establishes "help relationship" • promotes dependency	b. Unilateral benefit (illusion of growth) Short term benefit	Paternalistic mode Dependency
Recipient	a. Accepts interaction	a. Unconditional climate: responds and establishes "service relationship" b. Conditional climate: responds and establishes "help relationship"	a. Self development discovery, growth, transformation and responsibility b. External change and generally short-lived low commitment	Promotional mode Autonomy Paternalistic mode Dependency
	b. No interaction is established			

Figure 7.1. Matrix for Analysis.

to be considered for the study. The analysis of these interactions presents what could happen on both sides of the exchange, leading to either autonomy or dependency. Using this matrix for analysis and for coding the information, three distinctive methodological moments are presented:

1. *Initial.* The volunteer establishes his intention of his/her action using either a serving attitude or a helping attitude. The recipient may or may not respond to the relationship.
2. *Relationship and climate.* The volunteer establishes a specific kind of relationship with the recipient. Here is where the volunteers' intentions become evident as does his or her capability of establishing the kind of relationship originally intended towards the recipient.
3. *Outcome.* There are several possible end results as we observe results on both sides of the interaction.
   a. If the volunteer established a "service relationship" there are mutual benefits for both recipient and volunteer and this kind of interaction leads to growth and autonomy for both of the participants in the relationship. The changes that can occur will be long lasting and the result of a personal choice of both participants. They have attained a mutually promotional mode.
   b. If the volunteer established a "helping relationship" there is a strong possibility that only one of the participants received some personal benefit

from the interaction. It can be the volunteer, who feels satisfaction, or it could be the recipient, who may obtain a partial benefit conducive to some amount of change, but it is usually short lived being the result of a climate of control and the outcome is considered a dependent one. They have attained or produced paternalistic mode.

c. There has been an interaction and an exchange, but the outcome in terms of dependency or autonomy is not clear.

THE DYNAMICS OF THE VOLUNTEER-RECIPIENT RELATIONSHIP

Previous research on giving and volunteering using interviews with volunteers (Butcher, 1996)[1] suggested that, psychologically, volunteers obtain a series of personal benefits as they collaborate in community ventures. One finding of this research is that "service" became a key element that promoted openness, horizontal relationships, dialogue and encounters with others. A service mode offered individuals an opportunity of an equal and dignified exchange, allowing common human values to emerge. Assuming that values are restructured from both angles of any interaction, this principle could then be true for both participants in a relationship. Under the humanistic perspective, people not only enact their beliefs and values, but are transformed through their interactions with others. It seemed appropriate to use this same perspective to look closely at the quality of these relationships (Butcher, 1999), bringing forth a myriad of new questions. It was said that personal growth is one of the outcomes of voluntary participation. It then became important to find out if it extended to the beneficiary of the volunteer-recipient relationship as well. A starting point seemed to be the attitudes that volunteers portray in their work and the effects they could produce.

Looking at the diagram, we must remember that what is being studied is the volunteer attitude as he/she initiates a relationship with a recipient, thus eventually establishing a climate under which the relationship evolves. Human interactions and relationships are not chemical reactions where adding elements to a formula guarantees a specific result, so the idea of presenting three methodological moments is to illustrate progress throughout the relationship. The end results are seen as outcomes and either promotion or dependency. But what about the relationship

---

[1] A Masters thesis on giving and volunteering, The Art of Giving: The Forgotten Factor in Development, presented a theory on the factors that seem to be important in giving from a humanistic perspective, where active service to others while volunteering turns into a personal growth experience. Based on Humanistic and Transpersonal Psychology, a model is proposed: where service "S" becomes a key factor in providing an environment for actualization and self-development.

itself? In studying the attitudes of volunteers as they interacted with their recipients, insight provided an opportunity to observe the dynamics of the volunteer-recipient relationship. A certain predisposition or attitude towards the "other" was present. If the "serving" attitude was present, there were supposedly more chances of establishing a climate of growth for both sides of the relationship.

Change, personal growth, and awareness turned out to be some of the final outcomes, but other things also happened since, in reality, many volunteers are not consciously aware of their dispositions. They usually have no clear understanding of the difference between "helping" or "serving", these were conceptual differentiations established for the study. During exchange, participants spoke of: self-discovery, humbling experiences, understanding of others, frustration, elation, anger, joy, feelings of awe, and self worth enhancement. Attitudes in the beginning of the relationship can be altered by the experience and what was a helping attitude in the beginning, may be different by the end of the relationship, the person being "helped" or "served" could be the volunteer instead of the recipient. Here is where the richness of the lived experience lies. Learning and growth, for example, come from within each individual, since each person will "live" the experience differently based on their own internal perceptions.

Attitudes were extremely important in setting the tone for interaction. What was observed as the interviews were analyzed was that no matter what the initial attitude of the volunteer, be it to help or to serve, it was the experience of the relationship that enclosed the power of transformation. Some of the values and motivations held by some of the participants changed singnificantly. For one volunteer, the founder of a self-group, the volunteer-recipient relationship made her uncover what was really happening during exchange and interaction. After years of thinking that she was facilitating the group sessions, she realized that recipients had been the true facilitators throughout their meetings. One recipient, a potter in a small Mexican village, could not believe how a woman (the volunteer) could make him feel "a sense of freedom, not just to experiment, but to make mistakes as well . . . she never imposed a limit . . . ". His views on women changed because of this relationship.

In most cases, both participants became truly engaged. In the dynamics of a relationship, two elements are present: process and content. Processes are the steps we follow, a certain order of events. The content is the experience itself where both sides of the interaction participate. For all the volunteers, with no exceptions, there was an enhanced sense of gratitude. Every single one mentioned " . . . receiving much more than they were able to give." Their commitment grew as the relationship grew. On the other hand, the recipients also expressed a feeling of gratitude towards the volunteer. However, their comments were overwhelmingly geared towards feelings of discovery in self-reliance. The presence of those volunteers in their lives made a significant difference.

OUTCOMES AND CONCLUSIONS

1. The attitude and disposition of the volunteer as he/she began interaction with the recipient seems to be important in establishing a climate for interaction.

The volunteers articulated that as they became aware of their ability to sincerely be at someone else's disposition, there was more freedom of choice available on both sides of the relationship and less dependency was created; their actions reflected the established service concept that we have described. The non-judgmental and unconditional climate that emerged from an initial "serving attitude" of the volunteer, allowed self-discovery and growth on both sides of the relationship coinciding with the therapeutic Rogerian (1978) model of Interpersonal Relationships. There always was a "possibility of personal growth" for both the volunteer and for the recipient. In humanistic terms, a climate is established, but is the free choice and responsibility of the participants to take advantage of such a climate and act accordingly.

2. "Service relationships" outnumbered the "help relationships" nine to one.

In 18 open-ended interviews, both parties in the volunteer-recipient relationships studied stated that they experienced a sense of personal growth as the main outcome. Given our assumptions they established nine service relationships. As individuals described their interactions, other outcomes were also mentioned such as: learning from each other, feelings of improved self-worth, satisfaction, change and enthusiasm. It could be said that a values change occurs when we can observe new attitudes and different actions after, and presumably as a result of, an established relationship. The criteria to be able to classify a volunteer-relationship with an independent or autonomous outcome was based on what both participants expressed to be their "learning experiences." One case, for example, a recipient with HIV learned to look at her husband with respect, even though he had been the cause of her illness. Her actions after the experience were those of solidarity with her husband, appearing with him on TV shows and AIDS ad campaigns. It is one thing to say that we have changed, but our actions need to speak of our values. Another recipient, a prostitute, learned to care about and look after her three children, something she had not done before the volunteer-recipient relationship. She had never felt loving care in her own childhood and it was this particular relationship that changed her outlook on providing love for her children. A volunteer who works with the elderly revealed "a new sense of respect . . . and understanding of self . . . [I]t makes me keep my feet on the ground and touch reality." Another volunteer who teaches art to drug addicts and street children in a museum talked about the need for understanding, trust and, acceptance. Her learning experience had to do with accepting the kids as they were, without trying to change them, and perceiving the importance of always establishing equal terms.

3. Only one case was not able to establish an unconditional climate.

In one case, an obvious "help relationship" was recognized: there was no apparent change or perception of personal change, or self-discovery by the recipient.

Here, the volunteer set the rules within the relationship without taking the recipient into account. She had her mind set on what was "good" for the other person. Although a serving attitude was supposedly expressed by the volunteer at the beginning, the volunteer's actions reflected more of a helping attitude. This coincides with creating an "illusion of growth," where the volunteer felt satisfied of her participation and good about herself (one side benefits). However, the recipient did not express the same experience. Her interest in the relationship was for convenience. The reason she continued the sewing lessons for several years was because she received groceries every time she went to class. There was no mention of personal growth, although there was a feeling of gratitude towards the volunteer for the "help" provided.

4. *Culture and environment did not affect the volunteer-recipient relationship to the degree originally considered in the "cultural" hypothesis.*

In the Mexican community, most formal volunteer groups were classified in the Johns Hopkins Comparative study by Salamon, Anheier, List, Toepler, Solowski, and associates (1999) as belonging to social services area (education, health care, and economic development). Although some of these organizations provide direct goods and services that could be considered "paternalistic" in this country, the volunteers in the study that rendered their time and talents in formal organizations did not particularly create dependency in the individual scope of action. The kind of relationship established was independent of the nature of the organization.

In the one-on-one relationships, paternalism does not seem to be as active as originally thought, at least not to the point of influencing the individual volunteer attitude or the relationship. Since paternalism was considered the historically predominant cultural model in civil society participation, one would expect more "help relationships" than the ones actually found. It was originally thought that by creating a category to exclusively examine sociocultural aspects during the relationship, a consistent pattern of action or interaction would emerge as the relationship evolved. As the category was analyzed, "culture" was ever present: values, language, codes of conduct, etc., but not in the form of a pattern of behavior. Each relationship was unique, the socioeconomic and personal differences were major, but each volunteer that was able to establish a "service relationship" managed to relate to the recipient in his/her own personal style. The range of volunteer activities varied extensively: they included cultural programs, religious practices, health issues, education, skill building, and facilitation practices. Both genders were represented and included a broad span of organizations both in size and in scope were included: public and private organizations, traditional and longtime established or relatively new and self-initiated.

To conclude, these outcomes reflect the answers to the questions posed at the beginning of this chapter. In volunteering, close personal contact and the creation of volunteer-recipient relationships seem to be important to obtain results of well-being and personal growth for both parties as they interact with each other.

Attitudes that volunteers portray appear to determine a climate for this relationship to develop. The "lived experience" of volunteering appears as a factor of change and is reflected in how we enact our values.

More research is necessary to further understand the benefits and the signifi-cance of how service and voluntarism can provide as a pathway for participation in community issues. As we volunteer, we have the opportunity of becoming aware of our needs and the needs of others when we learn to relate and interact. From a hu-manistic perspective, it was seen that voluntary action and "service-relationships" can create conditions for personal growth and exchange. In developing countries, voluntarism can be regarded as an effective catalyst in social transformation be-cause it offers options to create horizontal type relationships adding elements to enhance environments of openness, choice, and liberty – the basic ingredients of a true and functional democracy. In first world countries, citizen participation and volunteering can hopefully continue to provide and promote an egalitarian social fabric for the building of stronger societies.

REFERENCES

American Red Cross. (1989). Taking Volunteerism into the 21rst Century, *The Journal of Volunteer Administration. III*, 1.
Assagioli, R. (1990). *The act of will.* (2nd ed). Sheffield, UK: Crucible.
Buber, M. (1970). *I and thou.* New York: Scribners.
Butcher, J. (1997). El arte de dar: Factor olvidado del desarrollo [The art of giving: The forgotten factor of development]. *PROMETEO. Mexican Journal of Humanistic Psychology and Human Development, 17*, 2–10.
Butcher, J. (2001). *Civil society and voluntary action in Mexico.* STEP Research Group on Social Economy and Civil Society, Social Economy in Countries of the South, International Seminar, March 28–30, Leuven.
Butcher, J. (2003). *Hacia una cultura de servicio* [Toward a culture of service]. Unpublished doctoral dis-sertation in Human Development, Psychology Department. Universidad Iberoamericana, Mexico.
Coreth, E. (1985). *¿Qué es el hombre ?* [Was is der Mensch?]. Barcelona: Herder.
Dass, R., & Bush, M. (1992). *Compassion in action: Setting out on the path of service.* New York: Bell Tower.
Denzin, N.K., & Lincoln, Y.S. (1994). *Handbook of qualitative research.* London, UK: Sage Publications.
Frankl, V. (1979). *El hombre en busca de sentido* [Man's search of meaning]. Barcelona: Herder.
Fromm, E. (1956). *The art of loving.* New York: Harper and Row.
Geertz, C. (1973). *The interpretation of cultures.* New York: Basic Books.
González, A.M. (1999). *De la sombra a la luz.* [From the shadow to the light]. México: Universidad Iberoamericana.
Guba, E.G., & Lincoln, Y.S. (1994). Competing paradigms in qualitative research. In N.K. Denzin & Y.S. Lincoln (Eds.), *Handbook of qualitative research.* Thousand Oaks, CA: Sage.
Luks, A. (1988). Helper's high. *Psychology Today, 21*, 39–42.
Mansbridge, J.J. (Ed.) (1990). *Beyond self-interest.* Chicago: University of Chicago Press.
Maslow, A. (1988). *El hombre autorrealizado.* [Towards a psychology of being] Mexico: Kairós.
Moustakas, C. (1990). Heuristic research, design and methodology. *Person Centered Review, 5*, 170–190.

Ritzer, G. (1995). *Social contemporary theory*. New York: McGraw-Hill.

Rogers, C.R. (1959). A theory of therapy, personality and interpersonal relationships, as developed in the client-centered framework. In S. Koch (Ed.), *Psychology: A Study of Science, Vol. III*. New York: McGraw-Hill.

Rogers, C.R. (1961). *On becoming a person*. Boston: Houghton Mifflin.

Salamon, L.M., Anheier, H.K., List, R., Toepler, S., Sokolowski, W.S., & Associates. (1999). *Global civil society*. Baltimore, MD: Johns Hopkins Centre for Civil Society Studies.

Schwartz, H., & Jacobs, J. (1979). *Qualitative sociology. A method to the madness*. New York: Macmillan.

Strauss, A. (1987). *Qualitative analysis for social scientists*. Cambridge, UK: Cambridge University Press.

Schmelkes, S. (1997). *Para entender la sociedad civil en América Latina* [To understand civil society in Latin America]. *Sociedad Civil, 3*, 113–141.

United Nations Volunteers (1999). *Expert working group meeting on volunteering and social development*. New York, November 29–30.

Chapter 8

From Restitution to Innovation
Volunteering in Postcommunist Countries

Stanislovas Juknevičius and Aida Savicka

INTRODUCTION

Active involvement in social actions and movements is widely recognized as a precondition for truly democratic society. Voluntary associations are the basic components of the civil society. Participation in voluntary associations such as political parties, religious organizations, trade unions, self-help groups, sports clubs, and other interest organizations is regarded as a very important factor integrating society as a whole and an important element of the participatory democracy.

Social observers from Alexis de Tocqueville (1835) to Robert D. Putnam (1993) stress the importance of networks of voluntary associations for the emergence and prosperity of democracy. According to Putnam, civil society is characterized by the active participation of citizens in public life, the search for the common good, solidarity, tolerance, and trust. In this paper, the issue of the dynamics of volunteering in a radically changing socio-political environment will be analyzed mainly from this theoretical perspective.

For a better insight into the complex relation between the rise of civil society and the development of voluntary activity in the postcommunist environment, we will employ the theoretical model elaborated by the Lithuanian sociologist Marius Povilas Šaulauskas (1998) which refers to the Lithuanian case but is also applicable (we believe) to the analysis of the social change in the whole region. According to him, it is possible to distinguish four orientations of social change in the postcommunist environment:

1. *Restitutive*: orientation to the restoration of old, nonexisting social structures and institutions

2. *Imitative*: orientation to the creation of social structures and institutions that originated in different social environments
3. *Continuative*: orientation to the development and modification of the existing social structures and institutions
4. *Innovative*: orientation to the autonomous creation of distinct and qualitatively new social structures and institutions

As Šaulauskas claims, the development of civil society after the breakdown of the communist regime was twofold. In the first, revolutionary, phase of social change, the development of civil society was extremely fast and guided first of all by restitutive and imitative orientations. In the second, evolutionary, phase, the pace of development of civil society decreased, restitutive and continuative orientations were constantly weakening, and innovative and imitative orientations were gaining in importance. Thus, the scholar concludes that "the development of . . . Civil Society took place as a transition from *restitutive* to *imitative* and then, backed by the growing *self-stigmatizing ressentiment*, up to the *innovative continuation*" (Šaulauskas 1996).

This approach may be applied to the analysis of the dynamics not only of civil society in general, but also of its specific forms, for example, voluntary activity. Volunteering is defined here as the carrying out of voluntary unpaid activities for the benefit of other people or the environment. A volunteer constantly renounces something—his/her time, intellectual or physical energy, money, etc. S/he receives something in exchange—moral satisfaction, the approval of other people, the hope of eternal life. The type and intensity of this exchange is conditioned by prevailing social attitudes, values, and the individual psychological or moral properties of the volunteer. An essential characteristic of voluntary organizations is that their members are not forced into membership and they can start their activities or close them whenever they wish, although, as Stein Kuhnle and Per Selle note accurately, "voluntary organizations are 'voluntary' to varying degrees" (Kuhnle & Selle, 1992: 7).

Three factors fostering voluntary action can be distinguished. These are, first, the specific characteristics of the social context; second, ideological incentives; and third, the personal characteristics of the volunteer. On the one hand, volunteering as a renunciation or giving away always means overstepping egoism by an individual. On the other hand, the replacement or collapse of ideologies has an impact on the state of volunteering throughout the country.

On the basis of these assumptions, the following hypotheses on the specifics of volunteering in Lithuania are proposed:

1. Since the ideology that had regulated nearly all spheres of human activity in postcommunist countries collapsed, it seems reasonable to expect an

essential transformation of volunteering in these countries. It is probable that in the Baltic countries (Lithuania, Latvia, & Estonia), which had experienced the strongest influence of the Marxist ideology, this transformation should be the deepest.

2. The decline of volunteering in the communist organizations is the most likely trend of this change.
3. Since the postcommunist countries (at least majority of them) are developing as democratic societies, there is potential for a new rise of the spirit of voluntarism.

For the verification of these hypotheses, data from the EVS 1990–1991 and 1999–2000 research were used. This article will focus mostly on the macro level analysis of the dynamics of volunteering in a postcommunist milieu. This does not mean that the authors are not aware of or neglect the importance of the factors of the micro level and the personal characteristics of volunteers. These are left aside for methodological reasons: the level of voluntary activity is so low in East European countries that it is not possible to establish statistically grounded associations between volunteering and the personal characteristics of volunteers. Therefore, we will focus mainly on the changing social and ideological contexts of voluntary activity and the effects of this change. We will also discuss the prospects of volunteering in the postcommunist milieu.

MARXIST THEORY AND THE PRACTICE OF VOLUNTEERING

Previous to the introduction of communist regimes in Eastern Europe, the state of volunteering was quite diverse in these countries. In those societies that remained traditional and mostly rural (such as Lithuania), volunteering was not a widespread phenomenon since social life was concentrated in rather narrow circles of family members and neighbors. Meanwhile, in the urbanizing countries, voluntarism was growing (for instance, in Czechoslovakia). The introduction of the communist regime, however, made all countries equal in this respect, quite successfully, since bridling of spontaneous civic action was seen as one of the major tasks of the totalitarian governments.

It would be incorrect to deny that certain forms of voluntary activity existed in the communist countries. The question that most concerns us here is whether volunteering in communist countries was related to the concept of civil society. Numerous commentators have claimed that under communism "civil society—everything which fills that amorphous sphere between the individual and State—ceased to exist" (Babiuch-Luxmoore, 1994: 242). Hence, civic action could survive only on the margins of society (for instance, in the case of opposition associations).

> The vision of a civil society which was created by democratic opposition groups under communist rule was based on the idea of a State whose role would be limited by independent social initiatives.... But it was a form of civil society created largely in negative categories and in opposition to the establishment (Babiuch-Luxmoore, 1994: 242–243).

Thus, civil society in communist countries was obviously too weak to serve the purpose of mobilizing citizens for spontaneous voluntary action, and the state was strong enough to restrain it. Nevertheless, volunteering was not absent in communist countries, and its roots could be found in Marxist ideology itself.

All postcommunist states have one feature in common, that is, all of them have experienced to a greater or lesser extent the influence of Marxist ideology. Therefore, it is worth addressing at length the main features of the Marxist attitude to volunteering.

Karl Marx distinguished two main stages of the perfect society of the future: the lower and the higher. The lower stage was later called socialism, and the higher, communism. As Marx wrote,

> [I]n the higher phase of communistic society, when the enslaving subordination of the individual to the division of labor, and with it the antithesis between mental and physical labor, has vanished; when labor is no longer merely a means of life but has become life's principal need; when the productive forces have also increased with the all-round development of the individual, and all the springs of cooperative wealth flow more abundantly—only then will it be possible to completely transcend the narrow outlook of bourgeois right, and only then will society be able to inscribe on its banners: from each according to his ability, to each according to his needs! (Marx, 1975: 119).

The importance of this definition is manifested by the fact that in 1961 it was integrated with no changes into the so-called program of communism builders of the Soviet Union.

Marx aimed to essentially change the attitude toward labor rooted in the Judaeo-Christian tradition from a disagreeable duty or even curse ("accursed be the soil because of you. With suffering shall you get your food from it every day of your life" (Jones, 1968: 8)) it had to turn into a source of enjoyment and pleasure. Since, in the communist society, commodity-monetary relations should disappear, all the labor should in fact become voluntary.

The first leader of Soviet Russia, Vladimir Lenin, developed the ideas of Marx and attempted to put them into practice. In April 1918, on a Saturday (*subbota* in Russian), a group of railway workers voluntarily did some unpaid work. They were followed by some other worker groups, mostly communists. In his comments on these events, Lenin wrote,

> ["C]ommunist subbotniks" are of such enormous historical significance precisely because they display the class-conscious and voluntary initiative of the

workers in developing the productivity of labor, adopting the new labor discipline, in creating socialist conditions of economy and life (Lenin, 1974: 423–424).

Although Lenin's idea of making volunteering the principal form of labor failed, the importance of unpaid labor during the so-called period of socialist construction (1920–1960) in Soviet Russia and later in the Soviet Union was constantly growing. The subbotniks (later they were called *red Saturdays*) became an indispensable part of the socialist way of life. At least one Saturday a year (usually it was the Saturday closest to Lenin's birthday, April 22), all Soviet citizens worked in their workplaces for free, or did some other socially beneficial work. Schoolchildren and students were highly involved in this kind of activity.

Another important field of volunteering in the Soviet Union was unpaid work in different social organizations and movements. Directly after the Civil War, there appeared a number of mass voluntary organizations such as the Society of Friends of Defense and Aviation-Chemical Construction (founded in 1926 and aimed at teaching the population about chemistry in general and about defense against chemical attack) and the Military Scientific Society (founded in 1920 and committed to scientifically studying the World War and the Russian civil war). Of the organizations of this kind, the Voluntary Society for the Support of Army, Aviation, and Marine (DOSSAF in Russian) had the most members.[1] Later, the role of sport became more important. In one of his speeches, Lenin called trade unions "the school of communism." Consequently, more and more people became engaged in the work of trade unions. A significant proportion of the population took part in the activities of cultural organizations, the so-called amateur culture.

The importance of volunteering in the Soviet Union is also shown by the fact that these activities involved children as well as adults. After the Second World War, in most schools, the organizations of the so-called young *Timurians* were set up. Their activities focused mainly on assisting the lonely, the elderly, and the disabled.

Volunteering theory and practice in the former Soviet Union should not be given a one-sided assessment. On the one hand, it played a decidedly positive role. First, the *subbotniks* brought certain economic gain. Following each of the *subbotniks*, mass media supplied information on the amount of money earned in order to excite a feeling of achievement (which is crucial in any voluntary action). Second, participation in the activities of social organizations and movements corresponded to social integration. Amateur artistic activities supported and, at times, helped to revive national cultures. Volunteering also contributed to the fostering of such character features as unselfishness, sacrifice, etc., in teenagers and youth.

[1] For a detailed historical analysis of the rise and development of mass voluntary organizations in the Soviet Union, see Odom (1973).

On the other hand, volunteering, like other types of activities in totalitarian states, was under state control and engineered by the state. Therefore, volunteering was quite frequently compulsory rather than voluntary. Here, we encounter the paradox phenomenon of "compulsory volunteering." The share of compulsion in voluntary activities has varied throughout history; it has probably, never been totally nonexistent. However, in no other instance was state control, and even coercion, of voluntary activities evident and straightforward to the degree it reached in Soviet society. For instance, the above-mentioned *subbotniks* were highly institutionalized. They became a part of the state tradition, and their meaning could not be questioned by the citizens, that is, the volunteers. Thus, participation in *subbotniks* was not a matter of free individual choice. For this reason, *subbotniks* vanished immediately after the disappearance of the state pressure.

Thus, state-controlled nonprofit organizations were essentially bureaucratic institutions, and this was how citizens conceived them. Membership of such organizations was usually limited to paying membership dues. Ordinary members were absolutely powerless to influence their activity. It was declared officially that membership was voluntary but the reality was completely at odds with these declarations. Thus, in the Soviet Union, there existed a unique form of voluntarism that might be called pseudo-voluntarism. Here, voluntary work, which is a matter of personal decision by definition, was imposed upon the citizens by the state institutions. Therefore, upon the liberalization of this society, particularly during the period of perestroika, the importance of volunteering dropped suddenly.

DYNAMICS OF VOLUNTEERING IN POSTCOMMUNIST COUNTRIES

After the breakdown of the totalitarian system, the situation of volunteering changed dramatically. One could say that two types of voluntary associations existed in the socialist society: those "truly voluntary" associations that emerged essentially in opposition to the system (for example, religious associations, underground political circles, green movements) and the "quasivoluntary" associations that were controlled by the state (e.g., professional associations). After the collapse of the socialist state, some associations of the first type dissolved gradually because they lost their guidelines: there was no longer a totalitarian state to oppose. Meanwhile, associations of the second type faded because they lost their main consolidating force, that is, state control. In this situation, new kinds of voluntary associations have to have the characteristics of Western democracies and form as an expression of the willingness of the citizens to cooperate for the achievement of public good.

Taking the above considerations into account, three basic scenarios of the development of voluntarism in the postcommunist milieu are possible. First, it could be assumed that volunteering in the countries incorporated into the Soviet Union and, therefore, most influenced by Marxism (but also with more suppressed "truly voluntary" associations) has decreased more significantly than in the so-called "people's democracies." To put it differently, the weakening of continuative orientation was greatest in those countries where voluntary activity was fostered first and foremost by the old ideology. Consequently, volunteering in Lithuania, Latvia, and Estonia should have declined more significantly than in Poland, Hungary, the Czech Republic, Slovakia, and Bulgaria.

Second, the fate of volunteering largely depends on the capacity of the population of these countries to adapt themselves to the new political conditions and to acquire the skills to operate under a democratic regime and cooperate for the achievement of public good; that is, it depends on their capacity to transform through imitation and innovation. As to this, the postcommunist countries applying for European Union (EU) membership were divided into two groups in 1998. Poland, Estonia, Slovenia, Hungary, and the Czech Republic were identified as carrying reforms more rapidly and thus better prepared for EU membership. Meanwhile, Latvia, Lithuania, Slovakia, Bulgaria, and Romania were included in the group of countries in which democratic reforms have not been so smooth and which are less well prepared for EU membership. In this case, volunteering in the countries of the first group should have decreased less significantly than in the countries of the second group.

Third, it is possible that neither the impact of the communist ideology nor the speed of restructuring of the economy and politics had a decisive influence on the development of civil society and, consequently, volunteering. Which of these assumptions comes closer to the truth?

Turning to the empirical data for the answer, the first thing to be emphasized is the extremely low level of volunteering in Eastern European countries when compared to Western European countries. The level of volunteering is the lowest in Russia, where we find only 8.8 per cent of the population doing unpaid work for voluntary organizations. The proportions of volunteers are somewhat higher in other Eastern European countries—Ukraine (13.1%), Lithuania (13.6%), Poland (13.7%), Hungary (14.8%), Romania (15.7%), Bulgaria (16.5%), Estonia (17.8%), Belarus (18.8%) and Latvia (22.4%).[2] Here, we do not observe a direct relationship between the level of volunteering in the country and its success in establishing or reestablishing a democratic regime. Quite unexpectedly, Poland and Hungary have lower proportions of volunteers than Romania, Bulgaria, and even Belarus and Slovakia. As to Belarus, a possible explanation is that continuative orientations remain quite strong in this country, and the nature of voluntary organizations did not change significantly after the dissolution of the USSR. There is no clear pattern as regards voluntarism in Eastern European countries.

---

[2] Data on the levels of volunteering in different countries in 1990 come from the source book of the 1999/2000 European Values Study Surveys (Halman, 2001).

However, the division between Eastern and Western European countries is strikingly obvious: Western European countries with prolonged stable democracies enjoy a much higher level of voluntarism than the newly established Eastern European democracies. This finding complies with our hypothesis that democracy is favorable to voluntary activities.

It is important to note that the developments in voluntary activity during the last decade in Western Europe and Eastern Europe are also quite contradictory. In Western European countries, the level of engagement in voluntary organizations either has not changed significantly or increased. Meanwhile, in Eastern European countries, the level of unpaid work for voluntary organizations decreased significantly (with the exception of the Czech Republic, where it remained practically unchanged). If volunteering in Western and Eastern Europe did not differ significantly in 1990, the difference was obvious in 1999. A probable explanation is that, in 1990, Eastern European countries were at the peak of social mobilization, which declined after the so-called "honeymoon of transition."

Thus, the numbers of people engaged in voluntary associations in postcommunist countries dropped during the nine years between the surveys. These findings lead us to the conclusion that the breakdown of the communist ideology and regime led to the downfall of voluntary activity in Eastern European countries (disregarding the "honeymoon" phase). However, this factor alone does not explain the diversity of voluntarism across postcommunist countries.

To better understand the complex phenomenon of the dynamics of voluntary work, a more detailed analysis of changes in specific fields of voluntary activity is needed. To aggregate the data, voluntary organizations were grouped into six main types:

1. Welfare organizations (here we include social welfare services for elderly, handicapped, or deprived people, organizations concerned with health, poverty, employment, housing, and racial equality)
2. Religious or church organizations
3. Trade unions and professional associations
4. Political parties and movements
5. Interest groups (youth clubs and movements, sports or recreation, education and cultural activities, women's groups)
6. Ideology-based movements (third world development, human rights, ecology, animal rights, and peace movements)

One can expect that the pace of development of the various types of voluntary organizations should be different. For instance:

1. It is reasonable to expect a decline in the activities of "pseudovoluntary" organizations that survived the breakdown of the communist regime with

only some minor changes in their rhetoric and organizational structure. To use Šaulauskas' terms, we hypothesize a decline in continuative voluntary activity. Here, trade unions are a good example.

2. On the other hand, one can expect a rise of the new forms of voluntary activity, that is, an increase in restitutive and imitative forms of voluntary action. Among the first, religious and church organizations should be mentioned as having the greatest potential for recovery. Among the latter, various welfare organizations, interest groups, and ideology-based movements could be listed, such as human rights and ecology movements or youth clubs and similar organizations.

3. As to the political parties, their situation is more obscure since communist parties, which were quite numerous (at least formally) at the dawn of the velvet revolutions, suddenly lost the majority of their members and were even banned; meanwhile, new political parties and movements started to appear. The first research was conducted exactly at the moment of turning.

It seems that the empirical data are supportive of our hypotheses. We perceived trade unions as a continuative form of voluntary activity and hypothesized the decline of their activity. This way of reasoning is grounded empirically. What we observe in all postcommunist countries is a rather sharp decline in the numbers of people working for trade unions and professional associations. This is especially true of the post-Soviet countries, where the proportions of citizens working for trade unions and professional associations were higher than in other Eastern European countries previous to 1990 and dropped very much during the decade of social reforms (from 13% to 2% in Estonia, from 12% to 3% in Latvia, and from 11% to 2% in Lithuania). This finding is not surprising if one keeps in mind that, under the communist regime, membership of trade unions was obligatory. These trade unions were degenerated, of course, in the sense that they had no right to bargain with the employer (i.e., the State) or to strike—what they could do and actually did was provide their members with some welfare facilities (which were also controlled). Thus, it is only natural that the breakdown of the regime also meant the dissolution of trade unions and professional associations of this type. Some new kinds of trade unions have appeared, of course, but the formation of trade unions in the postcommunist milieu is not a commonplace phenomenon. In the future, activation of the new type of trade unions in these countries does seem possible because there is a need for employees to cooperate for the protection of their rights against employers who quite often abuse the difficult situation in the labor market.

Turning to another significant actor in civil society, religious organizations, one should look for their roots in the more distant past. Therefore, they should be treated as restitutive rather than continuative institutions (although the Church managed to preserve some of its activities, they were forbidden). As we hypothesized, the importance of religious organizations rises in the postcommunist milieu, at least during the initial, revolutionary phase of social change. In all countries except Bulgaria and Poland, we observe the rise of voluntarism in religious organizations. The case of Poland is easily understood: here, religious activity was never successfully suppressed by the regime and augmented tremendously even before the first survey. Despite the sharp decline, the level of participation in religious organizations in Poland remains among the highest in the region. It seems that the activity of religious organizations (both traditional and nontraditional) has stabilized and there remains little room for growth. Some decline could even be expected in some of these countries (e.g., Lithuania & Poland) as these societies secularize.

Welfare organizations were almost absent under the communist regime. Old, precommunist voluntary welfare organizations were outlawed despite the fact that there was a need for them. As we mentioned above, some welfare facilities were provided by trade unions and by Young Pioneers or members of the Young Communist League, all of which were pseudovoluntary organizations. The main provider of all welfare facilities was declared to be the state itself. The situation changed dramatically after the 1990s. The state is no longer supposed to nor is it able to answer all the needs of its citizens. The previously unknown phenomena of unemployment and extreme poverty have become everyday issues. However, the state is too weak and too poor to handle these problems. Thus, the need for civil action to solve welfare problems is tremendous. The question is whether the civil societies in postcommunist countries are consolidated enough to mobilize themselves and take action. It seems that only some of them are. The proportions of people doing unpaid work for welfare organizations was not high in 1990 (from 3.5% in Lithuania to 8.7% in Poland; Latvia was an exceptional case with a very high proportion of volunteers) and they even dropped significantly till 1999 (from 1.7% in Lithuania to 5.1% in Estonia). We observe a slightly rising level of voluntary activity for welfare organizations only in the Czech Republic. We assume that this rise is stimulated by the need to cope with the new social reality first of all through innovative consolidation of the civil societies of these countries. Therefore, it is reasonable to expect a rise in this type of voluntary activity in other Eastern European countries as their civil societies strengthen.

Similar conclusions may be drawn with regard to the dynamics of voluntary work for interest groups and ideology-based organizations in Eastern European countries. As to the first, again, we observe a decline in voluntary activities for interest groups in all countries except the Czech Republic. As to the ideology-based voluntary organizations, their activities show the least decline in the Czech Republic. Thus, it seems reasonable to conclude that there is a potential for the activation of voluntary organizations based on imitative and innovative orientations in postcommunist countries along with the consolidation of their civil societies.

From this viewpoint, it seems that the postcommunist countries have successfully abolished the remnants of the old political system and, at present, their political parties also belong to the categories of imitative and innovative rather than continuative civil groups. It is not surprising, therefore, that identical patterns of development of activities can be observed as in the case of other imitative and innovative civic groups—welfare organizations, interest groups, and ideology-based organizations: voluntary activity for political parties was not widespread in 1990 (from 1% of respondents volunteering for political parties in Poland to 6% in Latvia) and decreased more or less significantly in all countries except the Czech Republic.

This is a very general overview of the developments in different spheres of voluntary activity in Eastern European countries. For a more detailed empirical exemplification of our theoretical assumptions, let us turn to the Lithuanian case.

VOLUNTEERING IN LITHUANIA

There is no ground to claim that the development of voluntary activity in Lithuania is exceptional in any way or to expect tendencies radically different from those that can be observed in other Eastern European countries. However, one thing that might be surprising is the very low level of volunteering in Lithuania in general, even compared to other postcommunist countries. Among the countries included in our analysis, the level of volunteering in Lithuania exceeds the level of volunteering only in Russia and Ukraine, and it is much lower than the level of volunteering in the neighboring countries—Latvia and Estonia—with which Lithuania shares its communist history. It is interesting to note that this difference in voluntary activity was not significant in 1990, when about 30% of the citizens did unpaid work for voluntary organizations in each of the Baltic countries. Even though the level of volunteering dropped in each of these countries in the period between 1990 and 1999, the most dramatic changes occurred in Lithuania, where the proportion of volunteers dropped from 30.2% to 13.6%. In Lithuania, volunteering increased slightly only in religious organizations (from 2.9% to 4.2%). In all other fields—welfare organizations, trade unions, political parties, and other ideology-based organizations, and even in interest groups – volunteering decreased significantly (see Figure 8.1).

Even though we do not have data about the dynamics of volunteering between 1990 and 1999, one can assume that this period of deep and radical changes in all domains of social life was marked also by important developments in the nongovernmental sector. We observed high levels of voluntary activity during the period of the "honeymoon of transition." It seems probable, however, that this euphoric period was followed by a sharp decrease in volunteering both because of the poor experience of the citizens in acting under the new conditions and because

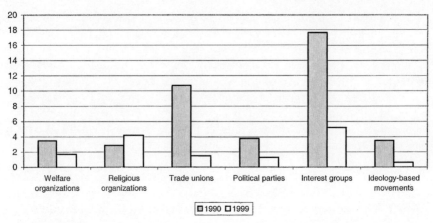

Figure 8.1. Unpaid work for different voluntary organizations in Lithuania, 1990–1999 (%). *Source:* EVS 1999-Lithuania.

the legal basis was inadequate for the formation of voluntary organizations. This assumption is supported by the data from several researches conducted by SIC Gallup Media at the request of the Non-Governmental Organization Information and Support Center (NISC). According to the data from the national survey "NGOs in Lithuania," conducted in 1998, only 9% of the respondents said that they were members of voluntary organizations compared to 13.6% of the respondents of EVS 1999–2000. Here, we can trace some growth in the number of volunteers. However, this comparison is not valid because the two surveys employed different methodologies. Still, it does not contradict our hypothesis that the dynamics of volunteering was not unidirectional.

It is interesting to note that the changes in the numbers of volunteers are different from the changes in the numbers of registered voluntary organizations (the latter being more easily assessed by the statistical measures). Whereas the number of volunteers was quite high in 1990, then dropped significantly, and later somewhat increased again, the number of newly founded (per annum) voluntary organizations was constantly growing during this period. According to the research of NonGovernmental Sector in Lithuania (NISC) conducted in 2000 and based on statistical data, the Lithuanian nongovernmental sector started to develop more actively (first of all in the sense of official registration) only after 1995 (see Figure 8.2). During the last few years, we observe a tendency toward stabilization of the process. In 2000, there were more than 5000 voluntary organizations in Lithuania. It has been estimated, however, that about one fifth of the registered organizations were inactive.

Among the voluntary organizations officially registered in Lithuania, there is a complex mix of more or less active, more or less institutionalized voluntary

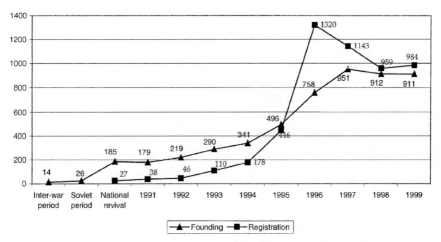

Figure 8.2. Number of newly founded and newly registered voluntary organizations in Lithuania.
Source: SIC Gallup Media and NISC.

activities that are fostered by continuative, restitutive, imitative, and innovative orientations.

Continuative tendencies are constantly weakening in voluntary activities since it has become unacceptable to associate oneself with the Soviet past. There still remain some trade unions and professional associations as well as political units that may be perceived as remnants of the communist regime, even though most would deny their continuative character and employ novel rhetoric. Of the restitutive orientations, traditional religious and church organizations are the purest examples. For instance, the Lithuanian Catholic Youth Federation traces its sources back to 1910. Its activity, like that of a number of other organizations of the same type, was halted by World War II, then restarted in emigration to return to Lithuania in 1989. Some restitutive tendencies may also be observed in the formation of trade unions and professional associations, such as the Lithuanian Labor Federation founded as a continuation of a Christian professional association initially formed in 1919. A special case of the restitution of prewar voluntary organizations is the Lithuanian Riflemen's Union, which is a civilian, voluntary paramilitary organization. The Riflemen aim to inform society about the mission of the Armed Forces and to prepare citizens for total and armed resistance in the event of war. The Union was initially founded in 1919 and enjoyed great popularity—the union had 62.000 members before World War II. One hundred and five orchestras and 72 riflemen's clubs belonged to this organization, and it had 350 libraries and 4 theaters. After the occupation of Lithuania by the Soviet Union in 1940, the Union was abolished and many of its members were killed or exiled to Siberia. In 1954, the Union was restored in emigration, and in 1989, it was restored in Lithuania. What is special about this voluntary organization is the exceptional government treatment of it and the institutional support for it. In 1997, even a special law passed that introduced the Union into the Lithuanian defense system.

Examples of imitative orientations in voluntary activity in Lithuania are the many international voluntary organizations working in different domains of social life—politics, religion, welfare—such as the Red Cross Society, the Green movement, the nonpolitical student organization AIESEC, the nonpolitical, nonreligious Children's Rights Protection Organization "Save the Children," feminist organizations, and so on. Some other organizations that do not have an international network were also formed as a result of imitative orientations. These are primarily interest groups, such as the Lithuanian Association of Country Musicians. Two organizations that may be mentioned as the most interesting examples of innovative voluntary initiatives differ significantly in their organizational structures. One is the Lithuanian Students Abroad, which is a self-support group oriented toward sharing academic information and takes the form of a virtual club. It is totally unstructured and has no hierarchical organization except for a moderator. The other is the Union of Lithuanian Political Prisoners and Deportees, which was formed in 1988 as a result of the shared experience of forced territorial replacement and political prosecution under the Soviet regime. At present, the Union has 60 divisions across the country and 50,000 members. It is a political organization that takes part in elections at all levels. The main aim of the activities of the Union is the securing of independence for Lithuania, justice, democracy, and self-sufficiency of the state system as well as neutralizing the consequences of Soviet occupation and the communist regime.

This picture is by no means representative of the whole voluntary sector in Lithuania. Rather, it sketches some aspects of the developments of voluntary initiatives taking place in the postcommunist milieu. It shows that the nongovernmental sector is young and weak in Lithuania. Such a situation is not adequate to the needs of a society in which there is an increasing demand for voluntary services. But for the time being, continuative orientations in voluntary initiatives are being superseded in Lithuania. Imitative and innovative orientations have still not been consolidated. It seems that, in the present situation, restitutive orientations alone are effective in mobilizing people for voluntary action. To help people to organize and co-ordinate their voluntary initiatives, different support centers were established to promote volunteering across all sectors by increasing public awareness, organizing volunteer training, and providing people with the relevant information, on the one hand, and improving the legal status of volunteers, on the other. This kind of institutional support for grass-roots voluntary initiatives might be a very important factor in the future development of the Lithuanian voluntary sector and some improvements are already manifest.

CONCLUSION: THE FUTURE OF VOLUNTEERING

In sum, continuative tendencies in voluntary activity are losing their initial strength in the postcommunist milieu, as it was hypothesized. Restitutive tendencies rise somewhat in the initial phase of social reformation. In the long run, however, there is little potential for a rise in voluntarism here. The most interesting developments can be expected in the domain of imitative and innovative voluntary activities. From what we see at the moment, their level of activity is growing only in the Czech Republic and in Hungary, that is, in those countries that are the most advanced on the road to democracy and civil society. The passivity of Poland is somewhat striking in this context since it is also acknowledged as one of the leaders of democratic reforms. There is ground to expect that the Eastern European countries which are less advanced in this respect will follow the example of the Czech Republic: strengthening democracy and consolidating civil society should lead to new forms of voluntary activity.

The difference between the kind of voluntarism that existed in socialist societies and the voluntarism characteristic of a society with a democratic tradition may be grasped by confronting two concepts of volunteering: unpaid labor versus active citizenship. The Lithuanian way to democracy, among a number of other things, manifests itself as a transition from the former conception of voluntarism to the latter. Empirical data about the dynamics of voluntary activity in Eastern European countries are supportive of our theoretical assumption that voluntary organizations should become more active along with and as a part of the wider process of building civil society. Thus, we can expect that an increase in voluntary action among Lithuanians is highly dependent on the success of democratization, in general, and the strengthening of civil consciousness, in particular.

REFERENCES

Babiuch-Luxmoore, J. (1994). Sociological obstacles to democratic stability. In A. Jawlowska & M. Kempny (Eds.), *Cultural dilemmas of postcommunist societies* (pp. 240–255). Warsaw: IfiS Publishers.

Halman, L. (2001). *The European values study: A third wave.* Tilburg: EVS, WORC, Tilburg University.

Jones, A. (1968). *Jerusalem Bible.* London: Darton, Longman & Todd.

Kuhnle, S., & Selle, P. (1992). Government and voluntary organizations: A relational perspective. In S. Kuhnle & P. Selle (Eds.), *Government and voluntary organizations: A relational perspective* (pp. 1–33). Aldershot: Avebury.

Lenin, V. (1974). A great beginning: The heroism of the workers in the rear, on communist "subbotniks." In V.I. Lenin, *Collected works. Volume 29* (pp. 409–434). Moscow: Progress Publishers.

Marx, K. (1975). Critic of the Gothic programme. In L.S. Feuer (Ed.), *Marx & Engels Basic writings on politics and philosophy* (pp. 113–132). New York: Basic Books.

Odom, W.E. (1973). *The Soviet volunteers: Modernization and bureaucracy in a public mass organization.* Princeton, NJ: Princeton University Press.

Putnam, R.D. (1993). *Making democracy work: Civic traditions in modern Italy*. Princeton, NJ: Princeton University Press.

Šaulauskas, M.P. (1996). Customizing iron cage: Postmodern postcommunism? Lithuania and the Baltics. In: Working Papers, Bergen: University of Bergen.

Šaulauskas, M.P. (1998). Postkomunistines revoliucijos želmenys: iš revoliucinio tarpsnio į postmodernią Lietuvą? [Shoots of the postcommunist revolution: From the revolutionary phase to Post-modern Lithuania?]. *Sociologija: Mintis ir Veiksmas, 2*, 77–95.

Chapter **9**

Volunteering in Romania
A *Rara Avis*

MĂLINA VOICU AND BOGDAN VOICU

INTRODUCTION

Citizens' involvement in unpaid civic activities, for others or for the common good, is often said to account for much of the effectiveness of liberal democracy as a way to organize society. Alexis de Tocqueville's journey in United States in the 19th century led him to make several observations that became classic touchstones in the social sciences. Americans proved to be more likely to participate and volunteer in associations than Europeans (while European associative life was seen as being richer than that of the Asians).

Differences in participation and/or volunteering between countries were often explained by cultural or structural factors. The present chapter tries to offer some explanation of the low frequency of volunteering in Romania compared to other European countries.

After a brief review of the literature in the first section, the second part of the chapter focuses on individual level determinants of volunteering in Romania. We argue that, as in other countries, in Romania, people with "dominant status" (Smith, 1984) are more likely to volunteer than others. Thus, education, income, bridging social capital, religious practice, and age are also important determinants of volunteering in Romania.

However, volunteers are fewer in Romania than in the rest of Europe. The second part of this chapter focuses on structural and cultural factors that may explain this. We argue that members of the more traditional Romanian society, fragmented in almost unconnected small social groups, lack opportunities to participate in voluntary associations and to volunteer. The collapse of civic society during the communist period also contributed to this. Low levels of education and poverty are other possible explanations, as is the label of "voluntary work," used as the official denomination for unpaid, mandatory activities, imposed by the communist state on its citizens, for the benefit of the state or of its companies. We argue that this induced some repulsion for volunteering.

CONCEPTUAL DELIMITATIONS AND THEORETICAL BACKGROUND

Definitions

The term *volunteerism* is used with a variety of meanings and it has quite different connotations. "There is no unified definition that properly defines the boundaries of volunteerism" (Cnaan & Amrofell, 1994: 337) and this makes it difficult to analyze volunteerism and voluntary activity.

Some authors stress the *altruistic character* of voluntary work, considering it to be beyond any concern for economic profitability (Wuthnow, 1991), while others underline its *un-altruistic dimension*. Smith shows that the volunteer is "motivated by the expectation of psychic benefits of some kind of result" (1982: 25) and that "material and solidary incentives are far more important for the most kinds of volunteerism than are purposive incentives"[1] (1982: 37). Tilly and Tilly (1994) define voluntary work as *uncommodified*, unlike the labor market and the informal sector, but other authors (like Karl)[2] do not exclude the monetary benefits and, implicitly, the *commodified aspect*. Shead (1995) emphasizes the *formal character* of voluntary work, arguing that it takes place in the context of one organization or agency. Wilson and Musick (1997) also include *informal* help in the notion of volunteering, although they treat it separately.

We define voluntary work by referring to its formal, nonaltruistic, and un-commodified character. We understand volunteering to be an activity through which the individual spends a part of his time, without any wage, by free choice, in a formal way, within an organization, working for the benefit of others or of the entire community.

---

[1] According to Clark and Wilson (Smith, 1982: 37) material incentives are goods, services, money, and equivalents; solidarity incentives are interpersonal rewards of various kinds: friendship and prestige; purposive incentives are various kinds of intrinsic, intangible satisfactions that result from a person's feeling that he/she is contributing to some purpose and helping to achieve some valued goal.

[2] B.D.Karl ("Lo, the poor volunteer . . . " *Social Science Review,* 58:493–522, see Cnaan & Amrofell, 1994: 337) points out that the American businessmen who entered the government during the war to run certain agencies considered themselves to be volunteers because they accepted governmental wages of only one dollar yearly.

Determinants of Volunteering

In the search for an answer to the question "Why do people volunteer?," social researchers developed two main approaches to volunteering. One is based on the investigation of the resources of those who volunteer. The other focuses on the beliefs and values that underlie volunteering.

Previous work on volunteering suggests strong associations between volunteering and availability of resources both at societal and individual level (see Smith, 1994; Wilson, 2000; Pearce, 1993 for reviews of the literature). People controlling more resources are more often volunteers: first, they have more resources to share (time, money, education and abilities, social connections, etc.); second, by having control over these resources, they are more attractive to voluntary organizations. Income and human and social capital are frequently reported as determinants for volunteering behavior, together with socio-economic status indicators (age, gender, religion, marital status).

Volunteering means participation and cooperation, and supposes trust in people who benefit from voluntary work. The presence of social capital[3] facilitates participation in voluntary activities and membership of voluntary associations. Voluntary organizations usually recruit members, not through publicity, but by using the social networks of those who are already members (Pearce, 1993: 67). Multiple social networks increase the probability of more people getting in contact with voluntary associations, participating, and volunteering in their activities (Wilson, 2000: 223; Wilson & Musick, 1997). Finally, there is a circular relation: participation in voluntary associations contributes to increasing both relational social capital and civic skills; implicitly, it increases the probability of getting in contact with other voluntary associations (Smith, 1994; Wilson & Musick, 1997; Putnam, 2001: 121 etc.).

One should note that not all types of social capital contribute to encouraging voluntary activities. If the positive relation between volunteering and bridging social capital[4] is reported by almost all studies dedicated to volunteering, evidences supporting the relationship between bonding social capital and volunteering is lacking. However, as bonding social capital consists mainly of strong informal ties developed within the membership group or within a small community, it does not

[3] For Coleman (1990), for instance, one of the forms of social capital consists in participating in the development and activity of organizations, especially of voluntary organizations, but also in the informal lives of those aiming for profit.
[4] Narayan (1999) and Woolcock (2000) distinguish between bridging and bonding social capital. The latter consists of relations and norms of trust developed within the main membership group, being a form of social capital that contributes to maintaining group cohesion. Bridging social capital consists in ties and mutual trust developed between groups, facilitating cooperation and collective action. In the absence of bridging capital social, bonding social capital acts as a separation factor, and it could be an obstacle to the formation and functioning of voluntary associations.

encourage the existence of formal associations, and directs volunteering behavior toward informal help. We expect that people who are involved in strong kinship relationships (spending much time with relatives, often helping each other etc.) will not have a higher propensity to volunteer.

Wilson and Musick (1997: 699) argue that people whose children are still living with them are more likely to volunteer than childless people are, as their children give them supplementary social contacts. Sundeen (1990: 492) shows that, among married people, those with children exhibit a higher probability to volunteer. On the other hand, Putnam (2001: 119–120) suggests that "schmoozers" volunteer more often. Entertaining friends at home frequently (Putnam's indicator for "schmoozing") represents a measure for a larger social network. Moreover, if those friends are not relatives, but, for instance, work-colleagues, this is a sign of a larger social network, of more possible connections and weak ties, of bridging social capital. These imply more possibilities and a higher probability to volunteer.

Trust is also important for voluntary association membership. As Tonkiss and Passey point out, "trust can be viewed as the basis for voluntary association itself" (1999: 262). Lack of trust in people and institutions could be an impediment in working in cooperation with others within an institutionalized system.

Fukuyama's (1995) argument that lower participation in associations and volunteering in fragmented societies increases, at societal level, the importance of bridging social capital. Fukuyama shows that, in familial societies lacking relations between social groups, people do not cooperate outside their main group (usually the extended family). Implicitly, in such societies, there are fewer volunteers. Similarly, Dekker and van den Broek (1996: 137) suggest that societies lacking trust present voluntary associations with fewer members. Curtis, Grabb, and Baer (1992: 150) use the same argument to explain inter-country differences in voluntary association membership. For ex-communist countries, Fukuyama (1995) notes that centralized government and political control over society break the links between various social groups and discourage the existence of voluntary associations. Although Fukuyama's explanation is built on the Chinese case, with its traditional centrality, it is partially relevant to Romania too. Strong political control over civic associations, labor unions, church associations, etc., almost destroyed Romanian civic society and discouraged voluntary activity, including volunteering.

Human capital is another determinant of volunteering reported by most papers dedicated to this topic (see Wilson, 2000; Smith, 1994 for reviews). An acceptable level of health is required to make volunteering fully possible. Being healthy increases the probability of volunteering. In addition, the more educated a person is, the more knowledge he/she can use in order to help a voluntary organization to achieve its goals. On the other hand, more education means a high probability of increased aspirations and interest in fulfilling superior needs, including more gratification from non-material rewards.

The positive relation between volunteering and income is explained similarly (Wilson, 2000; Smith, 1994).

There is no consensus in the literature on the effect of gender on volunteering. Several studies emphasize the high rate of volunteering among women (Wilson & Musick, 1997; Wilson, 2000). Wilson (2000: 227) shows that women are more involved in voluntary work because they "score higher on measures of altruism and empathy, attach more value to helping others." Women are less active on the labor market; therefore, they have more free time and a more flexible schedule, allowing them to volunteer. Dekker and van den Broek (1996), and Pearce (1993: 68) report that men are more likely to volunteer: being better educated they have more resources to share; they have more spare time as they are not responsible for domestic work; etc. However, there is evidence that the gender effect disappears when the control of socioeconomic status is imposed (Sundeen, 1988).

The relationship between age and volunteering is a controversial one (Pearce, 1993: 68). Some authors sustain that volunteering is high among teenagers, and decreases among young people, with a maximum for adults (40–55 years). From the opposite perspective, Wilson (2000: 226) shows that "rational choice theory predicts an increase in volunteering at retirement age because more free time becomes available," while exchange theory explains the increase in volunteering among retired persons because voluntary work can replace the social and psychical benefits derived from paid work. As volunteering is a new phenomenon in Romanian society, we expect it to have a higher impact on young Romanians, as they are more open to change.

The social environment, related to the locality, provides by itself a resource (for volunteering). The lack or abundance of material resources, the type of social capital, opportunities for education, and the level of education in an area were already discussed in this section. However, there are other characteristics of locality that can provide incentives to volunteer. Sundeen (1988: 555) suggests that, in smaller cities, there are fewer common needs to be met, face-to-face interactions are more frequent, and the problems find informal, mutual solutions. On the other hand, bigger cities manifest a greater need for public goods and services; therefore, they can offer more opportunities to volunteer. From a different perspective, Romanian analyses (Frunză & Voicu, 1997; Sandu, 1999b) argue that people in rural areas show less initiative, waiting for everything to come from the authorities (usually from the state). Participation in voluntary associations is also reported to be lower in villages (Grigorescu, 1999: 162). Our hypothesis draws on these findings and theoretical arguments: living in urban areas should increase the probability of volunteering. Unlike Sundeen (1988), we do not expect any relationship between the size of locality and the probability of volunteering. The reason for this is the smaller variation in terms of size among Romanian urban areas compared to American ones (for which Sundeen's conclusions were drawn).

Also, as voluntary associations were practically forbidden until ten years ago, the initial need for them was almost equal in all cities. Finally, as smaller, "peripheral" cities tend to follow the example of "core" cities, especially when new institutions are established, there is a chance that the level of volunteering may increase slightly with the size (and importance) of the city. This may be similar to the tendency towards higher levels of volunteering in medium sized localities reported by Sundeen.

Values are frequently mentioned among the many determinants of volunteerism. Although some authors sustain that "values fail to predict volunteering reliability" (Wilson, 2000: 219), values play an important role in determining the participation in voluntary activity. Kendall and Knapp (1995: 72) emphasize that the voluntary sector has an expressive function that expresses mainly the social, philosophical, moral, and religious values of those who support the voluntary sector. Religious values play a key role in determining and sustaining volunteerism.

Wilson and Musick (1997) found a relationship between religiosity and formal volunteering, especially between behavioral measures of religiosity and volunteering. Wuthnow (1994) indicates that religious organizations provide not only the possibility to volunteer within the organization, but also personal contact opportunities. This helps people to increase their social network, facilitating their involvement in other voluntary activities. Similarly, Cnaan, Kasternakis, and Wineburg (1993) point out that religious belief is not a key factor in explaining participation in the voluntary sector. In the Romanian case, we also expect that volunteering is linked to religious practice.

Pearce (1993), Cnaan and Amrofell (1994: 346–347), and Smith (1982) suggest that volunteering could be motivated by pure altruism, social connections opportunities, internal qualifications, or contextual rewards. However, they completely reject altruistic motivation as an incentive for volunteering. As an immediate consequence, one could reduce the determinants for volunteering to a set of social resources and socio-economic status indicators: a person who is looking for fulfillment of superior needs such as a positive self-image or other internal gratifications is likely to have at least a good material position, a good education, etc. On the other hand, once involved in voluntary work, a person's social relations increase because of meeting other volunteers.

These considerations, along with data restrictions (lack of information about volunteers' motivation and values) led us to opt for a resources-based approach to volunteering in Romania.

In sum, we expect to find a higher volunteering propensity among more educated and wealthier people, with stronger out-group relations, who are younger, with a higher frequency of religious practice, and who reside in urban areas. We do not expect gender differences in volunteering, nor differences because of locality size (apart from those between urban and rural areas).

INDIVIDUAL DETERMINANTS OF VOLUNTEERING IN ROMANIA

Data Source and Measurement

Romanian social databases do not provide much data on volunteering. With the exception of a survey dedicated to philanthropic behavior (unfortunately unavailable), only the Romanian versions of EVS/WVS 1990–1993 and EVS 1999 offer good measures for volunteering. EVS 1999 is the main data source for this chapter. However, we used data from other surveys, such as the Public Opinion Barometer series of the Open Society Foundation (the BOP-OSF 1998–2001 surveys); databases from the RIQL data archive; and data collected by the Foundation for the Development of Civil Society (FDSC) on non-profit organizations.

Our measure of volunteering was based on the respondents' claims that they do or do not do unpaid work for a set of specified organizations (see Table 9.1). Analyses were conducted for people volunteering in a) any type of organization except trade unions and political parties; b) any type of organization excluding those mentioned and religious organizations. As Curtis, Grabb, and Baer (1993)

Table 9.1. **Romanian Volunteers by Type of Organization**

	Number of cases	%
Social welfare services	11	1.0
Religious or church organizations	41	3.7
Education, arts, music or cultural activities	20	1.8
Trade unions	67	6.2
Political parties or groups	21	1.9
Local community action	7	0.6
Third world development or human rights	5	0.4
Conservation, the environment, ecology, animal rights	7	0.6
Professional associations	12	1.1
Youth work	6	0.5
Sports or recreation	14	1.2
Women's groups	4	0.4
Peace movement	0	0.0
Voluntary organizations concerned with health	7	0.6
Others	17	1.5
Total excluding trade unions and political parties	110	10.6
Total excluding trade unions, political parties, and religious organizations	83	8.0

Source: EVS 1999–Romania

suggested, each item indicates not an organization but a *type* of organization for which the respondent volunteers. An additive index indicates the number of types of organizations in which a respondent volunteers, not necessarily the number of organizations in which the respondent actually volunteers. Constrained by the very skewed distribution of the number of voluntary activities (80% of the volunteers volunteer for just one type of organization), we preferred to compute our indexes as dummy variables.

We have excluded the participation in labor unions and political parties from the analysis because, in Romania, work in this kind of association is not real voluntary work. Unpaid work in a union is sometimes mandatory and many of those involved in such activities are pursuing their own interests. The same reasons underlie the exclusion of respondents who do unpaid work for political parties. Religious organizations were excluded in order to check if the strong effect of religious practice on volunteering has deeper roots, as we argued above, or is due exclusively to the fact that some components of the volunteering index are religious organizations.

Among the predictors, we employed three measures for the different facets of social capital (see Table 9.2): "frequency of social contacts" represents the frequency of spending time with friends (4 point scale); "trust in people" was measured on

Table 9.2. Logistic Regression of Volunteering in Formal Organizations

	Religious associations included		Religious associations excluded	
	B	Wald	B	Wald
Income per capita (within household)	0.09*	8.85	0.11*	12.26
(Inverse of) Age	27.83*	6.76	41.79*	11.98
Religious Practice	0.33*	10.33	0.32*	7.12
Trust in people	0.42*	8.56	0.42*	6.22
Education	0.03	2.03	0.05*	4.15
Urban area	0.22	0.63	0.57	2.71
No. of children in household	0.11	0.88	0.19	1.94
Man	0.02	0.01	0.34	1.52
Frequency of social contacts	0.14	1.24	0.07	0.19
Size of Locality	−0.02	0.58	0.01	0.01
Constant	−2.34*	9.20	−4.049*	18.267
Nagelkerke-Pseudo-R2	9.9%		15.9%	
Goodness of fit	$\chi^2 = 44.3$; df = 10 (p < 0.0005)		$\chi^2 = 62.5$; df = 10 (p < 0.0005)	

Source: EVS 1999–Romania. *p< 0.05.

a 4 point scale;[5] "number of children within households" includes 17-year-old or younger children. For human capital, data limitation allowed us to use only "education," measured by the age when the respondent finished his/her studies. "Income per capita" was measured in hundreds of the Romanian currency (lei), while "size of locality" was measured in numbers (thousands) of inhabitants. "Religious practice" was measured on a 5 point scale, indicating the frequency of church attendance: "more than once a week," "once a week," "once a month," "Christmas/Easter day," less often. "Man" and "Urban" were dummy variables for gender and residence area, respectively.

Results

Logistic regression of volunteering confirms our hypothesis. "Dominant status," rich bridging of social capital, religious practice, location in urban areas, and younger age are positively associated with doing unpaid work in voluntary associations.

Income proved to be one of the strongest predictors. This is quite normal in a country where the majority considers itself poor: between 40% and 45% of the population declared between 1992 and 2001 that "they are not making basic ends meet," while around 30% declared that they "barely make basic ends meet" (RIQL data archive). The proportion of the population that considers itself as poor increased slightly in the last decade from 45% to 55%. EVS 1999 database does not provide a measure for subjective (feelings of) poverty. However, we used data from the BOP-OSF 1998 surveys in order to check if there is any influence of subjective poverty on voluntary association membership (BOP-OSF do not provide data on unpaid voluntary work). Self-perception as poor (10-point scale) seems to have the same effect on voluntary association membership as the per capita income has. This means that, along with the direct effect of income, people who perceive themselves as poor (the two measures are not collinear), are less likely to do unpaid work in voluntary associations.

Higher at younger ages, volunteering greatly decreases for adults and elderly people. For people above the age of 30, it remains almost constantly at a low level. The explanation can be found in the different attitudes toward voluntary activity. Younger people are more open to innovation, and voluntary associations are new and innovative in a society in which, during the communist period, any voluntary activity was forbidden or strongly controlled by the state.

Frequent religious practice determines higher volunteerism both in secular and religious activities. The data prove that there is no significant difference in religious belief for people who volunteer and those who do not. On a 0 to 5

---

[5] In our logistic model, we have treated both "trust" and "frequency of social contacts" as continuous variables. Because both variables are measured on 4-point scales, we reran our model treating them as categorical variables. The results were the same.

Table 9.3. Volunteering and Religious Denomination

Religious denomination	Volunteers (including religious associations)	Volunteers (excluding religious associations)	Total
Orthodox	9%	7%	89%
Catholic	7%	6%	8%
Protestant and Neo-Protestant	13%	8%	4%
Total	9%	7%	100%

Source: EVS 1999–Romania.

scale,[6] volunteers score 2.71 for religious belief, while non-volunteers score 2.62.[7] This supports our hypothesis that involvement in voluntary associations is linked to religious practice, but not to religious belief.

We also tested the hypothesis of the association between volunteering and religious denominations. We included in our analysis only affiliation to Christian Orthodoxy, Roman and Greek Catholicism, Protestantism, and Neo-Protestantism. Other religious denominations have very few members within the Romanian population. The data (see Table 9.3) indicate that there is no association between religious denomination and doing unpaid voluntary work.

Social capital is another strong predictor. Trust in people proved to have a strong association with volunteering when other determinants were controlled for, while the number of children and the frequency of social contacts were found to have a positive, but small, significant effect. For the frequency of social contacts, the low effect may be influenced by lack of fidelity in measurement. As Romanian society is quite traditional in many respects (Voicu, 2002a), especially in rural areas, social networks include predominantly relatives. Even those who prove to have intense interpersonal relations mostly have contacts within the kinship (Sandu, 1999a: 93). Under these circumstances, the frequency of spending time with friends could include not only contacts with non-relative friends, but also with relatives. Using a different data set (see Table 9.4), we checked for the relationship between the type of social contact and membership in voluntary associations. The only significant effect ($p < 0.10$) is that of frequently interacting with work/school colleagues (the only measure of bridging social capital in the table), which favors association membership. The same relationship is likely to exist between bridging social capital and volunteering.

Education has a stronger effect on volunteering when we exclude volunteering in religious associations. The explanation lies in the fact that Church attachment

[6] The indicator for religious belief is an additive index on which each respondent gets one more point if he/she answers positively to the following questions: Generally speaking, do you think that churches are giving, in Romania, adequate answers to the moral problems and needs of the individual; the problems of family life; people's spiritual needs; the social problems facing our country today.
[7] The index ranges from 0 to 5. When religious associations are excluded, volunteers score 2.46, and non-volunteers score 2.64.

Table 9.4. Voluntary Association Membership by Frequency of Types of Social Contacts

Frequency of interacting with		Membership in voluntary association	Membership in voluntary non-religious association
Relatives	Seldom[a]	7%	6%
	Often	8%	7%
Neighbors	Seldom	7%	6%
	Often	8%	7%
Colleagues	Seldom	7%	5%
	Often	12%	11%

[a] For each measure of relationships, we employed a set of four questions about the frequency of visiting, borrowing/lending money/things, spending time together, and discussing personal problems with neighbors, colleagues, and friends. All 12 items were measured on 4 points scales from which we computed "personal dominant opinion indexes" (adaptations of Hoffstaeder's dominant opinion index, computed as differences between positive and negative answers weighted with the total number of answers and items). In order to present the data, we recoded the three indexes as dummy variables.
Source: BOP-OSF-1998 (June and November merged files).

and trust in the Church are lower among those who are more educated (Gheorghiu, 2002). As expected, size of locality does not play any role in determining volunteering.

We did not find any significant effect of gender on volunteering when the socio-economic resources were controlled for. Men are involved in unpaid voluntary activities almost to the same degree as women are. The policy of the communist regime encouraged women to get waged jobs, even if it did not stimulate the sharing of domestic work with men (Voicu, 2002c). The trend remained the same during the transition period. In this context, women have less time to volunteer, as they are involved both in paid and domestic work.

We tried to test for a relationship between altruism and volunteering by using a very weak measure of altruism, or of benevolence and universalism: how important the respondents consider it to be that a society should "guarantee that basic needs are met for all" in order to be considered just (five points scale). We found no significant association either for the bivariate or for the multivariate case. However, recognizing the weakness of the measure, no definitive conclusions could be drawn.

CONTEXTUAL DETERMINANTS OF VOLUNTEERING IN ROMANIA

According to EVS 1999 data, only 9.5% of Romanians do unpaid work in at least one organization. With the exception of Russia and Ukraine, this is the lowest percentage of volunteers among the 32 countries in the data set. Other ex-communist countries also score low: 12% for Bulgaria, Poland, and Lithuania, 14%

for Hungary, 17% for Estonia, but 30% for the Czech Republic, 27% for Slovenia, and 22% for Croatia. In all Western European countries, except Spain and Portugal (17% and 13%, respectively), 20% of the population volunteer, while the UK, the Netherlands, and the Nordic countries score over 30%. EVS/WVS 1990–1993 recorded similar data.

No exact data exist on the proportion of Romanian volunteers. However, we can estimate the proportion of participants in voluntary associations. Social values surveys report figures between 13% and 15%: 13% in EVS/WVS 1993; 15% in RIQL's "Values"-1997; 13.8% in RIQL's "Democracy Consolidation"-1998; 12.9% in EVS 1999. For all these surveys, the list of types of associations presented to the respondents was almost the same.

The second source of data—the OSF Barometer series—does not offer comparative data. The 1998 Barometers included a reduced version of the list of types of voluntary association (without the "other type" option): 7.4% of the respondents claimed membership. The 2000 (May and November) and 2001 (May) questionnaires do not contain a list of types of associations, but a simple question about membership in "any" association. 9.4% and 11.9%, respectively, of the respondents answered the question positively. As the Barometer series' way of questioning is expected to produce underestimated figures,[8] membership of associations is likely to have remained constant (between 13% and 15%) during the last decade. This is lower than in any other country in Europe, except Ukraine.

There are several explanations for the low level of volunteering. The first proposed factor refers to the heritage of the communist period and the reduced number of associations existing in Romania. As we have mentioned, during the communist period, any association uncontrolled by the state was forbidden. The communist state did not allow the civil society to function and the law prohibited free association among individuals. The few existing associations, such as The Women's National Association and its local versions, were controlled by the state: central or local authorities named the leaders, excluded undesirable members, or forced people to participate and to do unpaid work in order to reach the association's goals. Even chess clubs and religious organizations were strictly regulated and directed by the communist party. The state and the party also controlled the labor unions (affiliation was compulsory for employees).

In addition, the communist regime promoted a kind of so-called "voluntary work," which was actually compulsory. People were forced to participate in "voluntary" "patriotic" activities, for the common good. These "voluntary—compulsory"[9] activities included work in agriculture (usually harvesting for state companies), cleaning public places, seeding plants, and gathering recyclables (there were even

---

[8] When the question specifies the exact type of association referred to, there is a higher probability that the respondent will actually answer and declare his/her membership in voluntary organizations.
[9] The expression was used informally, but on a large scale, during communism.

quotas of objects that had to be gathered monthly as "voluntary work" by every family). Not participating in these activities was severely punished. This compromised the meaning of volunteerism and fostered an attitude of reticence toward volunteering.

Before 1945, Romania was mainly a rural traditional country. Voluntary activities and associations functioned exclusively in urban areas, having either cultural, educational, caring, or sporting purposes. Members of these associations were usually active in political parties too, were better educated, and had a higher income than the average. During the first decades of communism, most of these people ended up in prison, while some managed to emigrate. The few survivors are quite old.

After 1989, volunteering was quite a new phenomenon in Romanian society. The present form of volunteering was "imported" during transition, having as a catalyst international NGOs. An "association boom" was immediately registered (UNDP, 1999: 59). In 1990, around 300 NGOs were established every month. Statistics about the total number of non-profit organizations are confusing, but they indicate a quite low level of associationism. Depending on the source, figures vary from 4,015 (FDSC, 1999), and 7,000 (Glinski, 1996: 2,[10] data for 1994) to over 30,000 (UNDP, 1999: 59, data for 1997). The last figure seems an overestimation and probably includes trade unions, political parties, private universities, etc. Among the European ex-communist countries, Romania has the lowest number of the NGOs. According to Glinski (1996), Poland had 47,000 NGOs in 1996; Hungary, 36.000; the Czech Republic, 31,500; and Slovakia, 10,000. Looking at the ratio between the number of NGOs and the number of inhabitants, the situation seems to be even worse, Romania being the second largest country in the group. In addition, less than 10% of the registered voluntary associations are active, the others reporting no activity, although they are not officially closed (UNDP, 1999:60). A lack of voluntary associations reduces one's possibilities to volunteer, despite one's willingness to do so.

As we showed in the previous section, volunteering is determined by income, education, and the existence of bridging social capital. With a GDP of roughly $4,000 ppp per inhabitant (UNDP, 1999:131), Romania is among the poorest European countries. Only 12% of the population has higher education, less than most European countries (OECD 2000). Finally, Romanians participate less in social life than other Europeans (Voicu, 2002a). On the other hand, as we have argued before, the structure of the social capital in Romania is not favorable to participating in and doing unpaid work for voluntary associations. Most social relations are developed inside the kinship. Several papers (Mihăilescu, 1996; Frunză & Voicu,

[10] Paper of P. Glinski, *Developing the third sector as a vehicle for civil society in Poland*, for the Second International Conference of the International Society for the Third-Sector Research. Mexico-City, 1996, quoted by Grigorescu (1999: 161).

1997) report the existence of a special form of "household" developed across the boundaries of towns and villages: the "mixed diffused household." People living in urban areas maintain strong ties with their parents/relatives who live in villages and share income and expenditure, either by explicitly having a common budget or through a continuous informal exchange of products, money, and work. Other studies (Stănculescu & Berevoescu, 1999; Sandu, 1999a) suggest that, in some villages in South-East Transylvania, once inhabited by a Saxon population,[11] specific neighborhood associations—with formal structures and governed by written rules—still exist, but their role is rather reduced. While once they governed the relationships within the community and contributed to the common good, now they limit their activity to helping on special occasions like baptisms, weddings, or funerals, and they function like closed societies, with membership sometimes being inherited.

Strong kinship networks act as an obstacle to the development of bridges between the kinship and other groups. Society becomes fragmented with small islands acting like independent, autarchic bodies. As Putnam indicates, in such circumstances, volunteering with others becomes obsolete, the low level of intergroup trust pushing volunteers to volunteer for others, in other words, to informal help.

The religious context is another factor which accounts for the low level of volunteering in Romania. Some authors have mentioned the impact of the type of dominant religion in the society and of religious pluralism on volunteering. Curtis, Grabb, and Baer (1992: 149) indicate that countries with a strong Protestant heritage have a high level of membership of voluntary associations, because Protestants are more likely to feel responsible for helping others than Catholics. Wuthnow (1991: 19) shows that the pattern of historic conflict between religion and other institutions, like the state, played an important role in modeling the voluntary sector. Countries with a pluralist religious tradition, where no religious organization had a special relation to the state, developed a pluralist voluntary sector.

In Romania, the large Christian-Orthodox majority (89% of the population at the 1992 Census) reduces the religious diversity. The relationship between the Orthodox Church and the state was generally very strong throughout history (Meyerdorff, 1996), especially in Romania, where the Church was highly involved in political life before communism (Voicu, 2002b). The social structure promoted by orthodoxy is predominantly hierarchic, even at its most informal. Centralized relations and the lack of material resources of ecclesiastic clergy prevented the emergence of a strong helping and caring role for the church. Intolerance and rejection of innovation did not allow the development of special relationships between voluntary associations and the church. However, during the last decade,

---

[11] These Saxons are a Germanic population living in South-East Transylvania. Many of them immigrated to Germany after 1970. The remainder represents less than 1% of the Transylvanian population.

several organizations (especially ecumenical and caring organizations) were built around religious establishments.

CONCLUSIONS

In this chapter, we argued that due to low levels of some universal determinants of volunteering (education, income, bridging social capital), the Romanian level of volunteering is among the lowest in Europe. Several cultural traits, many of them depending on the country's recent past, also contribute to this situation. In order to test our explanation, we ran a logistic regression on the entire EVS database (data for 32 countries; see Halman (2001) for details), controlling for education, income, social capital, age, gender, religious practice, and locality size,[12] along with dummy variables for each country (Romania was the reference category). The analysis revealed a clear East-West difference, with former communist countries scoring lowest. There are also differences between former communist countries. Romania scores lower than every other country in the sample except Russia. Ukraine presents no significant difference from Romania, while Poland does not differ if we include volunteering in religious organizations.

However, as we have showed, the profile of Romanian volunteers is similar to that reported in the literature for volunteers from other countries: they have a "dominant status" in terms of income and education, they are younger, they have of an extended network of social relations, and they exhibit a more frequent religious practice.

The differences between Romania and other CEE countries probably result from its recent history and social structure. The more hermetic Romanian communism, especially in its last two decades, did not allow the spread of voluntary associations as in Poland, Hungary, or The Czech Republic. The complete control of mass media (during the last decades of communism, people preferred to watch Bulgarian, Serbian, Hungarian, or Russian television channels) contributed to the maintenance of a closed society. With a large agrarian sector, and a delayed and partial modernization, Romania developed a hierarchical social structure, inhibiting individual and social initiative.

The prospects for the future are not very optimistic as far as volunteerism is concerned. Romanian society seems to be dominated by statism, and individual initiative is not encouraged. The idea of maintaining the traditional small isolated villages with fragmented land ownership (and bonding social capital) dominates public discourse and political action in relation to supporting community development. The instability of the law contributes to the lack of trust in institutions

---

[12] The data measurement was similar to that reported in the case of regression on Romanian data, except for trust, coded now as a dummy variable.

and people. On the other hand, the activity of international voluntary associations, along with the recognition of volunteering as a normal, not innovative, phenomenon, could help to increase volunteerism. Adding to this the generational change and economic growth, we expect a slight increase in volunteering for the next decade.

REFERENCES

Cnaan, R., & Amrofell, L. (1994). Mapping volunteer activity. *Nonprofit and Voluntary Sector Quarterly* 23, 335–351.

Cnaan, R., Kasternakis, A., & Wineburg, R. (1993). Religious people, religious congregations, and volunteerism in human services. *Nonprofit and Voluntary Sector Quarterly 22*, 33–51.

Coleman, J. (1990). *Foundations of social theory*. Cambridge, Mass.: Harvard University Press.

Curtis, J., Grabb, E., & Baer, D. (1992). Voluntary association membership in fifteen countries. *American Sociological Review 57*, 139–152.

Dekker, P., & Van den Broek, A. (1996). Volunteering and politics. In L. Halman & N. Nevitte (Eds.), *Political values change in Western Europe* (pp. 125–151). Tilburg, The Netherlands: Tilburg University Press.

FDSC (2000). *The Catalog of Civil Society*. Bucharest:. Foundation for Developing Civil Society.

Frunză, M., & Voicu, B. (1997). The state and the Romanian peasant. *Revista de Cercetări Sociale 4*, 118–130.

Fukuyama, F. (1995). *Trust*. New York: Free Press.

Gheorghiu, E. (2002). *Religiosity and Christianity in post-communist Romania*. In L. Pop (Ed.), *Values of transition. Transition of values* (forthcoming). Iaşi: Polirom.

Grigorescu, N. (1999). The associations. In I. Berevoescu et al., *Faces of change. Romanians and the challenges of transition* (pp. 160–165). Bucharest: Nemira.

Halman, L. (2001). *The European values study: A third wave. Source book of the 1999/2000 European values study surveys*. Tilburg, The Netherlands: Tilburg University Press.

Kendall, J., & Knapp, M. (1995). A loose and baggy monster. In D.J. Smith, C. Rochester, & R. Hedley (Eds.), *An introduction to voluntary sector* (pp. 71–90). London, New York: Routledge.

Meyendorff, J. (1996). *The Orthodox Church yesterday and today*. Bucharest: Anastasia.

Mihăilescu, V. (1996). Two villages in transition. *Revista de Cercetări Sociale 3*, 3–24.

Narayan, D. (1999). *Bonds and bridges*. Washington: World Bank (Working Papers Series WPS 2167).

OECD (2000). *Education at a glance*. Paris: OECD.

Pearce, J. (1993). *Volunteers*. London, New York: Routledge.

Pop, L., (Ed.) (2002). *Values of transition, transition of values*. Iaşi: Polirom (forthcoming).

Putnam, R. (1993). *Making democracy work*. Princeton, NJ: Princeton University Press.

Putnam, R. (2001). *Bowling alone*. New York: Touchstone.

Sandu, D. (1999a). *The social space of transition*. Iaşi: Polirom.

Sandu, D. (coordinator) (1999b). *Social capital and entrepreneurship in Romanian rural communities*. Bucharest, Romania: World Bank.

Shead, J. (1995). From lady bountiful to active citizen. In D.J. Smith, C. Rochester, & R. Hedley (Eds.). *An introduction to voluntary sector* (pp. 115–122). London and New York: Routledge.

Smith, D.H. (1982). Altruism, volunteers, and volunteerism. In J.D. Hartman (Ed.), *Volunteerism in the eighties* (pp. 23–44). Washington D.C.: University Press of America.

Smith, D.H. (1994). Determinants of voluntary association, participation, and volunteering: A literature review. *Nonprofit and Voluntary Sector Quarterly 23*, 243–263.

Stănculescu, M., & Berevoescu, I. (1999). Moşna, a village that reinvent itself. *Sociologie Românească 1*, 78–106.

Sundeen, R. (1988). Explaining participation in coproduction: A study of volunteers. *Social Science Quarterly 69*, 547–568.

Sundeen, R. (1990). Family life course and volunteer behavior. *Sociological Perspectives 33*, 483–500.

Tilly, C., & Tilly, C. (1994). Capitalist work and labor markets. In N. Smelser & R. Swedberg (Eds.), *Handbook of economic sociology* (pp. 283–313). Princeton, NJ: Princeton University Press.

Tonkiss, F., & Passey, A. (1999). Trust, confidence and voluntary organisations. *Sociology: 33*, 257–274.

UNDP. (1999). *National human development report—Romania 1999*. Bucharest, Romania: Expert.

Voicu, B. (2002a). Pseudo-modern Romania. In L. Pop (Ed.), *Values of transition, transition of values* (forthcoming). Iaşi: Polirom.

Voicu, M. (2002b). Religious modernity in Romanian society. In L. Pop (Ed.), *Values of transition, transition of values* (forthcoming). Iaşi: Polirom.

Voicu, M. (2002c). Equality, inequality and traditional roles. In L. Pop (Ed.), *Values of transition, transition of values* (forthcoming). Iaşi: Polirom.

Wilson, J. (2000). Volunteering. *Annual Review of Sociology 26*, 215–240.

Wilson, J., & Musick, M. (1997). Who cares? *American Sociological Review 62*, 694–713

Woolcock, M. (2000). Managing risk, shocks, and opportunities in developing economies. In G. Ranis (Ed.), *Dimensions of Development*, New Haven: Yale Center for International and Area Studies.

Wuthnow, R. (1991). The voluntary sector. In R. Wuthnow (Ed.), *Between state and markets* (pp. 3–29). Princeton NJ: Princeton University Press.

Wuthnow, R. (1994). *God and Mammon in America*. New York: Free Press.

Chapter 10

Generations and Organizational Change

DAG WOLLEBÆK AND PER SELLE

INTRODUCTION: WHERE HAVE ALL THE VOLUNTEERS GONE?

> The collective spirit among Oslo's inhabitants appears to have vanished. Housing associations, sports clubs and other voluntary organizations are struggling.—It has become much more trendy to sit around in cafés than to run around in the woods with a bunch of kids, says the Secretary General of the Norwegian Scouts' Association (*Aftenposten,* August 24th, 2000).

These concerns reflect the current mood in many traditional voluntary associations in Norway. Leaders in a wide range of fields within the sector seem to agree that the communal spirit is waning. It is commonly claimed that careerists, individualists and egoists with little time to spare represent an increasing proportion of the population. As a study of changing value patterns in Norwegian society shows, these values are difficult to reconcile with commitment to voluntary organizations (Hellevik, 1996). Furthermore, since young people distinguish themselves as the most egocentric and materialist age group of all (*op. cit.*), one might expect slow erosion of voluntary organising following the exit of older, more idealistic generations from the population.

On the other hand, recent research shows that volunteering in Norway is still very high in international comparison (Wollebæk et al., 2000). Over the past twenty years, the number of members, activists and organizations has remained remarkably stable (Andresen, 1999; Selle and Øymyr, 1995).

Why this discrepancy between statistics and experiences in the field? An article published in *Aftenposten* somewhat later—around Christmas—further complicates the picture. This time, the Salvation Army reported that, due to limited organizational capacity, they had to turn away a large number of people who had called in wanting to make an effort for people in need on Christmas Eve. The Blue Cross and the Church's City Mission had had similar experiences. At the same time, it was made clear that the influx of volunteers was considerably lower at other times of the year.

It is likely that most of the individuals wanting to volunteer for the Salvation Army are not members of the organization, as they do not participate on a year-round basis. The sense of community with the uniformed members is probably limited. The effort they make on Christmas Eve is mainly a relation between volunteer and recipient, whereas the organization is more peripheral. The organization's role is primarily to provide the necessary infrastructure for the activity to take place.

As in English, the word volunteering in Norwegian (*frivillig arbeid*) means work carried out "with free will" (*fri vilje*). It is possibly no coincidence that "volunteering" is increasingly replacing "active membership" (*aktivt medlemskap*) as the most frequently used concept to describe unpaid activities within the nonprofit sector. It may reflect that a shift towards new modes of participation is underway, in which individuals want to choose more freely which purposes s/he wants to contribute to at what times, rather than carrying out tasks as a mere function of their membership affiliations. The willingness to donate time and energy is still there, but the time-span is shorter. The ties normally present between a participant and an organization in the Norwegian voluntary sector, such as formal membership and occasionally serving on boards, are not necessarily integral parts of such relations. Clearly, this volunteering *á la carte* may still provide voluntary organizations with crucial resources in terms of unpaid labor, but it falls short of the type and degree of commitment the leadership of the Scout's movement senses is lacking.

Can the contrast between the demise of the Scouts and the advent of "one-off" volunteering be interpreted as an expression of a *modernization* of organizational society? Does the discrepancy between subjective experiences and statistical measures imply that a modern and individualist type of volunteering is expanding, while traditional participation forms are retracting? If these processes cancel each other out, the *amount* of participation may remain stable despite extensive changes. These changes may concern *where* and *how* one participates—what people are willing to take part in within what organizational contexts—to a greater extent than *how much*.

In order to penetrate the surface of apparent stability, one needs to focus on changes in the *margins*, i.e. differences between those who are entering and exiting organizational society. An analysis of *generational differences* helps to bring out the contrasts between the old and the new. At the organizational level this entails comparing newly founded associations with those formed in earlier periods. At the individual level it means to compare younger and older people. For reasons elaborated on below, if a modernization of organizational society is underway, we expect to find its clearest manifestations among young associations and individuals.

DESIGN AND DATA

By means of this strategy, we address two main questions:

1. *Do different generations relate to voluntary organizations differently?* Two sub-themes appear particularly relevant in light of the discussion above:
   a. Are younger people connected to their organizations with weaker ties than their older counterparts?
   b. Do younger people hold more pragmatic views on the value basis and types of activities carried out by voluntary organizations?
2. *Do variations between individuals of different age coincide with similar variations between generations of local-level organizations?*
3. *If there are differences between age groups, do they represent a life cycle or a generational phenomenon?* Will young people "outgrow" their possibly deviating attitudes, or hang on to them for the rest of their lives? If the first is the case, the consequences for voluntary organizations are negligible. If the latter is the case, and the differences are sufficiently large, they are likely to cause substantial change.

The data consist of a postal survey mailed to a random sample of the population aged between 16 and 85 in 1998 (*Survey on Giving and Volunteering*, see Wollebaek et al., 1998), in addition to a census of local associations in one of Norway's 19 counties (Hordaland) carried out on three occasions, 1980, 1990 and 2000.[1] In the analysis of the organizational data, we focus mainly on the development in the 1990s. Both data sources cover all types of organizations between state and market, including political parties, trade unions and other economic interest organizations.

Only the first of the three research questions above can be directly tested by our data. In the absence of time series at the individual level, we cannot decide whether possible differences represent life cycle or generational phenomena (q3).

---

[1] The individual survey is a part of the international *Johns Hopkins Comparative Nonprofit Sector Project* (CNP), in which Norwegian participation is financed by six ministries. The response rate was 45% (N = 1695). The unsatisfactory response rate increases the probability for sample biases. As in many other surveys, those with high education and middle age have responded most frequently. The analyses are thus weighted by education. This has not affected any of the findings reported in the chapter: Unweighted results deviate only marginally from weighted. The organisational data stem from the project "Organisations in Hordaland." The 1980 and 1990 data are presented and analyzed in Selle and Øymyr (1995). The 2000 survey, which was carried out as part of the CNP, was conducted in two phases. First, the names, addresses, and key information about each association (founding year, membership figure, organizational structure, etc.) were collected by the culture department of each municipality, in addition to the names of "extinct" associations. Then, all registered associations received a mailed questionnaire. The response rate was 60% (N = 2842).

However, the information from the organizational level (q2) will provide some indications. If related variations are found between younger and older organizations and younger and older individuals, it is, firstly, likely that they reflect the same, fundamental changes in their surroundings. This is elaborated on below. Secondly, the types of organizations which are retracting and expanding today indicate which experiences young people today will make in adulthood. These experiences may differ substantially from those of their parents and grandparents. The two levels may be *mutually reinforcing*; organizational changes may influence the attitudes of the participants and the other way around. Therefore, it is particularly interesting to study the development within organizations for children and young people, as they represent the arena in which many make their first, decisive experiences of voluntary organized activity.

Thus, a *generational perspective* on the modernization of voluntary organizations will be the central theme in this chapter. Let us therefore briefly review how this may be a fruitful approach to the study of organizational and social change.

GENERATIONAL DIFFERENCES REFLECT AND CAUSE SOCIAL CHANGE

Ever since Karl Mannheims (1980[1928]) seminal essay "Das Problem der Generationen," social science has regarded differences between generations as an important means of understanding changes in society. A common assumption has been that epochal watersheds influence the values of younger adults to a greater extent than older generations (Skocpol 1996). Value orientations among young people can, therefore, to some extent be used as an indicator of contemporary ideological currents. Furthermore, if young people retain values deviating from older generations in spite of maturing, we can speak of a *generational divide*. In such cases social and political change may occur, as older generations exit the population. Thus, generational differences may both reflect and cause societal change.

In this vein, Inglehart (1997, 1990) asserts that the material conditions experienced during childhood and adolescence decisively influence one's value orientations at a later stage in life. Building on Maslow, Inglehart argues that most weight is attached to goods that are in short supply. As a consequence of the scarcity of material goods, the pre-war generations developed predominantly *materialist* value orientations. In contrast, the younger generations, who were better off during childhood, became *post-materialist* to a greater extent. Liberated from basic economic concerns, they were free to care about ideals such as democracy, human rights, gender equality and environmental issues. According to Inglehart society changes as materialists exit and postmaterialists enter the population—old cleavages erode and new emerge.

Inglehart expresses optimism concerning the future of democracy. However, this position is challenged by Robert D. Putnam's (1995a, 1995b, 2000) important work on contemporary American society. Inglehart's image is reversed in Putnam's writings; it is precisely those born between 1910 and 1940—"the long civic generation"—who have kept American democracy alive. They voted more frequently at elections, read more newspapers, trusted each other more, and were more active in associations. They cultivated and reinvested the *social capital*, the most fundamental resource in order to carry out any concerted action at all, let alone maintain a vital democracy. The post-war generations, and their youngest representatives in particular, score lower on all the above indicators. One important reason is, according to Putnam (1995a, 2000), that they have almost literally become x-rayed into apathy by watching TV.

Putnam (2000) also argues that youths are *more*, not less materialist than their parents. This is corroborated by Hellevik's (1993, 1996) analyses of changes in the value patterns of the Norwegian population. Hellevik claims that the term *supermaterialists* fit many representatives of the younger generations better than *postmaterialists*. The study shows that Ingleharts scarcity hypothesis finds little empirical support. Rather, it appears to be the other way around—affluence generates materialism as those who have want more. But a generational and socialization hypothesis is central even in Hellevik's work: Today's youths have been raised to believe that needs can be met instantaneously, not to frugality and thrift. This has shaped their moral standards and value orientations. They emphasize indulgence and material possessions, and put their own needs above others' to a greater extent than older generations do.

Hence, there exists an extensive, thoroughly empirically documented literature demonstrating that generational effects are present and important. Values into which one is socialized during childhood and adolescence influence one's outlooks as adults. Furthermore, there are evident similarities between the above-cited perspectives, despite their varying degrees of optimism. Their portrayal of younger generations as less bounded by convention, with a critical view on authority and a pragmatic attitude towards moral and procedure, is omnipresent in the international and Norwegian literature: They live reflexive and modern "own lives" (Beck, 1997); they are a "self-reliant generation," who "(. . .) in the absence of collective solutions choose individual strategies" (Øia, 1995:106); they pursue their interests on "market-places of possibilities," where individual interests have priority over collective, but reject the "obligation society" of the past, in which it was the other way around (Almås et al., 1995).

All these perspectives are related to a development in which the position of the individual is strengthened at the cost of the collective, and in which authority and convention are challenged. There appears to be agreement that this process is gaining momentum, and that the younger generations display stronger individualist tendencies than their older counterparts. Obviously, this does not apply to *only* young people and not *everyone* below a certain age fit into this pattern. However, statistical differences between the value orientations of older and younger people are clear, consistent and difficult not to interpret in light of the historical epochs the different generations grew up in.

How do these changes manifest themselves in the organizational society? What are the possible consequences? These questions cannot be addressed without information about the development at the organizational level. Here too, generation may be important. A central hypothesis within organizational theory states that external influences largely determine the form an organization chooses at the time of foundation (Stinchcombe, 1965). This structure lives on, despite extensive changes in the environment. Because the local level of the organizational society is open and dynamic—an association is easy to create and easily put to rest—changes in the environment surface particularly quickly here (Selle & Øymyr, 1995; Wollebæk & Selle, 2002a).

The analogy between the organizational and individual level is evident. New organizations are less bounded by convention, institutional inertia and previous experience, much the same way as young people are more susceptible to new trends than older people. The basic structural characteristics of established organizations usually do not change much. Similarly, basic value orientation of individuals may remain relatively stable throughout life. But the relationship is also more direct. Changing inclinations of individuals influence which new organizations are formed, and changes in the composition of organizational society affect the socialization of new generations. The latter fact makes the study of changes in organizations for children and youth a particularly pertinent task in this context.

Thus, if similar development trends surface simultaneously at both levels, it is *more likely*, although not certain, that they express deep-seated changes in the environment rather than fleeting trends. This is important because not all changes that surface last. Many new types of organizations are ephemeral, and many observed differences between age groups prove to be life cycle effects and therefore relatively inconsequential.

Generational effects, on the other hand, are not. They not only mirror external development trends, but also cause social change. In what follows, we explore if and how this occurs.

THE RESULTS: ATTITUDES TOWARD VOLUNTARY ORGANIZING

Survey on Giving and Volunteering (1998) showed that 38% of youths (16- to 24-year-olds) spent one hour or more per week participating or volunteering in organizations, compared to 37% in the population aged 25 or above. The percentage with not even a passive membership or any volunteering in the past year, was 35 among youths compared to only 22 in the adult population. These results differ from surveys conducted in the 1970s and 1980s, in which young people were more active than older age groups (Wollebaek et al., 2000: 106–107). Young people have not yet abandoned voluntary organizations, but they may be on the verge of losing interest.

To what extent does this surface in attitudes towards organizations? Below, we approach this question guided by the two subthemes briefly mentioned in the introduction: Ties between member and organization, and status for values commonly attached to the traditional Norwegian organizational society.

A central characteristic of Norwegian organizations is that volunteers almost without exception also hold membership. The institution of the membership provides each participant with formal democratic rights, and has been instrumental in creating more durable, institutionalized ties between participants and organizations.

Against this backdrop, a strong support for the membership institution was expected. Accordingly, the results ((a) in Table 10.1) show that volunteers in all age groups consider membership important. However, there are also clear variations: The younger the volunteer is, the more reserved the enthusiasm. While membership is self-evident among older volunteers, it is alright among their younger counterparts. The responses to question (b) show that the minority is indifferent to which organization they volunteer for—it is important to contribute to a particular one. Again, however, the strength of the ties varies between the age groups: Young people place less emphasis on the organizational context of the activity, as long as the activity is there. The generational differences are smaller here than on the question of membership affiliation, mainly because a large proportion of young volunteers answer "don't know".

A related question concerns whether it is important to volunteer for an *organization*, or if this is relatively unimportant ((c) in Table 10.1). The question has acquired relevance in recent years, because new actors, such as public institutions, private enterprises and hybrid institutions mixing elements from all three sectors, increasingly make use of voluntary labour (Wollebæk et al., 2000). When faced with competition, the question arises whether organizations represent distinctive qualities volunteers want to promote, or whether the voluntary work itself is the center of attention.

Reviewing the responses to this question, we can no longer speak of differences in degree. The majority of volunteers aged above 55 think it is important that the activity takes place within the context of voluntary organizations, while this opinion is shared by only 23% of those aged below 25. Again, the relationship between age and degree of commitment to voluntary organizations is fairly linear, with the exception of an insignificant difference between the two oldest age groups.

Table 10.1. Ties to Organizations for Which One Has Volunteered. Percentage Among Those
Who Volunteered in 1998, by Age Group

	16–24	25–39	40–54	55–69	70+	Total
a. How important do you think it is be a member of the organization(s) for which you volunteer?						
Very important	31	34	42	60	60	43
Relatively important	44	41	33	28	22	35
Not very important or not important at all	20	21	23	10	10	18
Don't know	5	4	2	2	8	4
N (=100%)	94	234	242	114	58	791
b. Is it important to you to volunteer for the particular organization(s) for which you have volunteered, or do could you just as well have done the same work for different organization(s) carrying out similar activities?						
Important to volunteer for particular organization	57	67	61	69	79	66
Could just as well have volunteered for others	26	24	32	26	16	26
Don't know	17	9	7	5	5	8
N (=100%)	93	233	242	113	58	786
c. Is it important to you to have volunteered for voluntary organizations/foundations, or doesn't it matter much?						
important	23	33	44	59	53	41
doesn't matter much	77	67	56	41	47	59
N (=100%)	96	241	227	116	58	793

Source: Survey on Giving and Volunteering (1998).

The results show that the oldest volunteers express a stronger attachment to organizations in which they are active than the youngest volunteers do, with those aged between 25 and 55 in a middle position. Those aged above 70 years are more or less unison in the view that membership and volunteering are two sides of the same coin, and that the organizational context in which the activity takes place is far from irrelevant. They assign particular values to participation in organizations, which the younger generations attach less importance to.

The *unpaid effort* is one of these core values. There is extensive agreement in the population, both among volunteers and others, that, by virtue of contributing time without remuneration, volunteers represent important values that cannot be offered by paid professionals ((a) in Table 10.2). The younger age groups are more indifferent, even though the relatively uncontroversial statement is not met with any real disagreement. Among the elderly, by contrast, there is no doubt that

Table 10.2. Attitudes toward Volunteering and Internal Democracy by Age Group (%)

	16–24	25–39	40–54	55–69	70+	Total
a. Question to all respondents (including non-members): Unpaid workers represent important values which could not be replaced by paid professionals						
Strongly agree	40	51	58	71	73	58
Mildly agree	34	29	29	21	18	27
Strongly or mildly disagree	6	9	9	3	4	7
Don't know	20	11	4	5	5	8
N (= 100%)	203	456	425	259	182	1 636
b. Question to those who have volunteered in the past 12 months: What is your personal attitude towards partial payment for voluntary work?						
Very or slightly positive	33	30	21	18	8	23
Very or slightly negative	30	42	47	50	58	50
Don't know	37	28	32	32	34	27
N (= 100%)	80	235	232	122	66	792
c. Question to members of voluntary organizations: It is important to me that the organization is democratically structured						
Strongly agree	40	65	77	77	84	70
Mildly agree	28	20	14	13	12	17
Strongly or mildly disagree	5	4	3	1	1	3
Don't know/neither nor	27	11	6	9	3	10
N (= 100%)	109	293	287	158	85	1 003

Source: Survey on Giving and Volunteering (1998).

unpaid, voluntary work represents something different. As many as 73% strongly agree with the statement.

Even clearer is their rejection of partial, symbolic payment for voluntary work (b): 58% among the elderly are negative, and only 8% positive, presumably because they think this conflicts with the organization's fundamental values. Among the youngest, a narrow majority of those with an opinion support the notion of partial payment. It may be added that 21% among the youngest volunteers claim that such remuneration influences their choice to participate, compared to 7% among adults and the elderly.

Younger members also express a more lukewarm interest in internal democratic structures ((c), Table 10.2) than members in older age groups. A minority strongly agrees with the proposition that such structures are important, while the percentage among those aged 40 or more is twice as high. In contrast to other results reported here, there is no linear relationship between age and attitude towards this question, but a qualitative break between those aged below and above 25. However, there is little disagreement to be found among the youngest participants—their attitudes are more indifferent than critical.

The analyses above confirm that different age groups view participation differently. Young people deviate from older in two ways. First, they seem to be attached to particular *organizations* with weaker ties. They place less importance on the membership, and express weaker loyalty to particular organizations than their older counterparts. Secondly, they appear to be less connected with *organizational society* as a whole, and the values commonly attached to traditional, voluntarily organized activities in Norway. At the opposite extreme, we find the prewar generation, whose support for the values young people meet with doubt or indifference is almost unison.

WHAT DISTINGUISHES NEW ORGANIZATIONS FROM TRADITIONAL ONES?

Is it possible to find similar differences between the new and old in the local organizational society? Figure 10.1, which shows newly found and extinct associations in one of Norway's 19 counties in the 1990s, may point in that direction.

The number of associations has been stable over the past couple of decades, following an extensive growth from the World War II until 1980. But substantial changes have taken place in the 1990s. Traditional value-based movements are in decline—the large humanitarian associations with broad purposes, the mission movement, the temperance movement and the language movement. They are replaced by culture, leisure, and sports associations, associations for preservation of cultural artefacts, neighbourhood interest groups, and interest organizations for the handicapped.[2]

The expanding association types at the local level represent various purposes, but share one important characteristic—their activity is geared more toward their own members than toward society at large. The purpose is either to allow their members to pursue a leisure interest or to influence political processes in the interests of the members. Conversely, the organization types that are struggling have directed their activity outwards, worked for the "common good" or been strongly ideological. The expanding, extrovert associations for culture preservation represent an exception to the trend, but they are still a minor category.

Furthermore, the *turnover* of associations is significantly higher than in the 1980s. Twice as many associations were wound up during the 1990s than during the 1980s. This development is most noticeable among choirs and other musical

---

[2] The same types of associations display growth and decline when membership trends in the "surviving" associations are taken into account.

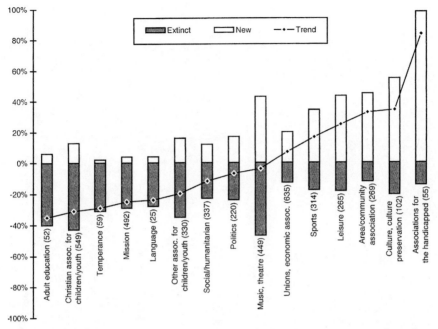

Figure 10.1. New and Extinct Associations in Hordaland in the 1990s. Percent of Number of Associations in 1990[a].

[a]Number of associations in 1990 in parentheses.

Note: Ten of the 33 municipalities excluded; five did not participate in the 2000 project and five could not account for the destiny of more than 80% of the associations registered in 1990. It is unknown if 4.5% of the associations registered in 1990 still exist in the remaining municipalities. These associations are excluded from the analysis.

activities, in which half of the population has been replaced. This mirrors that cultural expressions change form and content at a higher pace than before. However, the fact that several fields are experiencing increased turnover indicates that its causes are wide-ranging, structural changes within organizational society, which are addressed below.

When reviewing the development in the 1990s compared to the 1980s, many development trends have continued, while others are entirely new. The shift from political, humanitarian and religious activities towards culture, sports and recreation has been going on since the mid 1960s, when the post-war generation started to make its mark in associational life. This tendency is no weaker now. In particular, the decline of the three countercultures, temperance, mission and language purity, is very sharp. These movements played particularly important roles in the Norwegian nation-building and democratization processes, by mobilising the population in the periphery (Rokkan, 1967). There are approximately 30% fewer

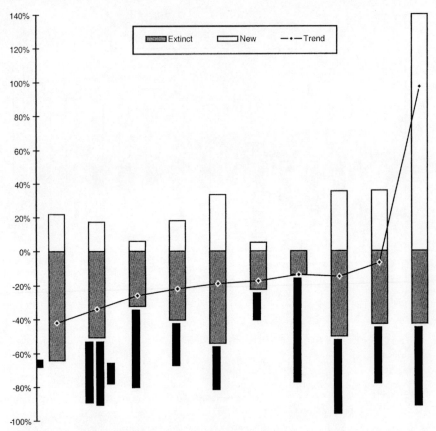

Figure 10.2. New and Extinct Associations for Children and Youth in Hordaland in the 1990s. Percent of Existing Associations in 1990[a].
[a]Existing associations in 1990 in parentheses.

mission and temperance associations today compared to ten years ago. Thus, previously dominant movements in the Norwegian organizational society are continuing to lose ground at a startling rate, and it is very unlikely that the generational differences at the individual level analysed above are unrelated to this development.

The *new*, negative development in the 1990s is that associations for children and youth are severely weakened after growing continuously from World War II until 1980. Figure 10.2 shows that most activity types are in decline—from play and arts groups organized by the homemakers' associations, to 4H, the worldly Youth League, the scouts' movement and youth clubs. Within musical and theatrical activities, there are fewer activities for children and youth today compared to ten years ago, while the supply of activities for adults has increased somewhat.

The political youth associations, which incarnate the type of ideological package deals youths seem to reject, are also struggling to attract members.[3]

There are few examples of growth among associations for children and youth beyond the small, but expanding group of informal, half-organized activities dominating "other categories" in the figure. New activities such as skateboarding, computer activities and roleplay have become organized to some extent, but in absolute figures the growth is modest compared to the decline in other associations for children and youth. Sports activities appear, on the other hand, to have a firm grip on the leisure time of children. The number of child members increased by ten per cent from 1991 to 1997 (Statistical Yearbook, 2000), but the proportion in the population aged between 16 and 24 with membership in a sports association shrank from 41 to 36% during the same period (Andresen, 1999).[4] These associations are not included in the figure, because they usually organize activities for both children, young people and adults, and therefore are not counted as children and youth's associations in this context.

The 16- to 24-year-olds described above have grown up in a situation where traditional activities, especially for children and youths, are in decline. Innovation takes place first and foremost within activities for grown-ups. It is in the early phase of a deterioration of the traditional, adult-run activities for children and youth—again with sports as an important exception—that the attitudes of today's young adults have been formed.

But it does not stop there. There are also other, important structural differences between new and old associations. The newly founded hold fewer meetings than old associations, quite often none at all.[5] Many of them are characterized by an informal organizational structure, with less of the "tedious paperwork".[6] The most important, however, is that *fewer of them are affiliated with regional or national mother organizations*. Among organizations founded before 1960, 86% are parts of such networks, as are 70% of the associations founded between 1960 and 1980. By contrast, this applies to only half of the associations formed after 1990. Organizations with the traditional, hierarchical structure are with few exceptions losing ground.

The organizational model in which the local level was connected to regional and national mother organizations held a near hegemonic position in Norway for

---

[3] The number of members aged below 25 in political youth associations fell from 41,318 in 1990 to 16,455 in 1999 (*Source*: Governmental Office for Youth and Adoption (SUAK)).

[4] Membership among children aged below 17 grew from 506,662 in 1991 to 555,664 in 1997.

[5] 24% of associations founded in the 1990s hold membership meetings once a month or more often. 26% holds no meetings at all. Among the associations founded before 1990, 31% hold meetings once a month or more frequently, while 18% holds no meetings.

[6] For example, 52% of associations founded in the 1990s have written statutes, 55% record minutes, and 65% hold annual conventions. Among associations founded before 1990, the corresponding percentages are 66, 71, and 75% respectively.

a long time. It was almost unthinkable to organize in other ways. As long as organizations were politically oriented, a structure providing membership activity locally, political strength nationally and internal channels enabling local branches to raise issues at the national arena was rational and instrumental. The dominant movements in Norway from the 1870s on, the mission, temperance, language, farmers', labor and sports movements, were founded at the same time as Norway was democratized, making them political in nature from the outset. It is no coincidence that almost all organizations founded before 1960 chose the same model as the political parties. The cultural heritage from the early mass movements decisively shaped the organizational options available for new organizations for a century. As a consequence, the Norwegian organizational society has traditionally been *integrated*, in the sense that the same organizations can be found at the local and national level, and not *two-part*, where local and national associations lead separate lives, as in many European countries and the United States.

Today, the linkages between the local and the national level is weakened on two fronts. Firstly, many new associations locally, often lacking a clear political or ideological agenda, see little point in joining national networks. This tendency is apparent in most fields, but the rapidly expanding area associations provide a prime example. Here, a national organization has existed for more than 25 years, which most local associations nonetheless refrain from joining. In the absence of common interests with other area associations in other locations and a national, political purpose, the organizational network becomes superfluous. Second, many new national organizations place less emphasis on having affiliated local branches. Internal democracy is for many a hindrance more than a resource and local branches friction in a streamlined organizational model.[7]

Purely local associations are less stable than associations that are parts of national networks. Among the associations registered in 1980, 43% of the former type survived until today, compared to 63% of the latter type. The difference is probably due to the buffer function of organizational networks during crises. They intervene in difficult periods, and contribute to institutionalizing associations to a greater extent. Associations with weaker networks become more vulnerable and dependent on the motivation of key members. Despite the more frequent dissolution of purely local associations, their numbers increase substantially, because the founding rate is much higher than within traditional organizations.[8]

While more vulnerable, associations with weak organizational networks are also more focused on specific activities and flexible. They may therefore be better

---

[7] Furthermore, the contact between the levels is weakened even within organizations with a hierarchical structure. The local branches tend to turn their attention toward conditions in the local community, while the national level orient themselves toward issues on the national agenda.

[8] Associations not affiliated with national organizations constituted 30% of local associations in 2000, compared to 20% in 1980.

equipped to meet the changes in individual motivation that seem to be underway. Many of them demand less from their members. They specialize in one activity or one purpose, so that the volunteer may use his/her energy for exactly that in which s/he is interested. The members are met with weak demands of loyalty to a particular organization and presented with little activity not directly related to the purpose of the association. Organizational activity becomes an individual relation between participant/volunteer and purpose, while the organization's role is to provide the required infrastructure.

TOWARD A NEW ORGANIZATIONAL SOCIETY?

Above, we have seen that voluntarily organized activity means different things to different age groups. Furthermore, the attitudes expressed by young people today correspond with the development among local associations.

The new *volunteer* wants to spend his time more purposefully, and to choose more freely between different activities. The main point is not what the organization looks like, but that it offers interesting and meaningful activities. If others can take care of the paperwork, it does not matter much if volunteers or professionals do the job. New *organizations* want to be independent of national structures in order to link the concrete activities as closely as possible to the purpose of the association. They are more specialized than before, and less often linked to larger, ideological projects. The new model of participation is therefore characterized by a strong activity orientation, short-term commitment, extensive turnover and a weak or contained value basis.

The data at hand does not allow us to decide whether the differences we have observed represent generational or life cycle phenomena. However, the analyses of the local associations indicate that it is more of the former than of the latter. *In a situation in which traditional, value based organizations deteriorate, it is improbable that today's youth will develop the attitudes today's elderly attach importance to, even if they should become just as active.* The organizations and structures that formed the attitudes of previous generations are weakened. Consequently, the organizational experiences today's young volunteers will make in adulthood will differ substantially from those of their parents and grandparents.

If the attitudes among young people actually represent a generational phenomenon, they point in the direction of a new organizational society with different social and political roles from today. Organizations will to a lesser extent be institutions nourishing durable, maybe even life-long commitments, as they detach themselves from larger movements, live shorter lives and have weaker ties to their participants. The activity here and now may still be considered important for volunteers and participants, but the new generation of organizations will have difficulties constructing the loyalty which comes from affinity to a greater cause.

However, while long-term commitment to organizations may belong to the past, *volunteering* (*frivillighet*) may not. One sign of this is the success of the half-public, half-nonprofit Volunteer Centers, where individuals contribute time and energy carrying out social work, while others take care of the paper work. Another is that people unprompted and in great numbers contact the Salvation Army and the Blue Cross on Christmas Eve to make an effort for people in need. The third, and most obvious, is that people still gladly volunteer in order to organize their own cultural and recreational interests.

The new volunteer, epitomized by today's young adult, is an individualist, but not necessarily an egoist. To drift from interest to interest, and actively choose what one wants to be a part of, is not only compatible with, but also the essence of the mantra of our times—to lead "reflexive" and modern lives.

If organizational society changes, does it really matter? In a neo-Tocquevillian perspective, wherein socialization through face to face interaction within horizontal, social networks represents the main contribution of voluntary organizations to social capital, and consequently to social integration and democracy (Putnam, 1993), a development in the direction sketched above is not necessarily negative. It does not inevitably entail less volunteering or less face to face contact, and the replacement of hierarchical, conflict-oriented movements by purely local, non-political associations is, if anything, regarded as positive for the production of social capital (e.g., Putnam, 1993: 90, 1995a: 71).

However, the changes in purpose, structure and value basis which appear to be underway will, in our view, weaken the democratic role of voluntary organizations in a way that micro-oriented approaches fail to capture. In our view, the democratic role of organizations cannot be reduced to what happens *internally*, i.e. socialization and the creation of social networks.[9] Equal attention needs to be paid to their *external* role in the democratic process. In this perspective, it is quite obvious that an organizational society modernized in the direction sketched out above will have great problems acting as *intermediary institutions* between individual and society and citizen and political system. A predominantly non-political and purely local organizational society with a diffuse value basis cannot successfully act as counterweights to the state and alternative channels of influence (see also Foley & Edwards, 1996; Rueschemeyer, 1998; Skocpol et al., 2000). Effective decision-making procedures may function locally without bonds to national organizations, maybe even without having members or meetings at all. But it is undeniably difficult to effectively mediate the views and interests of those affiliated when it comes to issues on a larger political scale through such a structure.

The findings above give little reason to expect that generational exchange will strengthen the hierarchical model and the membership institution. It is more

---

[9] Elsewhere, we discuss whether the internal effects of participation in nonpolitical associations may not be overstated in Putnam's work (Wollebæk & Selle 2002b).

likely that the individual and organizational levels become mutually reinforcing; that the exit of the pre-war generation from the pool of volunteers and the gradually growing importance of the younger generations will speed up the organizational changes that are already underway.

If the modernization of organizational society proceeds along the lines sketched above, its democratic importance will decline even though its volume may remain stable. Whether this is detrimental to democracy and social cohesion or not, depends on the ideals of the observer and the degree to which new forms of participation replace that which is lost. Whichever way one looks at it, however, it is an important infrastructure that is slowly eroding.

REFERENCES

Almås, R., Karlsen, K.H., & Thorland, I. (1995). *Fra pliktsamfunn til mulighetstorg.* Trondheim: Centre for Rural Research.

Andresen, Ø. (1999). *Organisasjonsdeltakelse i Norge fra 1983 til 1997.* Oslo-Kongsvinger, Central Bureau of Statistics.

Beck, U. (1997). *Risiko og frihet.* Bergen: Fagbokforlaget.

Foley, M., & Edwards, B. (1996). The paradox of civil society. *Journal of Democracy,* 7, 38–52.

Hellevik, O. (1993). Postmaterialism as a dimension of cultural change. *International Journal of Public Opinion Research,* 5, 211–233.

Hellevik, O. (1996). *Nordmenn og det gode liv. Norsk monitor 1985–1995.* Oslo: Universitetsforlaget.

Inglehart, R. (1977). *The silent revolution: Changing values and political styles among western publics.* Princeton, NJ: Princeton University Press.

Inglehart, R. (1990). *Culture shift in advanced industrial society.* Princeton, NJ: Princeton University Press.

Mannheim, K. (1980 [1928]). The problem of generation. [Das Problem der Generationen]. In P. Kecskemeti (Ed.), *Essays on the sociology of knowledge* (pp. 276–320). London: Routledge & Kegan Paul.

Putnam, R. (1993). *Making democracy work.* Princeton, NJ: Princeton University Press.

Putnam, R. (1995a). Bowling alone: America's declining social capital. *Journal of Democracy,* 1(January): 65–78.

Putnam, R. (1995b). Tuning in, tuning out: The strange disappearance of social capital in America. *Political Science & Politics, 28,* 664–83.

Putnam, R. (2000). *Bowling Alone.* New York: Simon & Schuster.

Rokkan, S. (1967). Geography, religion and social class: Crosscutting cleavages in Norwegian politics. In S.M. Lipset & S. Rokkan (Eds.), *Party systems and voter alignments.* New York: Free Press.

Rueschemeyer, D. (1998). The self-organisation of society and democratic rule: Specifying the relationship. In D. Rueschemeyer, M. Rueschemeyer & B. Wittrock (Eds.), *Participation and democracy: East and west. Comparisons and interpretations.* Armonk, NY/London, UK: M. E. Sharpe.

Selle, P., & Øymyr, B. (1995). *Frivillig organisering og demokrati. Det frivillige organisasjonssamfunnet 1940–1990.* Oslo: Det Norske Samlaget.

Skocpol, T. (1996). Unravelling from above. *The American Prospect* (no. 25, March-April).

Skocpol, T., Ganz, M., & Munson, Z. (2000). A nation of organizers: The institutional origins of civic voluntarism in the United States. *American Political Science Review, 94,* 527–546.

Statistical Yearbook (2000). Oslo/Kongsvinger: Central Bureau of Statistics.

Stinchcombe, A.L. (1965). Social Structure and Organization. In J.G. March (Ed.), *Handbook of organizations* (pp. 142–193). Chicago: Rand McNally.

Wollebæk, D., & Selle, P. (2002a). *Det nye organisasjonssamfunnet: Demokrati i omforming.* Bergen: Fagbokforlaget.

Wollebæk, D., & Selle, P. (2002b). Does participation in voluntary associations contribute to social capital? The importance of intensity, scope, and type. *Nonprofit and Voluntary Sector Quarterly, 31,* 2, 32–61.

Wollebæk, D., Selle, P., & Lorentzen, H. (1998). *Undersøkelse om frivillig innsats. Dokumentasjonsrapport.* Notat 9834. Bergen: LOS-senteret.

Wollebæk, D., Selle, P., & Lorentzen, H. (2000). *Frivillig innsats.* Bergen: Fagbokforlaget.

Øia, T. (1995). *Apolitisk ungdom? Sjølbergingsgenerasjonen og politiske verdier.* Oslo: Cappelens Akademiske Forlag.

Chapter 11

Volunteering, Democracy, and Democratic Attitudes

Loek Halman

INTRODUCTION

In this chapter, we investigate the relationships between active participation in voluntary organizations and democratic attitudes in contemporary Europe. Much has been said about the motives which lead people to take part in voluntary activities, but less attention is given to the consequences of engagement in voluntary organizations for democracy. Most often, these consequences are taken for granted or regarded as obvious and self-evident. "Democratic viability or longevity requires that there is a system of organizations that are independent of governments" (Lane & Ersson, 1996: 187).

According to Alexis de Tocqueville, democracy in America could emerge and grew because of the great number of Americans participating in numerous voluntary organizations. No wonder that there is a growing concern for the survival of democratic politics in contemporary Western societies. Putnam has argued that democracy is endangered in the United States because Americans are increasingly disconnected from social structures such as church, political parties, and bowling leagues. As a result, there is a growing deficit of social-capital with severe consequences for society, because it "threatens educational performance, safe neighborhoods, equitable tax collection, democratic responsiveness, everyday honesty, and even our health and happiness" (Putnam, 2000: 367). The decline in civic participation is often regarded as a consequence of ongoing individualization. The growing emphasis on the individual has eroded interest and participation in public life and led to a increasing search for identity and authenticity. To quote Sennett (1977), we are witnessing the Fall of Public Man.

179

Voluntary organizations are regarded as the bridges between citizens and the state. As Almond and Verba noted, "voluntary associations are the prime means by which the function of mediating between the individual and the state is performed. Through them the individual is able to relate himself effectively and meaningfully to the political system" (Almond & Verba, 1965: 245). Voluntary associations are seen as places where citizens learn social and civic skills and habits (Putnam, 2000: 338; 1993: 87ff). These skills and habits include collaboration, negotiation, feelings of responsibility and solidarity, shared goals, and public spiritedness. Involvement in voluntary activities is thus of utmost importance for society to become and remain democratic, but does this imply that people who are engaged in voluntary activities are more democratic than people who are not? This is one of the research questions investigated in this chapter.

Another research question deals with differences and similarities in the degree to which the various European populations are involved in voluntary work. The degree to which citizens participate in voluntary activities depends, of course, upon the opportunities available and the number of voluntary organizations present in a society. European societies differ in these respects, e.g., the voluntary sector was almost absent in Central and Eastern European countries and the development since the velvet revolutions took place are, according to some observers, still in "an embryonic state" (Crawford, 1996: 111). One of the requirements for voluntary organizations to emerge and develop is economic development. For example, efficient organization of the economy increases the opportunities for civic engagement, because working hours are reduced, while economic wealth increases people's opportunities to actually spend more time in all kinds of organizations. Religiosity may also be important in this respect, for religion is often regarded as being strongly associated with charity and solidarity. Finally, country differences in volunteering may be attributed to democratic experiences in the recent past because it is assumed that only in democracies can an infrastructure develop which is conducive to voluntary organizations.

A third issue we deal with in this chapter concerns recent trends in volunteering in Europe. On the one hand, it can be assumed that, as a consequence of ongoing individualization and increasing emphasis on personal autonomy, self-realization, and "calculative" behavior, people will be less inclined to do voluntary work (see also Dekker & van den Broek, 1998: 15). In America, however, Putnam observed the opposite; Americans seem to take part more frequently in voluntary actions. However, the increase was found particularly among older Americans while middle-aged Americans volunteered less (Putnam, 2000: 127–133). Also, the increase did not occur in all kinds of organizations, e.g., involvement in church-related activities declined in the United States. Thus, the trends appear to be dependent on age and kind of organization. Whether or not this is true will be further explored using the data from the European Values Study (EVS).

Thus, this chapter deals with three issues. The first issue focuses on the relationship between volunteering and democracy at individual level. The question addressed is are volunteers more democratic than nonvolunteering people? The second issue is what makes countries differ in the degree of volunteering? The third issue deals with trends in volunteering in Europe.

In the second section, the relationship between volunteering and democracy is elaborated and some theoretical considerations on the explanations of country differences in degree of civic participation and trends are presented. In the third section, we describe our data source and indicators, and in the fourth section we provide a brief summary of the main results of our analyses. The conclusions are formulated in the last section.

SOME THEORETICAL CONSIDERATIONS

There is widespread consensus that democracy is the best political system, and there seems to be also consensus that a strong civil society can contribute to a significant degree to the maintenance of democracy. Almond and Verba concluded that the civic culture is "particularly appropriate for a democratic political system" (Almond & Verba, 1965: 366). Democratic development and the maintenance of democracy requires that citizens participate actively in society, not only as voters but also in all kinds of civil and political bodies and organizations. Alexis de Tocqueville hinted already at the importance of civil organizations for the stability and effectiveness of democracy. In fact, in a democracy where people are free and their lives are no longer dictated from above, they have to organize simply to have their voices heard. Cooperation, thus, is almost a necessity to achieve personal ends and satisfy individual needs. The success of the democratic developments in Central and Eastern Europe is to a large extent dependent upon civil society in these countries. These groups, associations, and organizations which mediate between the individual and the state enable people "to defend their interests, which might otherwise be disregarded by a powerful state" (Fukuyama, 2000: 100).

Putnam demonstrated convincingly that, in Italy, the performance of regional governments could be attributed to cultural traditions, but also that differences in cultural traditions were historically rooted in different patterns of civic participation in associations. In the northern parts of Italy where "associationism flourishes, where citizens attend to community affairs and vote for issues, not patrons, there too we find leaders who believe in democracy, not social and political hierarchy" (Putnam, 1993: 102). Voluntary organizations contribute to democracy because in and through voluntary organizations people are able to express their interests and demands on government. Voluntary organizations not only teach citizens social and civic skills, but they also teach "the civic virtues of trust, moderation, compromise, reciprocity, and the skills of democratic discussion and organiza-tion" (Newton, 1999: 15). Volunteering is assumed to "lower the amount of drug use, criminal activity, teenage pregnancy and delinquency, to increase the success of schools and their pupils, to enhance economic development, and to make gov-ernment more effective" (Stolle & Rochon, 1999: 192).

Similar observations were made by Almond and Verba (1965). They found that members of voluntary organizations and associations felt more confident that they could influence government, and were also more politically active, more in-formed about politics, more open minded in their political opinions, and generally more in favour of democratic values. Thus, "the organizational member is . . . more likely to be close to the model of the democratic citizen" (Almond & Verba, 1965: 265). Our assumption, therefore, is that people who actually do voluntary work are more favorable toward democracy. Thus, the hypothesis (H1) states that volunteers will be more democratic than nonvolunteers.

At the aggregate level, one can then assume that the more volunteers a society has, the more democratic values are adhered to in that society (H2).

As noted before, Putnam observed important differences between Italian re-gions with regard to the degree of social capital in general and civic organizational structure in particular. Apparently, the context makes the difference. Social in-teraction depends to a large extent upon cultural and institutional settings, and societies and regions differ in respect of these settings. As Stolle and Rochon ar-gue, interactions "between people are characterized by the culturally embedded patterns of inclusion and exclusion of social groups. Those patterns are created by the tracings of social cleavages that themselves result from historical conflicts and tensions. The severity of these cleavages, and the extent to which they affect patterns of associational life, vary over time and space. Moreover, the density and style of associational life vary between countries, and even between regions within a country" (Stolle & Rochon, 1999: 193)

We search for explanations of country differences in religion, economic de-velopment, and democratic history. Religious involvement is regarded by some as conducive to social capital since it is often argued that religion connects people. Religious involvement can be seen as an important attribute, if not a prerequi-site, of voluntary activism because religious beliefs are assumed to produce an ethos that is trusting, altruistic, and cooperative (Whiteley, 1999: 37). "Faith cre-ates communal bonds that foster social connectedness, participation, and moral behaviour" (Uslaner, 1999: 216). Religion is considered a main reason to refrain from pure self-interest and religion is also regarded as creating a kind of moral duty to help others. Coleman (1990: 320) argued that religious ideologies may create dispositions that are favorable to attending to the interests of others. For example, Rokeach (1973: 128) demonstrated that people who attend religious services are often inclined to helpful behavior. More recently, Wuthnow (1991) has shown that religiosity promotes volunteering, while others have demonstrated the importance of religious involvement with regard to charitable contributions (see Uslaner, 1999: 216).

Thus, several researchers have suggested that religion encourages helping behavior, and thus the more religious a society is, the more its citizens will be inclined to help others and the more they will be inclined to become engaged in voluntary activities. Thus, the hypothesis (H3) is that the more religious the culture of a country is, the more volunteers the country will have.

Liberal democracy, says Giner "has been closely tied to civil society throughout modern history" (Giner, 1995: 302). Secondary associations and voluntary organizations are mediators between the individual and the state through which the individual can "relate himself effectively and meaningfully to the political system" (Almond & Verba, 1965: 245) and thus these associations and organizations are "a necessary part of the democratic infrastructure" (Almond & Verba, 1965: 244). The democratic infrastructure facilitates the formation of all kinds of organizations, not only political ones, and enables people to take part in social life and to express their preferences and satisfy their needs. Only in a democracy are there sufficient associations, organizations, and movements which provide people with the opportunity to meet, exchange ideas, and find support, collaboration, solidarity, and responsibility for shared goals. In Western Europe, a gradual shift has occurred from membership of older style or traditional social movements, such as churches, ethnic groups, unions, political parties, etc., towards membership of issue movements to protect or fight for certain causes, such as sexual liberties, feminism, environment, or even stopping the expansion of an airport or the building of a railroad or road (Barnes, 1998: 122). The establishment and development of such organizations and movements is strongly linked with the age of democracy. The older the democracy is, the more and better movements, associations, and organizations will have emerged and developed and thus the more people will become members of and or do voluntary work for such organizations, movements, and associations. The hypothesis (H4) is, therefore, that the older the democracy, the more people volunteer.

According to Giner (1995: 313), the "intimate affinity between permanent material progress and the traditional conception of civil society hardly needs to be spelled out." Volunteering and economic development, thus, are expected to be closely connected. Fukuyama (1995; 2000) has argued that civil society makes societies run more efficiently and as a consequence such societies are more prosperous and more wealthy. Putnam argues similarly, "a growing body of research suggests that where trust and social networks flourish, individuals, firms, neighborhoods, and even nations prosper" (Putnam, 2000: 319). People in networks can mobilize their network(s) to benefit from and achieve better lives. However, the relationship may also be reversed. Economic development may be an important prerequisite of the establishment and maintenance of voluntary organizations. In more prosperous societies, people have more opportunities to become involved in voluntary activities, simply because they have more leisure time. Further, more prosperous societies have more groups that can protect people's interests. In modern and/or postmodern societies, old cleavages have disappeared, but increasingly new arenas of conflict have emerged (Gundelach, 1995: 421). The new political arena is characterized by a great number of new issues, quite often related to concrete causes (Barnes, 1998: 122). Economic development increases this interest in new issues. Inglehart (1997) supports this idea: due to economic development and the development of the modern welfare state, there is an increasing interest in new issues which have to do with quality of life. People are less concerned with material wealth, and more and more concerned with the environment, emancipation, and personal interests. New groups and organizations will develop to protect these new interests. Thus, our hypothesis (H5) is that volunteering will be more widespread in rich and wealthy countries than in poor and less wealthy societies.

Putnam (2000) claimed that social capital is on the decline in the United States. According to him, Americans have become increasingly disconnected from family, friends, neighbors, and social structures, such as the church, recreation clubs, political parties, and even bowling leagues. This decline is thought to be a consequence of ongoing individualization which is assumed to have led to an unrestrained striving to realize personal desires and aspirations resulting in the giving of priority to individual freedom and autonomy and an emphasis on personal need fulfillment. Contemporary individualized people are interested mainly in their own lucrative careers and they are devoting their lives to conspicuous consumption, immediate gratification, personal happiness, success, and achievement. Meanwhile, they are neglecting the public interests and eroding civic commitment to the common good. Evidence of this is found in increasing crime rates, marital breakdown, drug abuse, suicide, tax evasion, and other deviant behaviors and practices.

A number of factors responsible for the erosion of social capital in general were suggested by Putnam (2000), and these factors may also explain the assumed decline in voluntary activities:

1. The increased pressure of time and money; people are simply so occupied with their work that they are unable to get civilly engaged, e.g., in voluntary activities.
2. There is an increased mobility. Americans move so often that it is difficult for them to get acquainted with their neighbors and to engage in voluntary activities.
3. The traditional family, the carrier of social capital, is on the decline, which appears from the increase in marital breakups and the decline in the number of children.
4. The impact of technology and mass media. People's scarce free time is increasingly devoted to watching TV, reducing the need for direct personal

contact. The TV programs people watch are increasingly associated with civic disengagement: entertainment as distinct from news (Putnam, 2000: 246).

Thus, increased mobility, time pressure, and the impact of technology decreases the likelihood of people being active in voluntary activities. Similar developments are taking place in Europe and it seems likely that Europe will experience a decline in volunteering as well. This is the sixth hypothesis we will explore in this chapter: (H6) volunteering has declined in Europe.

In analyzing data on volunteering in the United States, Putnam (2000: 128) did not find a decline as expected, but an increase in the 1975–1999 period. Confused by this unexpected observation, Putnam dug deeper and it appeared that particularly volunteering in charity and social service activities had risen, while involvement in churches and clubs had declined. An explanation for this unexpected and confusing result could be found in the age of the volunteers. Volunteering among older generations appeared to have grown tremendously. "Volunteering among seniors has nearly doubled over the last quarter century" (Putnam, 2000: 129). This shift can be understood if one realizes that the oldest people "constitute a 'long civic generation'—that is, a cohort of men and women who have been more engaged in civic affairs throughout their lives" (Putnam, 2000: 132). These generations were raised and socialized in times when civic values were highly valued, making these people more eager to get involved in voluntary activities. We assume this will also be the case for Europeans, and, therefore, the hypothesis (H7) is that volunteering among older generations has increased and volunteering among middle-age groups has declined.

DATA AND MEASUREMENTS

The empirical analyses are based on the survey data from the European Values Study (EVS). This project was launched at the end of the seventies in the member states of the European Union. In 1990, a second wave of surveys took place not only in Western Europe, but also in many Eastern European countries. The most recent wave of surveys was conducted in 1999/2000 in almost all European countries (Halman, 2001; see also *http://europeanvalues.nl*). The comparisons in time are based on data collection in the countries (12) which were included in all three waves, while the contemporary patterns of volunteering and democracy are based on data collected in 33 countries.

Volunteering is indicated by the number of organizations of which one is an active member. The respondents were asked whether they were active members, inactive members, or not members at all of a large number of organizations. Although a distinction can be made between different kinds of organizations (see, e.g., Selle, 1999: 146; see also Inglehart in this book), according to Putnam (1993: 173), it does not matter so much what kind of organization one is an active member of. Following his suggestion, we also simply added the number of organizations respondents did voluntary work for. This additive index indicates the general degree of voluntary activity in a country.

Democratic attitudes can be obtained from a series of opinions on democracy as a system of government. Two questions were asked. One asked respondents to evaluate democracy as a very good, fairly good, fairly bad, or very bad way to govern the country. The items were having a strong leader who does not have to bother with parliament and elections; having experts, not government, make decisions as to what they think is best for the country; having the army rule the country; and having a democratic political system.

The other question asked for the respondents' degree of agreement or disagreement with items like democracy may have problems but it is better than any other form of government; in democracy, the economic system runs badly; democracies are indecisive and have too much squabbling; democracies aren't good at maintaining order. The latter 4 items together with the item "having a democratic political system" of the previous question were included in a scale ranging from not in favor of democracy to very much in favor of democracy. The scores were calculated by means of factor analysis.

One of the hypotheses at aggregate level was that the degree of volunteering in a society varied according to the degree of religiosity or secularization. In order to investigate this macro-level issue, we developed a measure of the degree of religiosity or secularization of a country. For this purpose, we rank ordered the countries according to level of personal and public religiosity. *Personal religiosity* was measured using the answers to five items on various kinds of individual religious beliefs (respondent considers himself a religious person, he/she believes in a personal God, regards God as important, gets strength and comfort from religion, takes moments of prayer). By applying factor analysis, scores were calculated for this dimension.

Public religiosity was measured first by using a question on how often people attend religious services (answer categories ranged from 1 = more than once a month to 8 = never). It was also indicated by the degree to which respondents had confidence in the church. This item was included in a battery on trust in institutions. Finally, we included four items on the degree to which respondents felt that the churches give adequate answers to moral problems, family problems, spiritual needs, and social problems. By applying factor analysis, we calculated scores for public religiosity.

Both measures of religiosity were correlated ($r = .71$; $p < .001$), which is not very surprising. People who participate in religious services are often more religious than people who do not attend religious services.

At aggregate level, we also investigated the relationships between volunteering and democracy using additional features of the country. For democracy, we distinguished between *years of democracy* and *level of democracy*. A measure of the latter is available from Freedom House (*www.freedomhouse.org/ratings/index.htm*). It is indicated by scores on political rights and civil liberties, with one representing the highest degree of freedom and seven the lowest. Age of democracy is the number of years of continuous democracy since 1920 (see also Inglehart, 1997). *Economic development* was measured using GDP per capita purchasing power parity and taken from The World Factbook (2000).

ANALYSES

Table 11.1 gives an indication of the variety in European patterns of volunteering. Volunteering for sports or recreation organizations appears to be most popular, although it is still limited to less than 7% of Europeans. In the Czech Republic, Denmark, Finland, Ireland, Iceland, the Netherlands, Sweden, and Slovakia, more than 15% of the respondents indicated that they do voluntary work for sports or recreational organizations. In the Netherlands, education, arts, music, or cultural activities appear to be more popular than in other countries. 17% of the Dutch respondents do voluntary work in this sector, while the European figure is about 5%. In Sweden, 24% of the respondents said they did voluntary work for religious or church organizations while overall in Europe this is 6%. In the United Kingdom, voluntary work for social welfare services for elderly, handicapped, or deprived people, and involvement in youth work appears to be more widespread than in other European countries. 14% of Britons are active in social welfare services, compared with 4% of Europeans, and 15% of Britons do voluntary work in youth work organizations, compared with 3% of Europeans.

Given the small numbers of people doing voluntary work, it is useless to make further distinctions as, e.g., Selle (1999: 146) has suggested. Distinguishing between various kinds of organizations would result in such a small number of people being included in our analyses that it would be impossible to analyze these subgroups appropriately. This is an extra argument in favor of the advice of Putnam, who claimed that it does not matter what kind of organization one is an active member of (Putnam, 1993: 173). In Figure 11.1, we display the variety in Europe based on a simple count of the numbers of organizations respondents actually do voluntary work for.

Voluntary work is widespread not only in Sweden but also in Slovakia. In these countries, more than half of the respondents indicated that they did voluntary work for at least one of the organizations mentioned. In the Netherlands and in Great Britain, relatively large shares of the populations are also actively involved in voluntary organizations. At the other end of the scale we find Russia, where less than 10% of the respondents are active in the voluntary sector, followed by Hungary, Lithuania, Poland, Romania, and Ukraine, where large majorities are

Table 11.1. Percentages (Rounded) of Respondents in European Countries Doing Voluntary Work For

Country	Country code	Organizations[a]														
		a	b	c	d	e	f	g	h	i	j	k	l	m	n	o
Austria	At	2	7	7	2	3	1	1	2	2	2	9	2	0	3	4
Belgium	Be	6	6	9	2	3	3	5	3	3	4	8	3	1	4	7
Bulgaria	Bg	2	2	2	3	3	1	0	1	2	1	4	1	0	1	2
Belarus	By	3	4	2	5	1	1	1	2	1	1	1	1	1	2	1
Czech Republic	Cz	3	3	6	3	2	2	0	3	2	6	11	1	0	3	4
Germany	De	2	6	3	0	1	0	0	1	1	2	7	2	0	1	2
Denmark	Dk	4	3	5	4	3	3	1	2	4	5	14	1	0	1	7
Estonia	Ee	3	3	6	1	1	2	0	1	2	2	3	1	0	1	3
Spain	Es	3	4	3	1	1	2	1	1	1	2	4	1	1	1	2
Finland	Fi	7	8	5	4	3	2	3	2	2	5	12	2	1	4	6
France	Fr	4	3	5	1	1	2	1	1	1	2	9	0	0	2	6
Great Britain	Gb	14	6	3	2	1	2	4	8	8	15	4	1	4	10	[b]
Greece	Gr	8	9	9	4	3	7	3	5	4	3	5	2	5	5	3
Croatia	Hr	1	6	4	4	2	1	0	2	2	2	7	1	1	2	3
Hungary	Hu	3	5	3	1	1	1	0	2	2	1	3	0	0	1	2
Ireland	Ie	4	8	4	2	2	4	2	1	3	5	13	3	1	3	4
Iceland	Is	9	5	6	3	3	1	1	1	3	3	11	2	0	2	2
Italy	It	5	7	6	2	2	2	2	2	3	3	6	0	1	3	2
Lithuania	Lt	1	4	2	1	1	1	0	0	0	1	2	0	0	1	2
Luxembourg	Lu	7	6	8	3	3	3	5	4	1	6	9	2	1	3	2
Latvia	Lv	2	4	4	2	1	2	0	1	1	1	6	0	0	1	5
Northern Ireland	Ni	3	10	2	1	1	1	1	1	1	3	4	1	1	3	4
Netherlands	Nl	9	12	17	2	3	4	4	2	3	5	16	2	1	7	7
Poland	Pl	2	4	2	2	1	1	0	1	1	1	2	1	0	1	2
Portugal	Pt	1	3	2	0	1	1	1	0	1	1	4	0	0	1	3
Romania	Ro	1	4	2	6	2	1	0	1	1	1	1	0	0	1	2
Russia	Ru	1	1	0	4	0	1	0	0	0	0	1	0	0	0	1
Sweden	Se	9	24	11	10	4	6	4	4	4	5	18	2	0	3	10
Slovenia	Si	5	5	7	3	1	6	0	3	3	4	8	1	1	2	6
Slovakia	Sk	6	13	6	6	5	7	0	2	3	6	13	5	0	4	6
Ukraine	Ua	1	2	2	4	1	1	0	0	1	1	1	0	0	1	1
Europe (weighted according to population size)	Eur	4	6	5	3	2	2	1	2	2	3	3	1	1	2	4

[a]Organizations: a = social welfare services for elderly, handicapped or deprived people; b = religious or church organizations; c = education, arts, music or cultural activities; d = trade unions; e = political parties or groups; f = local community action on issues like poverty, employment, housing, racial equality; g = third world development or human rights; h = conservation, the environment, ecology, animal rights; i = professional associations; j = youth work (e.g., scouts, guides, youth clubs etc.); k = sports or recreation; l = women's groups; m = peace movement; n = voluntary organizations concerned with health; o = other groups;
[b]Item not asked.
Source: EVS 1999–2000 (see also Halman, 2001: 18–32).

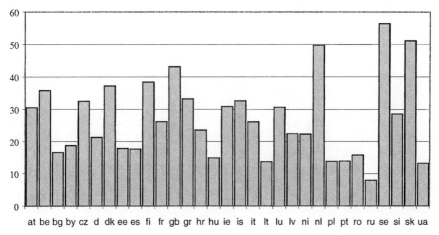

Figure 11.1. Percentages of volunteers in Europe in 1999/2000.
Source: EVS 1999–2000.

not active in voluntary organizations. In other Eastern European countries, the percentages of volunteers are also rather modest. The low levels of volunteering in Eastern Europe can perhaps be attributed to several cultural traits which are strongly determined by the recent histories of these countries (see also the chapters by Mălina Voicu & Bogdan Voicu and Stanislovas Juknevičius & Aida Savicka in this book). However, the cases of Portugal and Slovakia demonstrate that this is not a uniquely Central-Eastern European pattern. As we saw, many Slovaks do voluntary work, while very few Portuguese people are active in voluntary organizations. The Portuguese resemble the Hungarians, Lithuanians, Poles, Romanians, and Ukrainians. A clear east-west divide does not appear from such figures, nor does a clear north-south divide appear.

Our hypothesis on the relationship between volunteering and democracy at individual level was that volunteers will be more in favor of democracy than non-volunteers. In Figure 11.2, we have plotted the differences between the means scores on the democratic attitude for volunteers and non-volunteers. The scores of nonvolunteers in a country are subtracted from the scores of the volunteers in the country. A negative score indicates that nonvolunteers score higher on democratic values, while a positive score means that volunteers score higher than nonvolunteers.

In a majority of the countries, volunteers appear to be slightly more in favor of democracy than nonvolunteers. These differences between volunteers and non-volunteers remain if controlled for age, gender, and education. However, regressing the democratic attitude on volunteering, age, gender, and education reveals that the impact of volunteering on democratic attitude is rather modest. In most

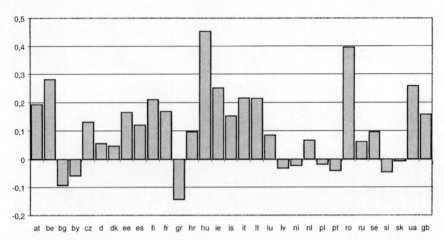

Figure 11.2. Differences in Democratic Values Between Volunteers and Nonvolunteers. *Source:* EVS 1999–2000.

countries, even where volunteering has a statistically significant impact on democracy, level of education appears to be a much stronger predictor of the democratic attitude than volunteering. The conclusion from these analyses is that, although volunteers appear to be (slightly) more democratic than nonvolunteers, in most countries, the differences in democratic attitude between these groups should not be exaggerated. At the individual level, the hypothesis that volunteering affects the democratic attitude cannot be substantiated.

At aggregate level, we did find some evidence for the link between numbers of volunteers and adherence to democratic attitude ($r = .469; p = .000$). Figure 11.3 illustrates this, but it also illustrates that the associations are modest. The numbers of volunteers are highest in Sweden, the Netherlands, and Slovakia, but these societies do not appear to be most in favor of the democratic attitude. Democracy is most favored in Germany, Austria, Iceland, and Denmark, countries where volunteering is less widespread. The cases of Slovakia, Portugal, and France seem to demonstrate that an east-west split does not appear. Generally speaking, volunteering is less widespread among the people of Central and Eastern European societies and democracy is less favored in these countries than in Western European societies, but this is equally true for France and Portugal, and as far as volunteering is concerned, not true for Slovakia. Democracy is most favored in Germany, but volunteering is less common there than in some less democratic societies.

Again, the pattern is less clear than expected, and thus we must conclude that the hypothesis cannot be confirmed, or can be confirmed only to a certain extent. Thus, Putnam's idea that the level of democracy is connected with involvement in networks cannot be substantiated.

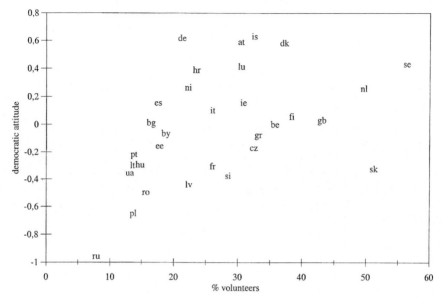

Figure 11.3. Country-Means on Democratic Attitude and percentage of Volunteers. *Source:* EVS 1999–2000.

Why, then, do countries differ in degree of volunteering? We assumed that it could be explained or understood from some country specific characteristics, such as level and age of democracy, economic development, and degree of religiosity.

In Table 11.2, these correlations are displayed. Private religiosity does not affect the degree of volunteering in society, but public religiosity does. The more people in a society attend religious services, the less people in that society are involved in voluntary activities (see also Hodgkinson in this book). Religiosity seems to generate lower levels of volunteering, which contradicts the hypothesis. Economic development, measured by GDP, is linked with volunteering: the higher the GDP, the more people are involved in civil society. The level and age of democracy are also associated in the expected direction with the degree of volunteering.

Table 11.2. Correlations between Country Characteristics and Degree of Volunteering

GDP	Public religiosity	Private religiosity	Political rights	Civil liberties	Age of democracy
.565***	−.251	.395*	−.411*	−.384*	.646***

Significance: *p < .05; **p < .01; ***p < .001
Source: EVS 1999–2000.

Table 11.3. Results Regression Analysis Volunteering regressed on
GDP, Religiosity (Public Religiosity Model 1; Private Religiosity
Model 2), Political Rights, Civil Liberties, and Age of Democracy

	Model 1	Model 2
GDP	−.310	−.317
Public religiosity	−.117	
Private religiosity		−.133
Political rights	−.852*	−.842*
Civil liberties	.716	.690
Age of democracy	.964**	.989**
R^2	.568	.573
Adjusted R^2	.481	.488

Entries are standardized regression coefficients; significance: *$p < .05$; **$p < .01$;
***$p < .001$.
Source: EVS 1999–2000.

The more political rights and the more civil liberties a population have, the more people in that society do voluntary work. The strongest association is found between age of democracy and degree of volunteering. The longer the democratic tradition of a society, the more people work for voluntary organizations and associations.

The impact of age of democracy appears strongest in a regression analysis (Table 11.3) in which the degree of volunteering was regressed on these country characteristics. Religiosity, private nor public, does have a significant impact when controlled for level of democracy and age of democracy. The same counts for economic development, measured by GDP.

Finally, we explored trends in volunteering, assuming that volunteering has declined. In Western Europe, trends can be observed from 1981–1999 (Figure 11.4), and they reveal that, in Western Europe as a whole, not much has changed. The percentage of volunteers has hardly changed, and the hypothesis of a gradual decline cannot be substantiated. However, it must be acknowledged that the trends are not uniform in Europe. From 1981 to 1999, volunteering decreased, although often only modestly, in West Germany, Spain, France, Iceland, Ireland, and Northern Ireland, and increased slightly in Belgium, Denmark, Italy, the Netherlands, Sweden, and Great Britain. In many cases, the trends differ between the 1981–1990 period and 1990–1999 period. A continuous increase was found in Belgium and the Netherlands while a continuous decline was found in Germany, Ireland, Northern Ireland, and Iceland. However, in the latter three countries, the decrease was strongest from 1981 to 1990, and modest from 1990 to 1999. The shifts in volunteering in France are hardly worth mentioning. Although volunteering increased during the eighties and decreased during the nineties, these changes are so small that the conclusion must be drawn that the degree of volunteering

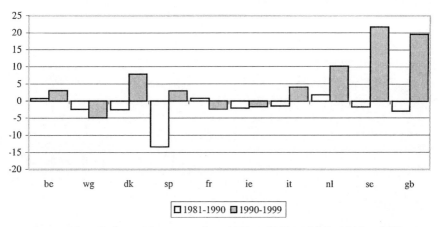

Figure 11.4. Shifts in Volunteering from 1981 to 1990 and from 1990 to 1999. *Source:* EVS 1981–1990–1999/2000.

remained more or less the same in France. Volunteering in the remaining countries, Denmark, Spain, Sweden, and Great Britain, decreased from 1981 to 1990 and increased from 1990 to 1999. Particularly in Sweden and Great Britain, volunteering increased significantly during the last decade. In Sweden, this was mainly caused by a sharp increase in voluntary work for religious organizations; in Great Britain, it was mainly due to increasing numbers of people who did voluntary work for recreational organizations. Although it is clear that the changes in degree of volunteering are not at all dramatic, there is no uniform pattern of change in Europe, and the trends are also not consistent over time.

According to Putnam, age has an impact on the degree to which people in the United States are engaged in voluntary work. It was assumed that in Europe the sharpest increase in volunteering would also be found among the older generations. And this appears to be the case, as is illustrated in Figure 11.5, where we have displayed the trends in volunteering in the last two decades for various age groups in 10 Western European countries.

The trends are not as clear as Putnam found in the United States. The US trend does not occur in Europe. In Great Britain, the Netherlands, and Sweden volunteering rose in all age groups, while in West Germany and Spain the opposite development occurred. The trends in the other countries do not resemble the American pattern either. Although the hypothesis that older age groups are increasingly involved in voluntary work can be substantiated in most European countries (Spain and Germany being important exceptions), the increase is not confined to these age groups but also occurred in younger age groups. Also the assumption that volunteering declined among middle aged groups cannot be confirmed in all countries.

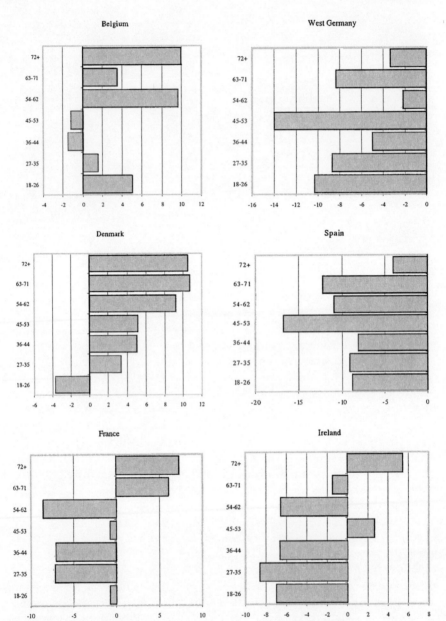

Figure 11.5. Trends in Volunteering in Various Age groups in 10 European Countries. *Source:* EVS 1981–1990–1999/2000.

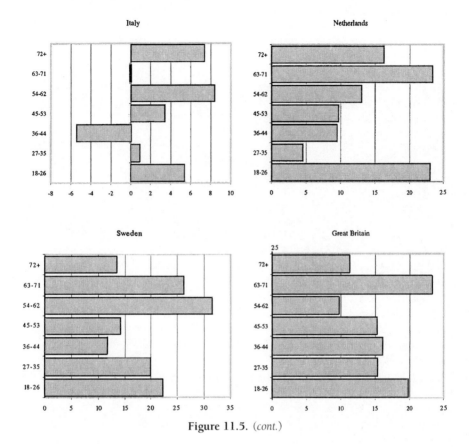

Figure 11.5. (cont.)

CONCLUSION

In this chapter, we explored the relationships between engagement in civil society and democracy, both at individual and at aggregate level. The literature on civil society suggests that there are strong links between volunteering and democratic attitudes. Volunteers are assumed to be democratic citizens, while societies in which many people are active in voluntary organizations are assumed to be more democratic.

We did not find much evidence to support these ideas. Volunteers in Europe do not appear to be more in favor of democracy than people who do not work for voluntary organizations and associations. In terms of predictive power, level of education appears to be more important for democratic attitude than being a volunteer. Also at aggregate level, we did not find much evidence for the assumption that support for democratic ideals is more widespread in societies in which volunteering is more common. Thus, volunteers do not appear to be the carriers of democracy. They do not appear to be more in favor of democracy than non-volunteering people. At aggregate level, the evidence is also not very convincing.

We also addressed the differences between countries in degree of volunteering. Most volunteers are found in Sweden, the Netherlands, and Great Britain, while volunteering is rather limited in many Central and Eastern European countries. Slovakia is an important exception to this rule. In this respect, Slovaks resemble Swedes and Dutch people. It is difficult to understand why this is the case. In Slovakia, the high number of volunteers cannot be attributed to one or two specific organizations. Religious and church organizations and sports and recreation have the most volunteers in Slovakia (about 15%), while voluntary work for other organizations is limited to 5%.

We explored if country differences in volunteering could be attributed to other country specific characteristics. From several theories, we concluded that perhaps volunteering was linked with economic development, level of religiosity, and level and age of democracy. The strongest association was found between volunteering and the political rights in a country. Age of democracy also appeared to be important, but GDP and factors related to religion appeared to be less important. It must, however, be admitted that the countries looked at do not differ much in political rights and or civil liberties. Besides, both measures appear to be heavily correlated, so that in a regression analysis spurious effects can occur. However, the longer the democratic history of a country, the more people are involved in voluntary activities. As such, theories which claim that democracy is important for volunteering to develop and be maintained, can be corroborated.

Finally, the analyses showed that trends in volunteering are far from uniform in Europe and the idea that particularly among the oldest and youngest age groups volunteering is rising can only be confirmed in a limited number of countries.

Thus, some of the hypotheses could be confirmed, and others could not. People who do not do voluntary work are almost as democratic as people who are actively involved in civil activities. The idea that democracy can only survive when many people are involved in voluntary organizations and associations is not strongly supported. This is not to say that volunteering is a hindrance to democracy or that people should not be engaged in civil society, but it raises a question about the importance of the voluntary sector for democratic values and perhaps even democracy to survive. Perhaps democracy can survive without an active voluntary sector because democratic feelings also exist among non participants. The number of volunteers is rather limited in most countries and declining very little if at all, even in those countries which have been democratic for a long time. Thus, from this point of view, the conclusion can be drawn that democracy is not endangered.

We did not differentiate between volunteers working for different organizations. On the one hand, it does not seem to matter what kind of organization one is involved in. There is no convincing evidence that volunteers working for a specific kind of organization are more democratic than volunteers working for other organizations or non-volunteering people. Thus, Putnam seems to be right in claiming that it does not matter. On the other hand, there may be differences in the kind of work volunteers are doing, independent of the type of organization. It seems obvious to assume that negotiating with authorities not only requires different skills of the volunteer, but also different democratic attitudes than checking cards at a rock concert or being a barkeeper in a club bar. Such differences cannot be investigated with the data set which was available to us, but it seems necessary to not only look at the kinds of clubs and organizations people do voluntary work for, but also to investigate the kinds of voluntary activities people are engaged in. For the moment, however, we cannot conclude more than that there is not much evidence to support the suggestion that volunteering and democracy are necessarily mutually connected.

REFERENCES

Almond, G.A., & Verba, S. (1965).*The civic culture*. Boston, Mass.: Little, Brown.

Barnes, S.H. (1998). The mobilization of political identity in new democracies. In S.H. Barnes & J. Simon (Eds.), *The postcommunist citizen* (pp. 117–138). Budapest: Erasmus Foundation and IPAS of HAS.

Coleman, J.S. (1990). *Foundations of social theory*. Cambridge, MA.: Harvard University Press.

Crawford, K. (1996). *East Central European politics today*. Manchester/New York: Manchester University Press.

Dekker, P., & van den Broek, A. (1998). Civil society in comparative perspective. *Voluntas, 8*, 11–38.

Fukuyama, F. (1995). *Trust*. London: Penguin Books.

Fukuyama, F. (2000). Social capital. In L.E. Harrison & S.P. Huntington (Eds.), *Culture Matters* (pp. 98–111). New York: Basic Books.

Giner, S. (1995). Civil society and its future. In H.A. Hall (Ed.),*Civil Society. Theory, history, comparison* (pp. 301–325). Cambridge, UK: Polity Press.

Gundelach, P. (1995). Grass-roots activity. In J.W. van Deth & E. Scarbrough (Eds.), *The impact of values* (pp. 412–440). Oxford, UK: Oxford University Press.

Halman, L. (2001). *The European values study: A third wave*. Tilburg: EVS, WORC, Tilburg University.

Inglehart, R. (1997). *Modernization and postmodernization*. Princeton, NJ: Princeton University Press.

Lane, J.E., & Ersson, S.O. (1996). *European politics*. London, Thousand Oaks, CA/New Delhi: Sage.

Newton, K. (1999). Social capital and democracy in modern Europe. In J.W. van Deth et al. (Eds.), *Social capital and European democracy* (pp. 3–24). London/New York: Routledge.

Putnam, R. (1993). *Making democracy work*. Princeton, NJ: Princeton University Press.

Putnam, R. (1995). Bowling alone: America's declining social capital. *Journal of Democracy, 6*, 65–78.

Putnam, R. (2000). *Bowling alone*. New York: Simon & Schuster.

Rokeach, M. (1973). *The nature of human values*. New York: Free Press.

Selle, P. (1999). The transformation of the voluntary sector in Norway. In J.W. Van Deth et al. (Eds.), *Social capital and European democracy* (pp. 144–166). London/New York: Routledge.

Sennett, R. (1977). *The fall of public man*. New York: Knopf.

Stolle, D., & Rochon, T. R. (1999). The myth of American exceptionalism. In J.W. van Deth et al. (Eds.), *Social capital and European democracy* (pp. 192–209). London/New York: Routledge.

Uslaner, E.M. (1999). Morality plays. In J.W. van Deth et al. (Eds.), *Social capital and European democracy* (pp. 213–239). London/New York: Routledge.

Whiteley, P. (1999). The origins of social capital. In J.W. van Deth et al. (Eds.), *Social capital and European democracy* (pp. 25–44). London/New York: Routledge.

Wuthnow, R. (1991). *Acts of compassion*. Princeton, NJ: Princeton University Press.

Chapter *12*

Cultivating Apathy in Voluntary Associations

NINA ELIASOPH

Recently, politicians, social theorists, citizens, and pundits alike have been looking to voluntary associations to heal many social ills. One of the many goods we imagine they provide is to "make democracy work" (Putnam, 1993), partly by broadening citizens' political and social horizons. But do they broaden citizens' horizons? How do they? Why don't they, when they don't?

In the ideal of the voluntary association, citizens gather as equals, carrying on free-wheeling conversation about a wide range of topics, openly airing issues of common concern (e.g., Tocqueville, 1831 [1968]). In this ideal, political questions easily flow in and out of conversation. For this ideal, the quality of conversation is key.

Yet, surprisingly, no one has seriously studied everyday conversation in volunteer groups, to discover how or if such groups work the magic that we attribute to them. This chapter attempts to remedy that strange absence. One important question for activism and research should be, "How do people create group contexts in which citizens can carry on free conversation about wide-ranging issues?"

Certainly, voluntary associations are necessary for democracy; without gathering in groups, people cannot cultivate the human affection and the infinite nuances of meaning that a humane democracy requires; without such associations, citizens do not experience the power that "springs into being" when people gather together (Arendt, 1958). There are many reasons that voluntary associations are good for society. But simply advocating "participation," is not enough.

Drawing on an ethnographic study of US volunteer groups, I argue that it is just as important to understand how civic groups limit engagement. Civic group participants in the United States learn how to care about the wider world, but they

199

also learn how to avoid caring. While they're learning how to participate in local affairs, they're also often learning how to *limit their imaginations* to a small circle of concern. I heard that volunteers find ample reasons to avoid talking politics in voluntary associations: members of the groups I describe assumed that talking politics would be demoralizing, and that the raison d'etre for voluntary associations was to convince fellow citizens that "you really can make a difference on issues that are close to home." With this prevalent cultural model of voluntarism, we can expect that while voluntary associations teach citizens to care about each other, the same associations can also teach them not to care about politics—or at least not to show in public settings that they care about politics.

So, the first surprise this essay unveils is that, in the United States, conversation in these civic groups is not as horizon-expanding as theory has it.

Second, when we do pay attention to conversation in these settings, we hear a strange reversal: behind the scenes, out of the group meetings, in small huddles of two or three, members could discuss their worries about the wider world, but in group meetings and other public settings the same people avoided talking politics. Drawing on the work of sociologist Erving Goffman, I show how useful it is to focus on the discrepancy between "backstage" and "frontstage" conversation in grassroots citizens' groups.

This discrepancy between back- and front-stage conversation shows just how much work it took to produce this appearance of apathy. Many volunteers had their own private analyses of social problems; many said in interviews that they had never voiced these ideas before. To understand this, we need to know what citizens assume the very act of speaking in a volunteer group means. I offer a method for understanding this basic "footing" in play in voluntary associations, and show what that footing is in the peculiar case of US civil society.

Third, I want to show how social workers, school authorities, and city officials aided this process of political evaporation.

And finally, I ask what is peculiarly American about this model of civic engagement, and whether it offers any lessons to the rest of the world. When the scholars, pundits and politicians point to voluntary associations' importance in upholding democracy, many of them hold up the United States—or at least the United States of a couple of decades ago—as a model of civic engagement. Here, I argue that yes, civic groups are crucial for democracy, but no, holding up the United States as the best model is a big mistake.

Examining where and how Americans can comfortably talk about politics might help us understand how so many manage to make the realm of politics seem so irrelevant to everyday life. Speaking gives political concern meaning and form, providing socially recognizable tools for thinking and acting. So if we want to know what to do to improve civic life, we need to understand how citizens create contexts for open-ended conversation, and we need to recognize what obstacles citizens face when creating such contexts.

THE IDEAL

The ideal of civic participation, for Tocqueville and others (Tocqueville, 1968 [1840]), Beem (1999) and Connelly (1994), is precisely that the border between "politics" and "life" is not set in stone; that sometimes volunteers might treat the issues they discuss as "political," sometimes they might treat those same issues as "not political." Historically, in the United States, associations that began as "civic" have transformed into "political" ones, and vice versa (Clemens, 1996). If this is so, then the boundary between political and personal is not fixed, not definable a priori, but defined as people in a hundred small conversations discuss their seemingly private worries, and discover how they are shared problems, and dream up social solutions to them. In this way, the category "politics" always remains permeable, as people constantly traverse the boundary between private and public and constantly draw more issues into public consideration. But in order for this to happen, citizens have to allow potentially political issues to air. And, in the US, that is the problem.

In American community life, volunteer groups are to good citizenship as apples are to fruit; they are the very model—what linguist George Lakoff (1987) would call an "Idealized Cognitive Model"—of good, productive citizen involvement. A great deal is at stake in the definition of the volunteer, and in the definitions of compassion, altruism, optimism, and everything else that goes along with volunteering. Here, we will see that volunteering is defined as the opposite of politics. When I interviewed volunteers who helped out at a local school, asking what they thought motivated some activists in town, one volunteer succinctly summarized my question as, "She's asking, 'Why do they choose politics instead of schools?'"

VOLUNTEERS ENCOURAGING EACH OTHER TO CARE

The volunteers I studied were unusually compassionate and optimistic, freely giving attention and care to their community, valiantly trying to create a community spirit. Even when someone got shot in the convenience store next door to the high school, no new parents came to the high school parents' meeting: As they put it, "just the same old bunch" showed up.

These volunteers were poised to combat the specter of futility and to convince all newcomers that "You really *can* make a difference!" and that "Everyone has something to offer," as they often put it. They hoped to communicate that message through the very act of volunteering and tried not to pay attention to problems that might undermine that message of hope. These citizens thought they could inspire feelings of empowerment within a small circle of concern, and they implicitly believed that helping people *feel* empowered was, *in itself*, doing something good for the community. Volunteers shared faith in the ideal of civic participation, but in practice, paradoxically, maintaining this hope and faith meant curtailing political discussion: members sounded less public-minded and less politically creative in groups than they sounded individually.

In my search for community involvement, I participated in two antidrug groups, one of which consisted entirely of volunteers and the other of which joined volunteers with social service program leaders from the local recreation department, the police, and other agencies. I attended meetings, rallies, antidrug parades, public hearings, and other events, and generally did what other members did. Incidentally, Tocqueville's example of Americans' zest for forming funny little groups is a campaign for abstaining from alcohol—perhaps not much has changed since then!

I also participated in a local group called the "Parent League"—about 12 parents—both moms and dads—of high schoolers, whose general purpose was to help the school out. Their main activity was running a concession stand at high school sports events that sold candy and burgers. I went to their meetings, festivals, parades, events, and generally did what all members did.

The two core volunteer groups on which I focused were remarkably similar, demographically speaking. They were typical of American volunteers, coming somewhat disproportionately from higher income and education groups, but including a wide range; the plurality (but not always the majority) of members was white.[1] I took part in the few rare meetings which drew these volunteers together with groups around town that were less racially or ethnically mixed—all African-American or all Filipino, for example.

As a volunteer myself, I had difficulty finding a niche that was not simply working alone on a predesigned project. I often asked what I could do to help: I could drive around town alone delivering hot meals to the elderly, meet an "at risk" child once a week to give support, supervise the playground before school, provide a "safe house" for kids who were in trouble, go to a street fair to sell raffle tickets for a volunteer group; maybe another volunteer would show up, but if not, I could do it by myself. These were projects involving only one volunteer, when I was looking for a group. If I were a citizen searching for a public forum in which to learn how to participate in and clarify my thoughts about the wider world, volunteer groups would not usually have been good places to search.

When I asked how I could get involved, all volunteers enthusiastically told me to contact someone (always a woman) whom they considered a "real super volunteer" or a really dedicated social service worker, saying that if I really want to know about volunteers, I should talk to this person, because "she does so much." No volunteer referred me to a "real super group." In all of the groups there were many members who never came to meetings but sent messages offering to help out with tasks. Volunteers did not think of themselves as doing good as a group, but as individuals.

---

[1] See Verba and Nie (1972: 99). Their term "communalists" comes closest to the category I call "volunteers."

Over tea one day, I asked one of those "real super volunteers," Julie, how people decided what projects to work on, where they got ideas, and when they discussed the overall big picture. People did not spin out those kinds of ideas "any more," Julie said, though she "personally thought it was fun." Maybe people got them "from the sixties," she speculated. Others said something similar, except for two who were on the school board, who told me they might meet now and then over coffee, on a *one-to-one* basis, for their "bigger picture" discussions—in private sessions, not in open meetings.

Volunteers said that meetings were a waste of time compared with the groups' real work. Though volunteers attended many meetings every week, each was very to-the-point, short, and task-oriented. When I said that I was studying "community life—what gets people involved in groups and how to get more people involved,—" many proudly recounted a long, long list of their volunteer activities, amazing me with how many evenings a week they devoted to volunteering. None mentioned why they were involved. Their point was that activity itself was a matter-of-fact way of demonstrating commitment.

Most meetings featured in-depth discussions of practical fund-raising projects, focusing attention on projects that were "do-able," as they put it. For example, in one meeting of the Parent League, a group of adults who had children in the local high school, participants lavished detail on the Royal Dog Steamer that they planned on bringing to school sports events: One parent exclaimed, with a bit of wry humor, "It can steam foot-longs, Polish dogs, hot links, regular dogs, sausages, you name it, about twenty at a time." (For readers who are not familiar with American cuisine, these are all different kinds of hot dogs.)

What is remarkable about this emphasis on fund-raising is that, for most volunteers, it would have been much easier and cheaper to pitch in money from their own pockets than to spend that enormous amount of time, money, and effort on fund-raisers and the elaborate equipment they required. But just chipping in money would have missed their point. The implicit moral of a fund-raiser was to show the community that common people care (Wuthnow 1991), not to show that only rich or educated or powerful people can effectively care. Fund-raising really seemed to be "doing something."

"WE ACCOMPLISH A LOT": WHAT "THE FRONTSTAGE" IS FOR VOLUNTEER GROUPS

When anyone came to a meeting to try to discuss issues that might be more overtly political than, say, a Royal Dog Steamer, members ignored them or quickly changed the subject. There was a prescribed cultural format for being a volunteer, and it did not include political debate. For example, a newcomer came to a meeting to tell members that a substitute teacher had called students racist names. In this meeting of mostly plump, pastel-clad parents, Charles came wearing a black leather jacket and skinny black jeans. A parent of a high school student himself, he was also the local representative of the NAACP, a national organization that promotes the interests of African Americans. He said that when the students complained, the authorities said they were "too busy" to deal with their complaint. And he also said there were often Nazi skinheads outside the schoolyard recruiting at lunchtime.

We all also already knew about the recent race riot at the movie theater down the block and the white hate group concert scheduled for later that month. But Parent League members remained calm. No one asked what the teacher had actually said, to judge for themselves whether it was racist. They just sat, blandly listening and very quickly ended the discussion.

Charles said he just thought more people should know about this incident, and that more parents should be involved, not just to accomplish things, but, as he put it, to talk.

Of course, the other members thought involvement was important, too. One parent exclaimed, "Don't underestimate us—we make efficient use of a small number of people! We get a lot done!" The notetaker's minutes for that meeting reported, "Charles Jones relayed an incident for *information*," as if it was obvious that there was nothing the group could do. Most of the minutes from the meeting described various fundraising projects:

> Someone said that the school principal said we should have bingo games. An extensive discussion on bingo operations ensued. Pam had the idea that we have one big fundraiser each year. . . . Trudy suggested a crab feed, Bob suggested a spaghetti feed.

This continued for half of a single-spaced page, indicating the real purpose of the group.

What was most taboo was speaking about a problem as an injustice, but addressing the same problem without referring to issues of justice was considered all right. Charles committed another big faux pas when he raised a principle for a group fund-raising activity at a Parent League meeting, in a discussion about raising funds to buy computers for the high school:

> First, has anybody tried going over to Microchip Lane (an area nearby, known internationally as a center for computer production) and *asking* for computers? The big corporations take our money but they don't give it back. *Unless you ask*. They'll even send people to train the kids to use the computers.
>   It's training them to work in industry, and the corporations need that as much as the kids. They should pay for the services the schools give them. Back in another fundraiser I worked on, we hit up Ford for 4 brand new cars. We raffled them off and made $2–3,000 per car. We also got "used trucks" from Seven-Up. The corporations will give if you ask.
> *Ron*: What "we" is this?

Charles: Excuse me?

Ron: What "we" got these things? What organization?

Charles (very slowly): At that point in time, it was 1969, I was in Texas. I was working with the (was I the only one who expected him to say Black Panthers?) YMCA (a mainstream nongovernmental organization). The second point is that you should put the money into an account to have it collect interest and just draw on that.

Bob: I really like your idea of putting some money away and just taking the interest.

They ignored the idea of "hitting up" the big companies. But later that evening they talked about "requesting donations" from small companies and mentioned a local politician who might be able to make a request from a computer company executive. "Requesting" was alright, but holding companies accountable was not. But raising a matter of principle and trying to discuss it publicly was considered unseemly.

The point is that allowing political conversation in their meetings would have given a different meaning to volunteers' work, even if volunteers had kept on doing *exactly* the same tasks.

BACKSTAGE COMPLAINTS AND RECOGNITION OF PROBLEMS

You might think that these parents did not care about politics, but not so. Behind the scenes, political issues relentlessly arose in the places that Goffman would call "backstage," away from the main group interactions. For example, while parents did not want to address the problem of the racist teacher in their meeting, they quietly celebrated group members' antiracist actions. In one case, a volunteer had signed up to host out-of-town visitors during a statewide football game. When she opened her front door, the visitors exclaimed, "Thank God you're not black!" And so the volunteer told her children to invite all their black friends over for a big slumber party. I heard this story when two volunteers recounted it with great pride, in a closet-sized office, after a meeting; it never would have arisen during a meeting. Volunteers also applauded this kind of direct action, but quietly.

Volunteers assumed, as one volunteer told me, that it was better "not to make an issue of including minorities but just treat them like everyone else." In other words, working together on concrete projects would do more good than talking about race.

Their efforts at ignoring race were also part of their general effort to avoid discouragement and snobbery; to be encouraging and welcoming meant treating everyone as an equal. Avoiding discouragement and snobbishness, though, had costs, among which probably was the community's ability to deal with race problems. Many parents of color came to one or two meetings and then never returned. I spoke to one who had come only once; she had concluded that the Parent League was "a bunch of white people who weren't interested in race."

Sociolinguist Teun van Dijk (1987) would agree, saying that this hesitation and circumlocution is clear evidence of "racism," but I do not think that would be a good explanation. Avoidance was the way the volunteers publicly treated *all* troubling social issues. The problem was not racism per se but volunteers' relation to political discussion in general, including discussion of racism. To talk about racism would have meant changing their political etiquette, to stop trying so hard to keep up that can-do spirit and let some frightening uncertainty in. Actively ignoring such tensions was considered a positive good, a moral act. It would be better to work on projects that illustrate how easy, effective, and enjoyable involvement is; then, they believed, everyone would get involved and race problems would dissolve in the busy harmony.

Racist *beliefs* or even subtly racist feelings were not the explanation for their silence, and more generally, volunteers were not unconcerned or unaware or lacking in democratic "values and beliefs." The volunteers did care about broader political problems; they just usually censored their concerns when speaking in public. They assumed that they had to, *given their definition of speech in the public arena.*

Behind the scenes I heard volunteers waxing indignant about funding for education, poverty, war, environmental destruction, racism, and a whole range of political problems that could not be solved locally by good citizens simply banding together with Royal Dog Steamers. When I asked them explicitly, in interviews, about these political problems, they labeled these problems "not close to home," and "not in our backyards," thus preserving the illusion that they could easily fix problems that were close to home.

But literally, environmental problems were in their backyards. All these volunteers were within a 20-minute drive of several chemical plants that had 4 major fires or spills within 2 years, a river so polluted that all aquatic life had died, a military station so toxic that all the worms in its soil had died, and more. Volunteers knew about these problems, worried about them, and dwelled on them *endlessly* in interviews, even when I tried to change the subject. They could also talk about them in small group conversations, outside of the main group gathering. But in meetings, they told themselves and each other that they did not care about such problems, instead of saying that they felt powerless to fix them. How different it would be if the volunteers could have said, in their meetings, that they did care but felt powerless! As it was, their assertions aided the cycle of political evaporation by preventing volunteers from voicing clear concerns, even to themselves.

OFFICIALS REINFORCE VOLUNTEERS' POLITICAL AVOIDANCE

The officials who worked with volunteers very strongly and frequently echoed and reinforced this assumption—that combating futility meant, above all, combating the *feeling* of futility. I heard the pattern broken only once, in an antidrug group meeting, when a social worker said that the penniless teenagers in her program had nowhere to go when they turned 18 and were out of the state's hands. There was silence, while everyone waited for her to tell us the solution.

After a long moment, she apologized with a giggle, "I just have a problem, not a solution."

The chair of the meeting said, "I'm sure someone'll be coming to talk to you figure out a solution." Perhaps volunteers and social service workers did indeed engineer a creative behind-the-scenes, quiet solution, but the general problem went undiscussed and unanalyzed in public.

A refrain among the social workers and volunteers said, "If a child is home alone with a problem, that child could go to any of the neighbors in the community, because they'd all be part of the Caring Adult Network (CAN)." In that way, adults could all share in raising the community's children, "so that the community is like an extended family for the children," in the words of one social worker; any mom on the block would poke her head out the kitchen window if she heard a child in trouble. The glowing image of the Caring Adult community contrasted sharply with the reality of the suburban city, with its empty streets, 7-lane strips, mobile nuclear families, and commuter parents. Portraits of this supportive, loving community always referred to the past, never to the present reasons that this type of community was absent. This "culture of nostalgia" (Skolnick, 1991) encouraged people to change their feelings about the community, as if the feelings themselves were the only problem.

In group meetings, officials echoed volunteers in their efforts at avoiding making connections between their everyday acts of charity and public issues. For example, an extremely active volunteer, Julie, made this announcement at a meeting of a group dedicated to preventing drug abuse: She said that a social services administrator was

> looking for volunteers to supervise the playground in the morning before school starts. A lot of parents have to leave for work at 6 or 6:30 AM, and there are no before-school programs even in the elementary schools, so the parents have no choice but to just dump their kids—first-graders, second-graders, even—on the playground, sometimes before it's even light out, and just hope for the best.

In making this request, Julie never wondered aloud whether there were any larger issues involved—perhaps long work hours and short vacations; perhaps the commuting patterns that left parents with an exhausting, sooty two-, three- or four-hour round-trip each day, with no public transportation alternatives;[2] perhaps the absence of paid positions for caregivers to watch the children on the predawn playground and at other times throughout the day—larger issues that made Amargo parents into "overworked Americans" (Shor, 1991) who hardly had time to see their kids.

But officials, like volunteers themselves, certainly did recognize the broad political aspects of the problems they faced, and they recognized the limits of their culture of political avoidance. Like the volunteers, the officials just left their worries backstage. One tale told at an antidrug meeting illustrates these tensions. The "really super volunteer," Julie, had told someone a story that was often recounted: "Julia Trenton Brooks was taking the bus one day," the story went.

> This particular bus she takes every day. On this bus is a little boy who gets on poorly dressed; sometimes not dressed warmly enough, sometimes he doesn't come at all.
>
> Well, over time, people on the bus have begun looking out for this young-ster, and making sure that he not only gets off at the right stop, but waiting till he gets from the bus stop into the school. Every morning, they made sure he made it into that school.
>
> Now, that's what we're after: a Caring Adult Network, so that the com-munity is like an extended family for the children.

The quaint story was full of archaic language: a sing-song storybook tone, with repetitive clauses like a nursery rhyme, old-fashioned words like "youngster," a child not dressed warmly enough—a stock image of a poor child from a fairy tale—and a character who rides the bus when normal people are insulated with their stereos in tinted-windowed, air-conditioned cars.

Backstage, a couple of days later, Julie and I were cleaning out the massive coffeemaker after another antidrug meeting. I told her I thought that that story was touching. She slowly turned toward me and said, "The poor little boy—he was so neglected, his hair uncombed, sometimes he looked hungry. He just stopped coming one day." I asked what happened to him. She said she didn't know. "That's the way it works. When the family does something, the kid will just disappear." I asked if there was any way to find him, to make sure he was all right. She sadly said no.

Volunteers knew that the care shown this child was unusual. Julie had been on the bus only because an eye impairment made it impossible for her to drive—the bus was an *in*-voluntary association for her. As in most car-centered American cities, adults who would want to be part of a Caring Adult Network would have

---

[2] One unusual Parent League member, said to me in the individual interview, "I used to tell people I had three jobs: driving to work, work itself, and then driving home, you know, because it takes two hours to get to downtown Pacific City and it's *not* relaxing."

to book a specific time and place to encounter a child. What if we were all alone in our cars—would we never notice the ragged, hungry child? Why were there not *more* public places like the bus? Who was responsible for the community's children? Could anything be done on more than one-at-a-time basis? What if the poor, small, young child had been a poor, violent, or foul-mouthed, big, old child? In this and other moments, volunteers publicly wanted to tell the uplifting story but not the sad ending; that part could be told only backstage.

THE CULTURE OF POLITICAL AVOIDANCE

One explanation of the public censorship I heard might focus on fear of disagreement. Elisabeth Noelle-Neumann (1985) coined the term "the spiral of silence" to describe the process in which people—who she says are by nature eager to get along with each other—refrain from expressing what they guess to be unpopular viewpoints to strangers. The spiral of silence sucks unpopular opinions out of circulation, by making them embarrassing to hold publicly. Noelle-Neumann bases her argument on experiments in which subjects are asked to imagine conversation between themselves and strangers on trains.

But Americans rarely go on trains or talk to perfect strangers. More often, people talk to people they already know, in familiar contexts, some of which could invite debate and other which could discourage it—the texture of public life is more varied than the flat experiment supposes. Elihu Katz (1988) shows that when people establish ongoing everyday contexts with friends, relatives, neighbors, and colleagues that are very different from the context of meeting a stranger on a train, then they can create spaces in which disagreement is not perceived as a risk to solidarity.

Context is all, here: over time, volunteers, unlike strangers on trains (or more precisely, unlike people talking in experiments about imagining strangers on trains), could have gotten to know each other's opinions, and could have developed a kind of trust that allowed for political disagreement. Instead, they worked together to establish contexts in which political debate itself was unpopular.

Volunteers' political etiquette systematically silenced some *types* of ideas than others: speaking with ambiguity, playing with ideas without an immediate solution, speaking about injustice and power was taboo. This is different from Noelle-Neumann's "unpopular opinions," a term that implies that we all already know what the range of opinion is and have staked out positions on that range. Here, it was not the opinion that was controversial but the style of discussing it. And even if people were trying to avoid disagreement, this, too, is a cultural style, not a rational calculation; Israelis, talking among casual acquaintances, for example, "use political talk the way Americans use talk about sports: to create common ground, with political disagreements only adding to the entertainment value" (Wyatt & Liebes, 1995: 21). So, the questions of observers and participants in civic life should be: "How do people create contexts in which disagreement is allowed or avoided?" and "How do people build a bridge, in conversation, between their local, personal affairs and broader political issues?"

Another explanation might focus on censorship coming from above. Usually, Americans imagine that any "restrictions" on public debate must come from outside of the groups themselves—from laws preventing freedom of assembly (Scott, 1990; Havel, 1988), or, more subtly, from propaganda that prevents people from learning about politics (e.g., Chomsky, 1988: Stauber & Rampton, 1996; Parenti, 1993)—or, even more subtly, from long-standing oppression that makes people unable to stand up for themselves (Gaventa, 1980).

Without a doubt, this is an important part of the story. But here, participants did *some* of the work of restricting communication themselves: They assumed that talking about politics would only sap vigor from the healthy tasks which volunteer groups realistically could set for themselves, and it would intimidate new members and make people feel bad. Paying attention to the dramatic shifts in discourse from frontstage to backstage makes it clear that citizens were not just lacking in public spirit, but lacked it only when speaking "frontstage." How did their public-spirited ideas evaporate out of public circulation? That is a question we, citizens and scholars alike, should be asking.

BRIDGING PRIVATE AND PUBLIC: THE STRANGE CASE OF CHILD-CENTERED CIVIC LIFE IN THE UNITED STATES

Frontstage, no one asked, for example, how other wealthy countries manage to support families with free health care, good and cheap education, year-long paid parental leave, short work weeks and long vacations, safe and plentiful child care, prenatal care, and other policies designed to support children and their caregivers. In practice, volunteers and officials took "a focus on children" to mean "a focus on private life," and "a focus on private life" to mean "a focus on feelings." That meant that the only real changes regular citizens could make were changes in feelings.

Deeply examining the *cultural and structural* bases for this footing offers a more promising explanation than those that focus solely on fear of discord or overt censorship. Here, among the volunteers I studied, we were all already presumed to know the solution: that everyone should be more like Julie, the extremely dedicated, gentle, full-time volunteer. Could even that generous flow of care offer as much attention and love as even one child needs in a dangerous social and physical environment, in an impoverished school system, in a society with longer work-weeks than any other, in an unwholesome wider world? For every child, the community would need at least one full-time Julie! Perhaps free, imaginative debate could have helped volunteers figure out whether any institutions might need to change. But no one was inviting average citizens to change anything more than feelings.

The irony in this US suburb was that social workers themselves had the same image of the social welfare bureaucracy that volunteers had: that only the spirit of voluntarism can revive the community; that bureaucracies should not replace the webs of care that go unspoken in a real community; that bureaucratic rationality cannot replace loving community. In this model of voluntary association, volunteering is the opposite of bureaucracy, instead of its complement. In this model, "volunteering" goes with "moral" and "private." This model of civic participation prizes heartfelt, kind, un-institutionalized volunteering over public institutions, and sets the two in direct opposition. It imagines care-giving as a private, moral act that has no relation to the discouraging world of politics and power. What would, in another country, be funded by the state (preschool) or outlawed by the state (mandatory overtime for workers, for example), is voluntary and private in the United States. As Joan Tronto and other feminist theorists argue (1996), what is needed is a *bridge* between the state and the local civic group, between what we understand to be "moral" and what we consider "political."

The American case offers the most unsteady bridge of all wealthy, Western nations. Compared to European children, American children benefit from a thinner social safety net, vaster economic inequality, parents who have fewer days off per year, fewer hours off per week, often gruelingly long commutes to work with no public transportation to ease the strain, no policies forcing denser development, and no paid parental leave for child-raising. On top of all of these problems that political policies could remedy, we deeply share a traditional belief that people do not normally need to take care of, or being taken care of by, others. People who volunteer in the United States often do so on behalf of the children, but the children need policy solutions to their problems.

Yet, there is a kernel of hope in this child-centered civic life. Taking care of children is *not* voluntary; it has to happen every day without fail; it is not something that the society can stop if doing it feels discouraging or not upbeat enough. It requires direct, one-on-one attention, but if it does not get done well, the whole society suffers. Bringing the intimate, involuntary, and public aspects of childhood zigzagging between the common sense boundaries separating public and private, voluntary and involuntary, moral and political, could have caused an explosion of political debate.

Tocqueville was right to say that there is something good about citizens who busy themselves fixing local problems instead of waiting for the hand of the state to do it for them. But when the cause of concern is something as involuntary, socially obligatory, and troubling as child-raising, this unbridged chasm between private, voluntary arrangements and public, political ones is not always as healthful as scholars and pundits often like to imagine. We need a better balance between the state and voluntary associations in the United States; our affection for voluntary solutions makes it harder for associations to imagine policy solutions (see Beem, 2000, on this point). With this powerful opposition in effect between politics and volunteering, volunteers can offer inspiration and a sense of camaraderie. I do not mean to dismiss this important function that volunteers serve. But they cannot offer steady help the very population on whose behalf they work the hardest: children, whose lives can rarely rely only on volunteers' good feelings.

What is a way out? Political structures and social inequalities make it hard to build that bridge, longstanding traditions of individualism make it hard to build the bridge, and civic etiquette make it hard to build the bridge. Social researchers and activists have devoted themselves to analyzing the first two variables here, but the third gets much less attention. Yet, theorists have long argued that regular political conversation is a defining feature of a healthy democracy; that in a democracy, the substance of political life is public discussion; that the ways we can talk about our concerns go far in shaping them. What they miss is that this discussion happens within a social structure and a political culture, that together tell us what the very act of speaking in a voluntary association means. Theorists imagine that civic associations provide a bridge between casual, informal friendship and political association; when good manners silence political speech in voluntary associations, the bridge is broken.

REFERENCES

Arendt, H. (1977). *Between past and present*. New York: Penguin.

Arendt, H. (1958). *The human condition*. Chicago: University of Chicago Press.

Beem, Ch. (1999). *The necessity of politics*. Chicago: University of Chicago Press.

Chomsky, N. (1988). *Manufacturing consent*. New York: Pantheon.

Clemens, E. (1997). *The people's lobby*. Chicago: University of Chicago Press.

Connelly, W. (1995). *The ethos of pluralization*. Minneapolis: University of Minnesota Press.

Gaventa, J. (1980). *Power and powerlessness*. Chicago: University of Illinois Press.

Goffman, E. (1959). *The presentation of self in everyday life*. Garden City, NY: Doubleday.

Katz, E. (1988). Publicity and pluralistic ignorance. In D. Whitney & W. Wartella (Eds.), *Mass communication review yearbook* (pp. 89–99). Beverly Hills, CA: Sage.

Lakoff, G. (1987). *Women, fire, and dangerous things*. Chicago: University of Chicago Press.

Noelle-Neuman, E. (1984). *The spiral of silence*. Chicago: University of Chicago Press.

Parenti, M. (1993). *Inventing reality*. New York: St. Martin's Press.

Putnam, R.D. (1993). *Making democracy work*. Princeton, NJ: Princeton University Press.

Schor, J. (1991). *The overworked American*. New York: Basic Books.

Scott, J. (1990). *Domination and the arts of resistance*. New Haven: Yale University Press.

Stauber, J., & Rampton, S. (1996). *Toxic sludge is good for you*. Monroe, ME: Common Courage Press.

Tocqueville, A. (1969 [1831], ed. J.P. Mayer). *Democracy in America*. Garden City, NJ: Doubleday,

Tronto, J. (1994). *Moral boundaries*. New York: Routledge.

Van Dijk, T. (1987). *Communicating racism*. Newbury Park, CA: Sage Publications,.

Verba, S., & Nie, N. (1972). *Participation in America*. New York: Harper & Row.

Wuthnow, R. (1990). *Acts of compassion*, Princeton, NJ: Princeton University Press.

Wyatt, R., & Liebes, T. (1995). Inhibition: Factors that inhibit talk in public and private spaces in three cultures. Paper given at Annenberg School of Communication, University of Pennsylvania, Philadelphia, PA.

Index